Green Roof Retrofit

Green Roof Retrofit:
Building Urban Resilience

Edited by

Sara Wilkinson

Associate Head of School Research & External Engagement
Faculty of Design Architecture and Building
University of Technology Sydney
Australia

and

Tim Dixon

Professor of Sustainable Futures in the Built Environment
School of the Built Environment
University of Reading
UK

WILEY Blackwell

Library of Congress Cataloging-in-Publication data applied for

ISBN: 9781119055570

A catalogue record for this book is available from the British Library.

Wiley also publishes its books in a variety of electronic formats. Some content that appears in
print may not be available in electronic books.

Cover Image: Courtesy of the Author

Set in 10/12pt Sabon by SPi Global, Pondicherry, India
Printed and bound in Malaysia by Vivar Printing Sdn Bhd

1   2016

Contents

Notes on Editors

Associate Professor Sara Wilkinson

Sara is Associate Head of the School of Built Environment for Research and External Engagement, a Chartered Building Surveyor, a Fellow of the Royal Institution of Chartered Surveyors (RICS) and a member of the Australian Property Institute (API). She has worked in UK and Australian universities over 25 years. Her PhD examined building adaptation, whilst her MPhil explored the conceptual understanding of green buildings. Her research focus is on sustainability, adaptation of the built environment, retrofit of green roofs and conceptual understanding of sustainability. Sara sits on professional committees for RICS to inform her research and to ensure direct benefit to industry. She sits on the editorial boards of five leading international journals and is Regional Editor for *Structural Survey* in Australasia. Sara has published over 100 articles and books. Her research is published in academic and professional journals, and mostly recently a RICS Best Practice Guidance Note on Green Roofs and Walls for RICS practitioners.

Professor Tim Dixon

Tim Dixon is Professor of Sustainable Futures in the Built Environment at the University of Reading (School of the Built Environment). With more than 30 years' experience in education, training and research in the built environment, he leads the Sustainability in the Built Environment network at the University of Reading and is co-director of the TSBE doctoral training centre (Technologies for a Sustainable Built Environment). He led the Urban Foresight Laboratory work package of EPSRC Retrofit 2050, and is currently working with local and regional partners to develop a 'Reading 2050' smart and sustainable city vision, which connects with the UK BIS Future Cities Foresight Programme. He is working on a smart cities and big data project for RICS Research Trust. Tim is a member of the Climate Change Berkshire Group and a member of the All Party Parliamentary Group on Smart Cities. He is also a member of the editorial boards of four leading international real-estate journals; a member of the Advisory Board for *Local Economy*; and a member of the review panel of the RICS Research Paper Series. He has written more than 100 papers and books in the field. He is also a member of the international scientific committee for the national 'Visions and Pathways 2040 Australia' project on cities.

Notes on Contributors

Assistant Professor Lu Aye has over 35 years of engineering experience in university teaching, research, development, demonstration and commercialisation of renewable energy and energy efficiency technologies. He is a leading expert in modelling, simulation and optimisation of energy systems.

Dr John Blair heads the Master of Sustainable Development course as part of UNSW's Sustainable Built Environment programme. He is currently undertaking research on greening rail corridors to secure a range of benefits, particularly carbon storage and sequestration.

Dr Tijana Blanusa completed a PhD in Plant Biology and joined the Royal Horticultural Society where she is Principal Horticultural Scientist, based at the University of Reading. Her research interests are in understanding the provision of ecosystem services by urban vegetation. She runs projects investigating the contribution of green roofs, green walls, garden hedges and other forms of green infrastructure to the moderation of air temperatures, capture of rainwater and aerial particulate pollutants.

Dr Ross Cameron is a horticultural scientist who specialises in urban green infrastructure and leads a research team covering various aspects of ecosystem service delivery and climate change adaptation in landscape plants. This includes research on green roof and green wall plants and their impact on the thermal properties of built structures.

Dr Renato Castiglia Feitosa has a Civil Engineering degree from the State University of Rio de Janeiro (1996), an MSc (2003) and a PhD (2007) in Coastal and Oceanographic Engineering from the Federal University of Rio de Janeiro. He is a lecturer at the University Estacio de Sa and a researcher at the National School of Public Health (ENSP) – Oswaldo Cruz Foundation (FioCruz).

Dr Sumita Ghosh is an academic, architect and urban planner who focuses on responsive urban design and spatial planning in the School of Built Environment at UTS. She has over 20 years' teaching, research and professional experience for government, local councils, research organisations and universities in Australia, New Zealand and India. Her research focuses on urban sustainability and green infrastructure planning (urban forestry and local food production).

Dr Angela Giovanangeli teaches in the School of International Studies at the University of Technology Sydney. Her research examines cultural initiatives and urban regeneration.

Dr Dominique Hes is an academic at the University of Melbourne specialising in multidisciplinary approaches to complex questions. Her recent book *Designing for Hope: Pathways to Regenerative Sustainability* explores the power of projects that provide social and ecological benefits; green infrastructure is a key element of this.

Dr Matthias Irger is an architect and urbanist who specialises in climate-responsive design and planning. His research interests focus on the effect of the built environment on the urban microclimate to improve the heat resilience and carbon footprint of cities.

Chris Jensen draws on his 12 years as an ESD consultant to provide industry-relevant research in architectural science and construction innovation. He has a particular interest in new technology for passive performance.

Sarah Kemp is undertaking a PhD in the School of Agriculture, Policy and Development, where she is investigating the impact of plant species choice on green roofs and the ability of green roofs to sequester rainwater.

Dr Jessica Lamond is Associate Professor in the Centre for Floods, Communities and Resilience at the University of the West of England. Jessica's research focuses on understanding the socio-technical aspects of structural and non-structural responses to flood risk and climate adaptation in the built environment. This includes work on the multiple benefits of blue green infrastructure as a flood and stormwater management approach. Jessica has published widely, including in leading journals such as *Housing Studies*, *Urban Design and Planning* and *Journal of Risk Research*, and is co-author of the World Bank integrated handbook *Cities and Flooding*.

Dr Tanya Latty is an entomologist with a special interest in insect behaviour and ecology. She has a BSc in Biology and Environmental Science from Trent University (Canada) and a PhD in insect ecology from the University of Calgary (Canada). Her highly interdisciplinary work involves local and international collaborations with researchers in a broad range of fields including mathematics, computer science, forestry and operations research.

Dr Paul Osmond is Director of the Sustainable Built Environment Programme at the University of New South Wales in Sydney, Australia. His research interests cross a range of topics in the broad domain of built environment sustainability.

Professor David Proverbs began his academic career in 1994, following 10 years of project management experience in the UK construction sector. He is Associate Dean – International in the Faculty of Computing, Engineering and the Built Environment at Birmingham City University. From 2013 to 2014 he was Co-Director, Centre for Flooding Communities and Resilience, University of the West of England. He has published widely on the topic of flooding and disaster prevention and management. David chairs the UK Council of Heads of the Built Environment (CHOBE) and co-edits *Structural Survey – Journal of Building Pathology and Refurbishment*.

Dr Fraser Torpy AssDipAppSc (STC), BSc (Hons) (UTS), PhD (UTS) started at UTS in 1991 and currently lectures in the School of the Environment. He has been undergraduate programme director for all environmental courses since 2013. His research focuses on the relationship between plants and urban environmental quality, with a current emphasis on several aspects related to green wall technology and urban greening. He has over 15 years' experience in horticultural biotechnology and has been instrumental in broadening our understanding of how plants can contribute to improved air quality in cities. He is director of the Plants and Environmental Quality Research Group at UTS.

Dr Ilaria Vanni is a teacher and researcher in the School of International Studies at the University of Technology Sydney. Her research is in the field of cultural history, with a focus on urban activism.

Dr Madalena Vaz Monteiro's PhD investigated the impact of plant structure and function on temperature regulation and the surface energy balance. Currently, she is involved with research aiming to better understand ecosystem services delivery by urban trees.

Foreword

When British Land first started creating green roofs on various London office buildings in 2004, it was challenging to take the idea from an ecologist's vision to the reality of a planted, healthy landscape. As a client, we were testing a new idea. We often needed to introduce our architects, structural engineers, contractors and property management partners to the concept – and then develop and test strategies together to deliver quality natural habitats on commercial buildings.

Over the years, as we have installed different green roof styles and commissioned studies, we have learned and shared many lessons. Today, we know more, for instance, about drainage and the potential for (or, more often, lack of) water retention. We understand the need for roof and terrace access to align with internal floor levels. We know which substrates last through British winters and how to plan for rooftop winds. We recognise issues and opportunities relating to visibility from surrounding buildings, and more. Happily, we have not been the only ones to recognise the benefits of green roofs and to learn these lessons.

Green roofs have gone mainstream around the world over the past 10 years. From London to Sydney, Hamburg to Istanbul, Singapore to Rio de Janeiro, they are a recognised strategy for urban green infrastructure. In London, there are now about 700 green roofs, covering 175,000 m². I am pleased that British Land has played a small but important part in this success story – creating green roofs on 12 new buildings and retrofitting three on existing buildings, with more on the way. Green roofs are no longer an unusual concept, and there are standard design formats and green roof types that architects and others understand and can design or install.

However, many of the technical benefits of green roofs remain to be analysed and understood. And so this book and the research it describes are much needed, particularly at a time when strengthening urban resilience is a critical policy issue.

Of particular relevance to cities and property owners are the prospects for retrofitting green roofs and the infrastructure benefits that all green roofs provide. Given the acres of existing roof space in cities around the world, what kind of buildings are particularly suitable for the additional structural load of retrofitting green roofs? With increasing incidence of flooding in many areas, how much rainwater can a 50 cm soil substrate attenuate, and can we make basement flood attenuation tanks correspondingly smaller? Also, how can we deliver green roofs that fulfil multiple functions, such as biodiversity, human enjoyment, aesthetics and food production?

Approaches to modelling urban heat island impacts are particularly useful for policy-makers. As climate change increasingly affects city temperatures, with knock-on effects on people's health and energy consumption, it is important to be able to calculate the benefit of green roofs for temperature management. Likewise, the proposed methodology for calculating the attenuation potential of green roofs should be of immediate assistance in factoring green roofs into strategies for our changing weather futures.

In addition, this book helpfully advances research on the social and biodiversity functions of green roofs for organisations interested in strategies to support human health, ecology and food production in urban areas. An in-depth analysis of a range of case studies explores how green roofs fulfil a range of functions – adding visual interest, creating garden spaces, growing food, introducing habitats for animal biodiversity and contributing to healthy environments through air-quality filtration, water management and temperature control. My colleagues are particularly interested in this social potential of green roofs. Following examples in the USA and Asia, we are exploring how to use our roof spaces to further promote people's health and wellbeing in the places we create.

I am delighted to recommend this book for its timely and substantial contribution to industry practice, and for improving our understanding of green roofs and their multiple benefits. The editors (Sara Wilkinson and Tim Dixon) have drawn together a diversity of authors to provide technical analysis of the practical and policy advantages of green roofs for cities facing climate change, with diverse case studies from Australia, the UK and Brazil. The research insights can also be tapped by property owners and designers to realise the commercial, social and environmental benefits of green roofs – from improving resource management in our cities to creating opportunities for bees, butterflies, birds and people to flourish in the built environment.

Green roofs have enormous potential in urban areas around the world. I hope that this book will aid cities and organisations in developing and growing acres of delightful and valuable habitats for people and the planet.

Sarah Cary
Head of Sustainable Places
British Land

Acknowledgements

Multidisciplinary projects are always challenging, exciting and fun, and working on this book together with our contributing authors has been no exception. The starting point was an increasing recognition that green roofs can really make an important difference in helping build 'urban resilience' (or the ability of our urban areas to be flexible and agile enough to bounce back from the anticipated and unanticipated environmental shocks stemming from rapid urbanisation, climate change and resource depletion). This is at the heart of the book, and is one of the key reasons so many cities globally are engaging with city-wide projects to green their environments – particularly so that they can adapt and mitigate for climate change.

The inspiration for this book arose from Sara Wilkinson's membership of the City of Sydney Technical Advisory Panel from 2012 to 2014. During that time, Sara met with a multidisciplinary group of academics, practitioners and policy makers to work on ways to increase the uptake of green roofs within the City of Sydney. Lucy Sharman was the City of Sydney Green Roof & Green Walls Officer, and being a member of the group really raised awareness of the multiple benefits of green roofs. Sara wishes to thank Lucy for that. As a building surveyor she was well aware of the need to retrofit our urban environments, but being part of the group increased the belief that collectively, we can create and deliver change. Membership of the group led to a number of new and exciting green roof research collaborations and projects with mental healthcare professionals, disadvantaged groups and sustainable urban agriculture entrepreneurs. Sara wishes to thank the RICS Research Trust, City of Sydney and NSW Environmental Trust for funding some of that research, which features in this book. Sara still works with other academic members of the Technical Advisory Panel group, who have contributed to this book. The Technical Advisory Panel has evolved and broadened now into the National Green Infrastructure Network (NGIN), comprising academics and practitioners from several Australian universities and national research organisations as well as NSW state policy makers.

Writing a book is always a journey, and we were fortunate on this particular journey to have the company and wise counsel of a truly international and multidisciplinary group of 20 academics. The geographical spread of knowledge and expertise ranged from Brazil to the UK, Europe and Australia, covering a wide range of climates and temperature zones. We really wanted to create a resource that covered every type of green roof retrofit and as many professional, technical, legal and stakeholder aspects as possible. The disciplines that have contributed include Building Surveying, Horticultural Science, Civil Engineering, Urban Planning, Architecture, Urbanism, Environmental Sustainability Consultancy, Entomology, Flood & Disaster Prevention Management, and Social Sciences. This is a rich and empowering environment in which to work, and we would like to thank all our contributing authors for their expertise and inputs to the text. This is the first book we are aware of that covers such a breadth of reasons to adopt green roofs from the retrofit perspective, and our aim is to facilitate the retrofit of greater numbers of green roofs as a result.

We also wish to personally thank the staff at Wiley Blackwell, Madeleine Metcalfe and Viktoria Vida for their support and help in delivering the book, and Sarah Cary of British Land for her foreword.

Finally, writing a book always takes time. Without the support and encouragement of family and friends the task would be much harder, so Sara would like to thank Ted, Ruskin, Maureen and Lindsay. Tim would also like to thank his family for all their help and support during the editing and writing process.

Sara Wilkinson and Tim Dixon

Building Resilience in Urban Settlements Through Green Roof Retrofit

Tim Dixon[1] and Sara Wilkinson[2]
[1] University of Reading, UK
[2] UTS, Australia

1.0   Introduction

The 'challenge of achieving sustainable development in the 21st century [will] be won or lost in the world's urban areas' (Newton and Bai, 2008: 4) and a major issue is the contribution that the built environment makes to greenhouse gas (GHG) emissions and global warming. Typically each year 1–2% of new buildings are added to the total stock; it follows that informed decision-making in respect of sustainable adaptation of existing stock is critical to deliver emissions reductions. Within cities, local government authorities are encouraging building adaptation to lower building-related energy consumption and associated GHG emissions. Examples include San Francisco in the USA and Melbourne in Australia. For example, the City of Melbourne aims to retrofit 1200 commercial central business district (CBD) properties before 2020 as part of their strategy to become carbon neutral (Lorenz and Lützkendorf, 2008). Office property contributes around 12% of all Australian GHG emissions and adaptation of this stock is a vital part of the policy (Garnaut, 2008). Whilst Australian cities date from the early 19th century, the concepts of adaptation and evolution of buildings and suburbs are not as well developed or entrenched as in other continents like Europe. However, the issue of the sustainable adaptation of existing stock is a universal problem, which increasing numbers of local and state

Green Roof Retrofit: Building Urban Resilience, First Edition.
Edited by Sara Wilkinson and Tim Dixon.
© 2016 John Wiley & Sons, Ltd. Published 2016 by John Wiley & Sons, Ltd.

governments will endeavour to address within the short to medium term. In most developed countries we now spend more on building adaptation than we do on new construction. Clearly there is a need for greater knowledge and awareness of what happens to commercial buildings over time.

There are a range of definitions for 'urban resilience', and a marked lack of agreement as to what the concept means. However, there is an underlying meaning which covers the ability to bounce back from external shocks, and Meerow's et al's (2016: 39) definition provides a comprehensive and up to date focus: 'Urban resilience refers to the ability of an urban system....to maintain or rapidly return to desired functions in the face of a disturbance, to adapt to change, and to quickly transform systems that limit current of future adaptive capacity'. Green roofs therefore not only offer an important element in developing urban resilience across a range of scales (building, neighbourhood and city), but also in helping create adaptive capacity to deal with future environmental disturbances, both of which are key themes explored throughout this book.

This book is intended to make a significant contribution to our understanding of best practice in sustainable adaptations to existing commercial buildings in respect of green roof retrofit by offering new knowledge-based theoretical and practical insights, and models grounded in results of empirical research conducted within eight collaborative construction project team settings in Australia, the UK and Brazil (see Section 1.6 below). The results clearly demonstrate that the new models can assist with informed decision-making in adaptations that challenge some of the prevailing solutions based on empirical approaches, which do not appreciate and accommodate the sustainability dimension. Hence, the studies collectively offer guidance towards a balanced approach to decision-making in respect of green roof retrofit that incorporates sustainable and optimal approaches towards effective management of sustainable adaptation of existing commercial buildings; from strategic policy-making level to individual building level.

1.1   Background and Context: Green Infrastructure

Green infrastructure (GI) is a term used to describe all green and blue spaces in and around our towns and cities, and as such is very much a collective term embracing parks, gardens, agricultural fields, hedges, trees, woodland, green roofs, green walls, rivers and ponds (RTPI, 2013). The concept evolved for thinking in the USA and the 'greenway' movement, which highlighted the importance of using networks to manage green space and achieve multiple aims and objectives (Roe and Mell, 2013). In the North American context, therefore, GI was originally based around conservationist principles, and in Europe it has evolved into a holistic and cross-cutting agenda. In the UK, GI principles have now flowed into a range of policy, practice and guidance for built environment professionals. In England, national planning policy (through the National Planning Policy Framework, NPPF) (Communities and Local Government, 2012) places an emphasis on local planning authorities to plan strategically for networks of green infrastructure, and to take account of the benefits of GI in reducing the risks posed

Table 1.1   Examples of GI assets (TCPA, 2012)

Natural and semi-natural rural and urban green spaces	Including woodland and scrub, grassland (e.g., downland and meadow), heath and moor, wetlands, open and running water, brownfield sites, bare rock habitats (e.g., cliffs and quarries), coasts, beaches and community forests.
Parks and gardens	Urban parks, country and regional parks, formal and private gardens, institutional grounds (e.g., at schools and hospitals).
Amenity green space	Informal recreation spaces, play areas, outdoor sports facilities, housing green spaces, domestic gardens, community gardens, roof gardens, village greens, commons, living roofs and walls, hedges, civic spaces, highway trees and verges.
Allotments, city farms, orchards, suburban and rural farmland	
Cemeteries and churchyards	
Green corridors	Rivers and canals (including their banks), road verges and rail embankments, cycling routes and rights of way.
Sites selected for their substantive nature conservation value	Sites of Special Scientific Interest and Local Sites (Local Wildlife Sites and Local Geological Sites); Nature Reserves (statutory and non-statutory).
Green space designations	Selected for historic significance, beauty, recreation, wildlife or tranquillity.
Archaeological and historic sites	
Functional green space	Such as sustainable drainage schemes (SuDS) and flood storage areas.
Built structures	Green (or living) roofs and walls, bird and bat boxes, roost sites within existing and new-build developments.

by climate change. The NPPF defines GI as: 'a network of multi-functional green space, urban and rural, which is capable of delivering a wide range of environmental and quality of life benefits for local communities' (Communities and Local Government, 2012: 52). Similarly, the UK's natural environment white paper (HM Government, 2011) offers explicit support for green infrastructure as an effective tool in managing environmental risks such as flooding and heatwaves.

GI is seen very much as a multi-functional asset therefore and so relates to making the best use of land to provide a range of valuable goods and services (see Table 1.1). GI is also underpinned by the concept of 'ecosystem services', which are provided by the range of GI assets. Work by the UK National Ecosystems Assessment, for example, includes the following as key ecosystem services:

■ Supporting services – those necessary for all other ecosystem services such as soil formation and photosynthesis.

- Provisioning services – such as food, fibre and fuel.
- Regulating services – including air quality and climate.
- Cultural services – such as recreational activities and wellbeing, aesthetic values and sense of place.

By thinking in this way about assets and services, it requires us to think more closely about the overall costs and benefits of GI as a service-producing infrastructure (UKGBC, 2015). One of the key attractions of GI is its multi-functionality, or its ability to perform several functions and provide several benefits on the same spatial area (EC, 2012). These functions can be environmental, such as conserving biodiversity or adapting to climate change, social, such as providing water drainage or green space, and economic, such as jobs creation or increasing property prices for owners.

As the European Commission (EC, 2012) suggests, a good example of this multi-functionality is provided by the urban GI of a green roof, which reduces stormwater runoff and the pollutant load of the water, but also helps reduce the urban heat effect, improves the insulation of the building and provides increased biodiversity habitat for a range of species. Thus it is this multi-functionality of GI that sets it apart from the majority of its 'grey' counterparts, which tend to be designed to perform one function, such as transport or drainage without contributing to the broader environmental, social and economic context (Naumann *et al.*, 2011; EC, 2012). In this way GI has the potential to offer 'no regrets' solutions by dealing with a range of important problems and producing the maximum number of cost-effective benefits.

GI has a wide range of health and wellbeing and environmental benefits, through improved mental wellbeing and better physical activity, as well as reduced exposure to pollution and high urban temperatures (POST, 2013). Although in the UK some local authorities (such as Birmingham, London, Manchester and Plymouth) have developed GI strategies, this is variable, and with the exception of SuDS, new GI is not *required* by national legislation. In Australia, the adoption of GI is at state and city level and varies between states and cities. Plans and strategies have been made and adopted, only to be amended and moved to other agencies. As such, no coherent national policy exists currently.

1.1.1   Green Roofs

Green roofs are an important and growing element of GI. Green roofs have existed throughout history. Some of the earliest examples include the Hanging Gardens of Babylon in 500BC (Figure 1.1), the ziggurats of Mesopotamia and early Roman architecture (Berardi *et al.*, 2014). Early Viking housing and mediaeval buildings also employed green roofs, with the technique also popular during the settling of the American west and in the vernacular tradition of Scandinavia. During the 20th century Le Corbusier also included them in his five points of modern architecture before the technology gained a real foothold in Germany (from the 1880s), then latterly in France and Switzerland (Magill *et al.*, 2011; Berardi *et al.*, 2014). In comparison, the UK is a relatively recent innovator in green roofs (although the

Figure 1.1   The mythical Hanging Gardens of Babylon.
Source: Wikimedia.

technology was used to camouflage airfield buildings during World War II)
with some good examples in London (St James Tube Station), Manchester
(Metropolitan University), Edinburgh (Royal Bank of Scotland) and Cardiff
(Interpretation Centre).

1.2   Extensive and Intensive Systems

Green roofs (also known as vegetation or living roofs) are an example of
a 'no regrets' adaptation measure that can serve multiple societal goals
(Mees *et al.*, 2013). For example, they can offer a number of improved
public ecosystem services (or benefits), such as increased biodiversity,
improved air quality and mitigation of the urban heat island effect, as well
as having the ability to harvest rainwater and reduce surface runoff.
Similarly, they offer additional private benefits to property owners through
improved energy savings, thermal comfort and aesthetics, and can potentially increase property values.

1.3   Valuing Green Infrastructure and Wider Economic Benefits

There are clearly a range of benefits that green infrastructure can bring to
bear in adapting to, and mitigating for, climate change. Often these may be
indirect, through reduced flooding risk, which can increase property values

Table 1.2   Potential benefits of green infrastructure in a retail centre (NRDC, 2013)

Green infrastructure improvements	40,000 sq. ft green roof with 90% green coverage 50 strategically planted medium-sized trees Bioswales and rain gardens that manage an inch of runoff from 2000 sq. ft adjacent impervious area 72,000 sq. ft permeable pavement parking lot Cisterns to capture runoff from 5000 sq. ft of roof area and use for irrigation
Building assumptions	Area: 40,000 sq. ft One storey with 40,000 sq. ft roof Lot area: 128,000 sq. ft Permeable area: 5000 sq. ft (covered in turf) Number of storeys: 15 Annual rent: $17 per sq. ft Annual retail sales: $2.182m per store
Potential benefits	Energy savings (reduced demand for heating/cooling): $3560 p.a. Avoided costs for conventional roof replacement: $607,750 NPV over 40 years Tax credit: $100,000 for installation Increased retail sales: $1.2m p.a. Stormwater fee reduction: $14,020 p.a. (with projected 6% increase) Total benefits (over 40 years) > $24,202,000
Non-quantified benefits	Water conservation (increase in net benefits) Increased property value (significant increase in net benefits) Reduced infrastructure costs (possible increase) Reduced crime (possible increase) Improved health and employee satisfaction (increase in net benefits) Reduced flooding costs (uncertain impacts)

(Molla, 2015), or perhaps contributing to, for example, a higher sustainability assessment rating through BREAAM[1] or LEED[2] (Berardi *et al.*, 2014). Perhaps key to understanding how cities could create real change in the built environment to bring about more sustainable outcomes is the commercial property sector, comprising offices, retail and industrial properties. Theoretically, at least, GI (including green roofs) could help increase property values, sales, save energy and increase workplace productivity. Research by NDRC (2013) highlights how, in an office building, the total present value of benefits can approach $2m and in a retail centre, $24m (with $23m of this in increased sales). In the case of the retail centre, present value benefits were calculated over a 40-year period using a 6% discount rate, and projected inflationary rates with the location assumed as being Philadelphia (Table 1.2).

GI can, in a general sense, also reduce lifecycle costs associated with private property improvements. Green roofs do not need to be replaced as

---

[1] Building Research Establishment Environmental Assessment Methodology.
[2] Leadership in Energy and Environmental Design.

frequently as conventional roofs – they are typically considered to have a life expectancy of at least 40 years, compared with 20 years for a conventional roof. For example, in a midsize retail building (with a 40,000 sq. ft roof), a green roof could avoid a net present value of over $600,000 in roof replacement costs over 40 years; a medium-sized office building, with a roof half that size, could save over $270,000. In some instances, green roofs can also reduce air conditioning system capital costs by allowing for use of a smaller heating, ventilation and air conditioning (HVAC) system.

1.4   Measures of Greenness in Cities and the Growing Market for Green Roofs

The Inter-American Development Bank (2014) suggest that Latin American and Caribbean cities need to measure and benchmark the amount of green space within their boundaries. A key indicator is suggested as being the amount of green space (in hectares) per 100,000 inhabitants, with a green rating as >50 ha, orange as 20–50 ha and red as <20 ha. Similarly, the World Health Organisation (WHO) has suggested that every city should have a minimum of 9 m² of green space per person. An 'optimal' amount would sit between 10 and 15 m² per person. Indeed, one of the greenest cities in the world is thought to be Curitiba in Brazil, with 52 m² per person, followed by Rotterdam and New York (Karayannis, 2014).

This increasing focus on green space and its role within a specific measure of urban sustainability has come at a time when there has also been an increasing focus on how cities can become more self-sufficient in terms of food production. Urban agriculture, which focuses on the development of localised food systems within and close to urban areas, has been a frequent feature of sustainable thinking in many cities (Hui, 2011). This is not surprising, given that cities occupy only 2% of the global land surface but consume 75% of the world's resources (Giradet, 2008), although by the same token cities can also be relatively efficient in terms of per capita consumption and emissions. There are many examples of what has been termed 'zero acreage farming' (Z farming), which implies the non-use of land/acreage, and which is a subset of the wider term 'urban agriculture' (Specht *et al.*, 2013; Thomaier *et al.*, 2014). Examples include open rooftop farms, rooftop greenhouses, productive façades and indoor farming. Clearly, green roofs which produce food are a key example of this growing phenomenon.

1.5   A Growing Global Market for Green Roofs

In contrast to other markets such as photovoltaics (PVs) or biofuels, the growth of green roofs and green walls (building-integrated vegetation, BIV) is often driven by city-level actions rather than national policies. Green roofs tend therefore to be driven by building code requirements and mandates or financial incentives (or both).

Previous estimates (Ranade, 2013) suggest that the green roof market globally will be $7bn, comprising a $2bn market for suppliers of polymetric materials and the balance for vegetation, installation and operations. This reflects falling costs, and also the use of incentives and regulation. By 2017, costs for green roof installation are expected to be cut by 28%, from an average of $38 per sq. ft in 2012 to $23 per sq. ft in 2017. Green wall growth is expected to be $680m by 2017. Europe has led the growth of the green roof market over the last 20 years: for example, Germany has 86 million m² of green roofs out of a total of 104 million m² and already 10% of flat roofs are green. Similar growth levels have occurred in Switzerland, where for example in Basel 70% of its green roof target has been met. Despite this, there is considerable opportunity for green roof growth in other European cities, such as London and Copenhagen. Wilkinson and Reed (2009) estimated that 15% of commercial office roofs in the Melbourne CBD could be retrofitted as green roofs. Despite this growth, the sector faces key challenges. Generally speaking, most green roofs globally have used sedum or drought-friendly irrigation, but green thinking is moving towards greater diversity in species – with payback periods of 30 years.

1.6   Overview of the Structure of the Book

As this chapter and the book as a whole emphasises, roofs can fulfil a multitude of objectives: attracting biodiversity, improving thermal performance, attenuating stormwater runoff, mitigating the urban heat island, providing space for urban food production, providing space for social interaction and engagement, and possibly space for the reintroduction of endangered species of flora and fauna. In most climates, therefore, green roofs can make a positive contribution to building resilience to climate change and help to arrest the speed of that change.

Furthermore, in addition to the primary reason for the retrofit, other benefits co-exist. For example, a green roof retrofit in northern Europe for improving thermal performance and saving energy not only results in less GHG emissions but also attracts biodiversity, reduces stormwater runoff, mitigates the urban heat island, and could provide space for the reintroduction of endangered species of local flora and fauna. Where access is provided, the roof could also provide space for urban food production and/or space for social interaction and engagement. These multiple benefits make it an attractive option.

In Chapter 2, structural issues are taken into account by Renato Castiglia Feitosa and Sara Wilkinson. Retrofit of the existing stock of buildings is vital, as only 1–2% is added annually to the total stock of buildings, and around 87% of the buildings that we will have by 2050 are already built (Kelly, 2009). With regard to green roofs, the overriding issue is one of structural capacity to accommodate the additional loads that a retrofit brings. This chapter considers the technical and engineering considerations that stakeholders need to consider when evaluating green roof retrofit potential. For example, existing structure, load-bearing capacity, access, power and water supply, orientation, exposure to sunlight and overshadowing, and occupational health and safety. In short, how to determine what type of green roof is suited to the structure.

Issues of urban heat islands are raised in Chapter 3 by Paul Osmond and Matthias Irger. The global climate change and the urban heat island (UHI) phenomenon – whereby cities absorb and release more heat than the surrounding countryside – carry growing potential to make urban life at particular times and places an exercise in low-grade misery. The mitigating role of urban vegetation and green spaces, reflective materials and strategies for reducing the release of heat from human activities like transport and air conditioning are increasingly well understood. Green roofs have also been widely recognised as playing a part in UHI mitigation. This chapter reviews the literature around the microclimatic effects of green roof retrofitting and presents a model based on detailed remote-sensing data for metropolitan Sydney, Australia. We apply this model to explore the effects of installing extensive green roofs on 100% and 50% of rooftops across the variety of urban form typologies which characterise Sydney's built environment. The results suggest a modest but real reduction in heat island effects.

Thermal performance is the focus of Sara Wilkinson and Renato Castiglia Feitosa in Chapter 4. Green areas have diminished in big cities and with increasing temperatures, deterioration of air quality is a common result. Consequently, there is a rise in air pollution and GHG emissions, the costs of air conditioning, and mortality and heat-related illness. Due to the lack of space in urban areas, green roof retrofit is a feasible alternative to this problem. Green roofs improve the insulating qualities of buildings, attenuating heat exchange through inadequately insulated and poorly sealed roof structures. After a review of the literature, this chapter reports an experiment on two small-scale metal roofs in Sydney (Australia) and Rio de Janeiro (Brazil) to assess the thermal performance of portable green roof modules. In each site, two identical roofs, one covered with modular lightweight trays planted with succulents and the other not, had their internal temperature recorded simultaneously and compared. Green roofs were showed to attenuate housing temperatures, indicating that green roof retrofitting could lower the cooling energy demand considerably.

In Chapter 5, Jessica Lamond, David Proverbs and Sara Wilkinson describe research demonstrating the assessment of whether to retrofit with green roofs as a means of attenuating stormwater runoff. The problem of pluvial flooding in terms of financial costs and the impact on our urban settlements is the starting point for a discussion on the potential of retrofitted green roofs as a mitigating measure. A range of technical specifications for stormwater roofs, and critical issues to consider in retrofit of existing buildings, are evaluated. Theoretical frameworks of the distributed benefits of green roofs are presented, and a methodology to estimate the potential for stormwater attenuation of green roof retrofit at the city-scale level is described in detail. The chapter reports on recent empirical research undertaken in two cities with very different climatic conditions: Melbourne, Australia and Newcastle, UK, at city-scale level. Having examined the city-scale level, a second illustrative case study at an individual building scale outlines stormwater performance and the assessment process in Portland, Oregon. The chapter concludes by describing how the stormwater effectiveness of green roofs may be limited in certain conditions by the availability of suitable buildings and the source of floodwater. A summary of the potential benefits of green roof retrofit for stormwater attenuation is made.

The focus of Chapter 6 is the changes to biodiversity associated with green roof retrofit and based on work by Tanya Latty, an entomologist. Green roof retrofits have the potential to increase urban biodiversity by providing animal habitats within highly urbanised areas. Indeed, many municipalities explicitly list 'benefits to biodiversity' as part of the rationale for building or retrofitting green roofs. But do green roofs actually increase animal biodiversity? Although green roofs can provide food sources for bats and birds, there is little evidence that the presence of green roofs actually increases bird or bat populations; in at least one case, green roofs appear to act as an ecological trap, attracting birds to build nests in habitats that cannot support their offspring. In contrast, green roofs support a wide variety of invertebrate species, but at levels that are usually below those of other urban green spaces such as parks or bushland fragments. Nevertheless, green roofs may play a role in urban conservation by creating corridors through urban areas, effectively connecting otherwise isolated populations. Future retrofits can increase invertebrate biodiversity by providing structurally complex habitats, providing a mixture of pollen and nectar-producing plants, and by using diverse substrates.

Plant survival and green roof installation/maintenance costs will long remain prime considerations in planting choices for green roofs, and this is covered in Chapter 7 by Tijana Blanusa, Madalena Vaz Monteiro, Sarah Kemp and Ross Cameron. If low levels of funding, lack of horticultural knowledge/experience and the need for reduced maintenance limit the options, then developing a roof with succulents and grasses might be a way to introduce some ecosystem benefits. However, in scenarios where a semi-extensive substrate depth can be afforded and an investment in sustainable irrigation (recycled rainwater, greywater) is possible, considering and using a wider range of low-growing perennial species with light-coloured leaves, higher leaf area indices (LAIs) and evapotranspiration (ETp) rates would likely provide more benefits. The total direct cost of roof installation may well be higher in that case but the argument in support of a more diverse plant choice should be linked to the direct and indirect savings and benefits which this planting produces over and above the simple extensive green roof. These benefits include building insulation and temperature reduction, localised air cooling effects, greater rainfall capture, more pollutant capture per square metre, greater biodiversity support, etc.

In Chapter 8, John Blair and Paul Osmond consider the potential for green roof retrofit to provide space for reintroducing or increasing the amount of indigenous or endangered species. The multiple environmental, social and economic benefits of green roofs are increasingly well understood among built environment practitioners and in the broader community. However, the issue of biodiversity protection and conservation of endangered flora in our densifying cities has received much less attention than benefits such as stormwater detention or building energy savings. This chapter provides a brief strategic overview of urban biodiversity conservation before examining the current state of play regarding the application of roof greening in the protection of endangered flora, including the identification of key knowledge gaps. The Eastern Suburbs Banksia Scrub – a threatened plant community indigenous to the coastal zone of Sydney, Australia – is introduced here as the focus for a proposed five-year research programme aimed at evaluating the role of green roofs in the management of this particular community and, it is hoped, helping to address the more general research gaps around roof greening as a viable flora conservation strategy.

Food security is an issue that we need to be conscious of, and in Chapter 9, Sara Wilkinson and Fraser Torpy examine the potential of green roof retrofit for urban food production. Human populations are becoming increasingly urbanised and thus distanced, both physically and psychologically, from the sources of their food. Decentralising food production from remote rural regions to within urban centres will address both the growing sense of disconnect and the growing costs associated with food transport. This chapter describes the social, environmental and economic aspects of local-scale urban food production, as well as setting out typical specifications and considerations in respect of bed systems, with a focus on the health and safety, technical, environmental and economic aspects of larger-scale rooftop food production. Our empirical observations demonstrate that there is great potential in most cities for the expansion of urban rooftop farming, and that many of the traditional barriers to growing food in cities – such as fears over food safety – can be overcome in virtually all situations.

As well as environmental sustainability, green roofs can provide social sustainability. Sumita Ghosh, Ilaria Vanni Accarigi and Angela Giovangeli report on the social aspects of rooftop gardens in Chapter 10. Rooftop gardens have a long history, dating back many centuries. In the contemporary context, the rooftop garden reflects a concern for the natural and built environment in terms of sustainability, community and food production. This chapter explores the social aspects of rooftop gardens by examining mainly two Sydney inner-city rooftop gardens in Australia: the University of Technology Sydney, an educational institution in Ultimo and 107 Projects, a permaculture garden that is part of a multidisciplinary creative space in Redfern. Eight rooftop gardens in different universities from other parts of the world are also considered. Through interviews, sensory ethnography and comparative analysis, this chapter highlights that rooftop gardens in different types of institutional settings revolve around shared interests in growing food as well as a shared ethos in creating community links in the workplace and beyond.

In Chapter 11, Dominique Hes, Christopher Jensen and Lu Aye consider an alternative to green roofs, where thermal performance and a reduction of building-related GHG emissions is the goal; this option is the cool or white roof. Cool roof paint (CRP) is a practical, low-cost and retrofit option for improving the thermal performance where there are significant cooling loads. This chapter looks at their viability in cool-temperate climates, where there is a higher heating load. The chapter presents the results of four experiments investigating a CRP roof retrofit of a 20-year-old metal roof; the extension of this data through modelling to test the sensitivity of CRP to changes in shading, roof pitch, insulation levels, insulation location and building roof-to-surface area ratios; the testing of the CRP against a green roof retrofit; and the benefit of white roofs on electricity production through photovoltaics. There is a benefit to CRPs used in a residential sense in Melbourne, reducing the cooling loads depending on ceiling insulation levels. The research shows that the CRPs are most beneficial for the retrofit of short (high roof area to overall surface area) industrial buildings. Other effective retrofit scenarios are discussed. Compared with CRP retrofits, the green roof reflected less energy back into the external environment and provided an additional reduction in internal temperature of up to 3°C on a hot summer's day (based on the retrofit of a 20-year-old metal roof with insulation of less than 1 R-value). CRP treatments have a valuable role to play in adding to the retrofit options when a green roof may not be appropriate.

In Chapter 12, Sara Wilkinson and Tim Dixon review the preceding chapters and highlight the importance of green roofs in the context of cities, neighbourhoods and individual buildings.

1.7   Conclusion

This chapter has outlined the context in which green roof retrofit can be seen to provide a means for reducing the environmental impact of the built environment on climate change and global warming. The structure of the book has been outlined to show how empirical research in three continents is being developed and implemented to address a range of social, environmental and economic issues related to sustainable development. For many practitioners this is a new area of practice, and the aim of the book is to raise awareness of the primary and related benefits that occur with green roof retrofit, as well as increasing knowledge to reduce risk and increase uptake of the technology.

References

Berardi, U., GhaffarianHoseini, A. H. and GhaffarianHoseini, A. (2014) 'State of the art analysis of the environmental benefits of green roofs', *Applied Energy*, 115, 411–428.

Communities and Local Government (2012) *National Planning Policy Framework*. Communities and Local Government: London.

EC (2012) *The Multifunctionality of Green Infrastructure*. European Commission: Brussels.

Garnaut, R. (2008) *Garnaut Climate Change Review*. Cambridge University Press: Cambridge.

Giradet, H. (2008) *Cities, People, Planet: Urban Development and Climate Change*. John Wiley & Sons: Chichester.

HM Government (2011) *The Natural Choice: Securing the Value of Nature*. HM Government: London.

Hui, S. (2011) 'Green roof urban farming for buildings in high density urban cities', Hainan China World Green Roof Conference, 18–21 March, Hainan, China.

Inter-American Development Bank (2014) *Annex 2: Indicators of the Emerging Sustainable Cities Initiative*. Inter-American Development Bank: Washington D.C.

Karayannis, G. (2014) 'Dissecting ISO 37120: Why shady planning is good for smart cities', available at: smartcitiescouncil.com/article/dissecting-iso-37120-why-shady-planning-good-smart-cities.

Kelly, M. J. (2009) 'Retrofitting the existing UK building stock', *Building Research & Information*, 37(2), 196–200.

Lorenz, D. and Lützkendorf, T. (2008) 'Sustainability in property valuation: theory and practice', *Journal of Property Investment & Finance* 26(6), 482–521.

Magill, J., Midden, K., Groninger, J. and Therrell, M. (2011) *A History and Definition of Green Roof Technology with Recommendations for Future Research*. Research Papers No. 91, available at: opensiuc.lib.siu.edu/gs_rp/91.

Meerow, S., Newell, J., Stults, M. (2016) 'Defining urban resilience: a review', *Landscape and Urban Planning*, 147, 38–49.

Mees, H., Driessen, P., Runhaar, H. and Stamatelos, J. (2013) 'Who governs climate change adaptation? Getting green roofs for stormwater retention off the ground', *Journal of Environmental Planning and Management*, 56(6), 802–825.

Molla, M. (2015) 'The value of urban green infrastructure and its environmental response in urban ecosystem: a literature review', *International Journal of Environmental Sciences*, 4(2), 89–101.

Naumann, S., Davis, M., Kaphengst, T., Pieterse, M. and Ratment, M. (2011) *Design, Implementation & Cost Elements of Green Infrastructure Projects. Final Report to the EU Commission*. Ecologic Institute and GHK Consulting.

NDRC (2013) *The Green Edge: How Commercial Property Investment in Green Infrastructure Creates Value*. National Resources Defence Council: New York.

Newton, P. and Bai, X. M. (2008) 'Transitioning to sustainable urban development'. In Newton, P. (ed.), *Transitions: Pathways Towards Sustainable Urban Development in Australia*. CSIRO Publishing/Springer-Verlag: Berlin; pp. 3–19.

POST (2013) *Urban Green Infrastructure*. PostNote No. 448. POST: London.

Ranade, A. (2013) *Building Integrated Vegetation*. Available at: cityminded.org/building-integrated-vegetation-mitigating-urban-environmental-challenges-with-building-material-technologies-8238.

Roe, M. and Mell, I. (2013) 'Negotiating value and priorities: evaluating the demands of green infrastructure development', *Journal of Environmental Planning and Management*, 56(5), 650–673.

RTPI (2013) *Building on Green Infrastructure in the UK*. Available at: www.rtpi.org.uk/media/499964/rtpi_gi_task_group_briefing_final.pdf.

Specht, K., Siebert, R., Hartmann, I., *et al.* (2014) 'Urban agriculture of the future: an overview of sustainability aspects of food production in and on buildings', *Agriculture and Human Values*, 31, 33–51.

TCPA (2012) *Planning for a Healthy Environment: Good Practice Guidance for Green Infrastructure and Biodiversity*. TCPA: London.

Thomaier, S., Specht, K., Henckel, D., Dierich, A., Siebert, R., Freisinger, U. and Sawicka, M. (2014) 'Farming in and on urban buildings: present practice and specific novelties of zero-acreage farming (ZFarming)', *Renewable Agriculture and Food Systems*, 30(1), 43–54.

UKGBC (2015) *Demystifying Green Infrastructure*. Available at: ww.ukgbc.org/sites/default/files/Demystifying%20Green%20Infrastructure%20report%20FINAL.pdf.

Wilkinson, S. J. and Reed, R. (2009) 'Green roof retrofit potential in the central business district', *Journal of Property Management*, 27(5), 284–301.

Technical and Engineering Issues in Green Roof Retrofit

Sara Wilkinson[1] and Renato Castiglia Feitosa[2]

[1] UTS, Australia
[2] FioCruz, Rio de Janeiro, Brazil

2.0   Introduction

It is necessary to retrofit the existing stock of buildings as only 1–2% is added annually to the total stock of buildings, and the result is that 87% of the buildings we will have by 2050 are already built (Kelly, 2008). However, the overriding issue here is one of structural capacity to accommodate the additional live and dead loads that a retrofit brings. Live loads are loads which move about or change, for example, the people in a building. Dead loads, in contrast, are the intrinsic weight of a structure. This chapter considers the technical and engineering considerations that stakeholders need to consider when evaluating green roof retrofit potential. For example, existing structure, load-bearing capacity, access, power and water supply, orientation, exposure to sunlight and overshadowing, and occupational health and safety. In short, how to determine what type of green roof is suited to the structure.

Using some typical building types, case studies show how to determine whether an existing roof has sufficient load-bearing capacity to support a retrofit green roof. Initially it may be worth considering whether the roof is intended to have people using it regularly and spending extended periods of time there. Equally, does the owner have a preference for a thermal or a biodiversity or a stormwater roof, for example? If so, this will affect the roof design and the depth of substrate, and hence the additional dead loads the original roof will need to support.

2.1   Technical and Engineering Considerations

This first section identifies the key factors to consider when evaluating the green roof retrofit potential of existing buildings. When analysing an existing building to determine its structural and physical suitability for a green roof retrofit, it is necessary to consider the following:

1. roof structure and covering typologies
2. available space
3. structural capacity
4. waterproofing membranes and insulation
5. drainage
6. heritage
7. green roof access
8. other issues
9. how to determine which green roof type is best suited to different structures
10. access for maintenance.

2.2   Roof Structure and Covering Typologies

Roofs can be either pitched or flat, and comprise a variety of impervious coverings described below. Whatever the form of the roof structure and covering, it is essential to undertake a thorough visual inspection to ascertain the condition of the structure and membrane and to identify any building defects. Any defects must be taken into account with retrofit, as if left untreated, they may undermine the integrity and/or lifespan of the green roof. Some defects are minor and superficial and can be repaired in situ, whereas others are more extensive and may involve substantial repairs and additional costs.

2.2.1   Pitched Roof Structures

Pitched roofs are often found on smaller, older and residential buildings. In traditional forms of construction the roof structure is independent of the structural frame (Riley and Cotgrave, 2014) and is usually of modest spans. Another option is for the roof structure to be part of, or integral to, the structural frame – such as a portal frame. This type of construction is typically found in industrial-type buildings. In domestic buildings, the structural material may be timber, or sometimes steel or aluminium in locations such as Queensland, Australia, where termites are an issue, for example. These materials have different physical qualities and age in different ways. For example, timber may be affected by rot, which can weaken the structure and cause deflection (Douglas, 2013). Some metals, however, can corrode and weaken when exposed to moisture or sea breezes. Roof structures, whether they are timber or metal, if covered adequately and if the building remains unaffected by differential settlement, can last for many decades, if not centuries.

Pitches can be as much as 50°, however the maximum degree for retrofitting extensive green roofs is said to be 35° (ZinCo, 2015), although other studies concluded that shallower pitches of 32° were considered maximum (Wilkinson and Reed, 2009). In intensive green roof systems, surfaces must be relatively flat. With pitched roofs, it is necessary to consider the degree of pitch. Where the pitch is too steep, the substrate will move over time and this will be exacerbated in heavy rain. Proprietary systems for pitched roofs do include support brackets, known as 'shear brackets', which are installed to prevent slippage of the substrates. The shear brackets are anchored to the roof substrate and sealed separately. They sit slightly below the surface, so that the vegetation is not visually interrupted. A similar detail is provided at the eaves. Various details are available to accommodate different eaves designs. Where applicable, snow loadings should also be taken into consideration.

Other systems are manufactured from recycled polyethylene (HDPE) and come in small 540 mm square units, which interlock. A benefit of this system is that it is lightweight and speedily erected. With pitched green roofs, irrigation may be integrated for use during dry periods to ensure that erosion does not occur due to plants dying off. Finally, all designs have to take into account that access for maintenance is more challenging.

2.2.2   Pitched Roof Coverings

Profiled metal sheeting is typically provided as a roof covering to pitched metal-framed roofs, and also to residential timber-framed roofs in some locations (Figure 2.1). In some locations, a plastic coating is applied to protect the metal from corrosion (Riley and Cotgrave, 2014). The metal sheets are steel or aluminium and are fixed with self-tapping screws to the

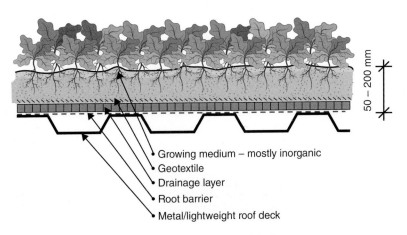

50 – 200 mm

• Growing medium – mostly inorganic
• Geotextile
• Drainage layer
• Root barrier
• Metal/lightweight roof deck

Figure 2.1   Extensive green roof on metal sheet roof deck.
Source: Your Home (2013).

purlins (horizontal beams that span across the rafters). Different proprietary systems are available with various profiles and fixings. For example, the purlins can be 'Z', 'C' or 'M'-shaped sections. In general, these roofs are unable to support people walking across them, so any green roof system has to take this into consideration with regard to planting selection and maintenance access issues. Typically, the metal sheeting systems are designed for a 25-year lifespan. Some proprietary green roof systems are designed to fix onto profiled metal sheet roofing systems (see Figures 2.2 and 2.3). Extensive green roofs are more suited to this form of lightweight roof construction, with the following characteristics:

- Shallow growing medium – typically less than 200 mm.
- Roof structure similar to conventional roof coverings.
- Weight 60–200 kg/m².
- Vegetation generally limited to low, shallow-rooting and groundcover plants that are tolerant of drought, wind exposure and temperature fluctuations.
- Not suitable for general access.
- Relatively economical.
- Some thermal and acoustic insulation benefits.
- Relatively easy to retrofit on existing roofs.
- Low maintenance.

In summary, pitched roofs are usually retrofitted with low-maintenance extensive green roofs. The shear forces, which create a downward movement

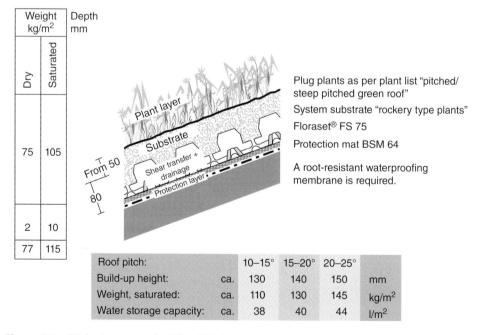

Figure 2.2   Pitched green roofs, 10° to 25° pitches.
Source: ZinCo (2015).

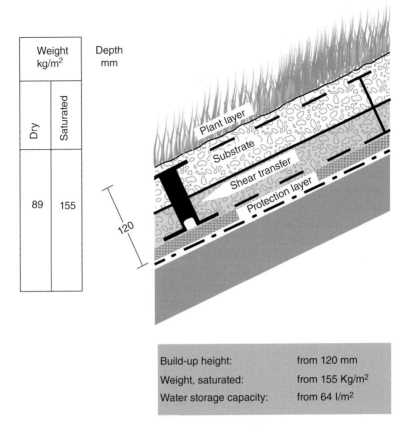

Weight kg/m²		Depth mm
Dry	Saturated	
89	155	120

Build-up height: from 120 mm
Weight, saturated: from 155 Kg/m²
Water storage capacity: from 64 l/m²

Figure 2.3   Steep pitched green roofs, 26° to 35° pitches. *Source*: ZinCo (2015).

of the substrates, are channelled into stable eaves edgings and, where necessary, into additional shear barriers using load-absorbing elements (see Figure 2.3). On account of the faster runoff of rainwater on pitched roofs, the substrate layer is increased and the possibility of additional irrigation should be considered. Furthermore, to prevent erosion on pitched roofs, plants should be applied in higher densities; where steep pitches exist, pre-cultivated vegetation mats are recommended to prevent soil erosion. It is said that the planting selection on pitched roofs is more important because of the runoff issue (ZinCo, 2015). A final consideration on pitched roofs is the orientation of the roof area (north/south depending on hemisphere) and how this might affect vegetation development.

2.2.3   Flat Roof Structures

The term 'flat roof' is a little misleading, as all roofs have some slope or pitch to ensure the effective discharge of rainwater. Flat roofs are defined as those who pitch is less than 10° (Riley and Cotgrave, 2014). In commercial buildings, typically the construction of the roof structure is supported by the building's structural frame and the roof deck, which forms a base on which the roof covering is applied. The roof structure provides support and transfers the live and dead loads to the building structure. In commercial buildings, the structure is either reinforced concrete or steel, although some newer sustainable buildings are using cross-laminated timber frames. In smaller, and in residential buildings, timber-framed decks may also be used.

Where concrete roof decks are provided, they may be cast in situ, or comprise 'pot and beam' (where concrete beams sit between concrete pots with flanges to support the beams), or they may be pre-cast concrete planks. An alternative is to use woodwool slabs to support the covering, or timber or profiled steel sheeting. The profiled metal sheeting can be covered with insulation and timber decking prior to the application of the waterproof membrane (see below), or it may be covered with reinforced concrete with the sheeting acting as permanent shuttering. Each material can carry a different amount of live and dead loads, and this is further influenced by the spacing of the supporting structure (e.g., columns). Live loads are defined as a moving, variable weight added to the dead load or intrinsic weight of a structure, whereas dead loads are defined as a constant load in a structure (such as a building) that is due to the weight of the members, the supported structure, and permanent attachments or accessories.

For both pitched and flat roofs, a structural engineer should be engaged to determine the additional loads that the existing roof structure can support safely. At this point, these estimated loads of the retrofit roof should be considered and then, a decision is made as to whether strengthening works are required. Additional structural works can be expensive and may render the retrofit not viable economically.

2.2.4   Flat Roof Coverings

There are a number of options regarding coverings, such as bituminous felt, or roofing felt, which is built up over multiple layers. This is an economical covering, which has been widely used over many decades. It has a lifespan of typically 20–25 years, depending on the degree of exposure and foot traffic, and other issues such as building movement and differential movement (which is where two or more different materials, in close proximity, move at different rates when exposed to heat and cold) (Douglas, 2013). That is, they expand and contract at different rates and the result is the formation of cracks, splits or tears in adjoining materials. Typically, differential movement is seen at junctions such as parapets (Douglas, 2013). Over recent years, felt coverings have been replaced increasingly with a single-layer covering of polymer-based material, which has a longer lifespan and is more able to cope with differential movement. Another traditional flat roof material is asphalt, which has a long lifespan of up to 40 years in some cases, is very durable and considered a good choice where foot traffic is expected. It is applied in a liquid form and therefore does not have any joints, which makes it a very good form of covering. However, it is expensive, is affected by solar degradation and can creep around up-stands (Riley and Cotgrave, 2104).

In terms of suitability for retrofit, it is necessary to determine the type of covering, its age and condition. Again, an assessment of its remaining life is undertaken to determine whether replacement is needed prior to the green roof retrofit. It is stated that green roofs extend the life of the covering by 100%; that is, a felt roof with a typical lifespan of 25 years will last for 50 years. The lifespan is extended because the roof covering is no longer exposed to the degrading effects of rainfall and water, ultraviolet (UV), sunlight or the effects of temperature changes, cooling at night and getting hot during summer months in daylight periods.

These, then, are the typical roof types, structures and coverings, which are the basis on which a green roof may be retrofitted. The typical construction of a green roof has six layers, on top of the structural roof and covering as follows:

1. Root barrier (polyethylene sheeting, copper or copper compounds in the membrane).
2. Insulation (optional).
3. Drainage layer (synthetic drainage mesh, granular aggregate).
4. Filter fabric (geotextile).
5. Growing medium – also known as planting medium or substrate (manufactured soil, crushed brick or other inorganic material, which may be supplemented with organic material such as coconut fibre or coir).
6. Vegetation (shallow rooted on extensive roofs, deeper rooted on intensive roofs).

2.2.5   Other Roof Designs

Green roofs can be retrofitted to other roof shapes or designs, for example barrel roofs and curved roofs. Here the proprietary systems developed for pitched roofs can be used in many cases. Roof coverings for barrel and curved roof designs tend to be polymer and asphalt applications, which are applied in liquid form, and the comments made above with respect to lifecycle apply here also.

2.2.6   Green Roof Modular Systems

In these systems (Figure 2.4), plants and substrate are gathered in trays or boxes with a water storage system, which provides water to the soil through evaporation, enhancing the plants' survival, even during extended dry periods. The soil is separated from the drainage system by a permeable fabric (Geotextile), which allows water flow but prevents soil passage into the water chamber.

As regards their applicability, modular systems are suited to either pitched or flat roofs. These extensive modular systems enable a reduction

Figure 2.4   Examples of modular systems applied in different types of profiled metal sheeting.

in maintenance and installation costs, since the soil and plants are previously planted offsite in containers made of plastic or any other recycled material, which are then applied directly onto the roof covering – be it existing slabs, profiled metal sheeting or tiles. Additionally, modular systems provide better initial conditions for plant growth than rooftops, due to the possibility of green roof cultivation in plant nurseries (gardens) or greenhouses (in cold climates).

2.3   Available Space

Many rooftops accommodate mechanical equipment, such as air-handling units and plant rooms. When retrofitting a green roof, it is necessary to undertake a survey of the roof space to ascertain the amount of available space for the green roof. Furthermore, some plant rooms vent emissions, which may make the roof, or parts of it, unsuitable for a social amenity space for building users. In this case, however, it may still be possible to install a thermal or stormwater green roof. At this point, it may be worthwhile to determine whether any mechanical rooftop units can be reduced in size or repositioned, as was the case with the UK case study described in this chapter. Where a more extensive retrofit of the building and services is occurring it may be possible, and economic, to reduce the size of the plant and relocate it. This factor will have an impact on the type of green roof that can be retrofitted.

2.4   Structural Capacity

Before designing any green roof system, it is critical to first conduct a structural investigation to determine the building's existing structural load-bearing capacity and to check for any damage. Damage would be in the

Table 2.1   Extensive green roof

Vegetation	Depth (mm)	Weight (kg/m²)
Extensive green roof with sedum, grass, moss, etc.	50–100	10 70–140*
Extensive green roof with soil, plants and small shrubs (below 0.5 m tall)	100–150	15 140–225*

Source: RICS Green Roofs and Green Walls Best Practice Guidance Note, 2015.
*Dunnett and Kingsbury (2008) rain loaded but not including plants.

Table 2.2   Intensive green roof

Vegetation	Depth (mm)	Weight (kg/m²)
Intensive green roof with larger plants and small shrubs (below 1 m tall)	150–200	20 225–300*
Intensive green roof with larger plants and small shrubs (below 3 m tall)	200–400	30 300–600*
Intensive green roof with larger plants and small trees (below 6 m tall)	400–1000	60 600–1500 up to 2600
Intensive green roof with larger plants and small trees (below 10 m tall); one tree weighs more than 150 kg	Over 1000	150 when one tree is 1000 kg/m²

Source: RICS Green Roofs and Green Walls Best Practice Guidance Note, 2015.
*Dunnett and Kingsbury (2008) rain loaded but not including plants.

form of deflection due to overloading of the structure. The building's structural capacity will determine the type of vegetation and substrate depth that can be grown. Also, the age of the building will influence the type of construction methods adopted. If available, original drawings or building information modelling data should be reviewed. This information, the thickness of the structural slab and the span between columns gives an indication of the load-bearing capacity of the roof structure.

Essentially there is a choice to be made between intensive and extensive green roof systems, with each having different load-bearing implications. Intensive green roofs are significantly heavier than extensive green roofs (see Tables 2.1 and 2.2), and are therefore more challenging and expensive to retrofit on existing roofs. If the structural capacity of the building is deemed insufficient to support the proposed green roof system then structural reinforcements may be made, but these can be prohibitively costly and will involve certification from the authorities responsible for building regulations and codes. Tables 2.1 and 2.2 show typical loads/weights for extensive and intensive green roofs, but caution must be exercised when designing a green roof retrofit to consider the structure of the existing building. In all cases, an independent analysis of the design loadings will need to be carried out by a certified structural engineer. Furthermore, as well as the weight of all additional structures, membranes, frames, walls, trellis, cables, mesh, finishes and so on, storm loading must be taken into account and the plants at maturity and soil loads.

Based on a conservative perspective and considering a typical sandy loam, it is estimated that the worst-case situation of loading on the roof would occur at 2000 kg/m³ for soil depths varying from 5 to 100 cm. On this basis, for green roofs with soil depths from 5 to 100 cm, the loading per square metre would be equivalent to 100 and 2000 kg/m², respectively. As the design load of existing roofs varies between 50 and 200 kg/m², it is expected that a structural upgrade is not necessary for soil depths up to 10 cm (Liu, 2011). However, lightweight-substrate materials with depths slightly higher, such as pumice and expanded clay, may reproduce the same loads as a single soil component. As noted by Peck and Kuhn (2003), the 36 cm depth green roof on the new library in Vancouver (Canada) weighs, under saturated conditions, 293 kg/m², and according to the British Columbia Building Code does not require a structural upgrade. Comparatively, the same depth of saturated sandy loam soil weighs 720 kg/m². In most existing buildings, high extra loads are not supported by the structure and thus, structural reinforcements are necessary. This circumstance is leading to an initial trend in the use of extensive systems for retrofits.

2.5   Waterproof Membranes and Insulation

A thorough inspection of the existing roof waterproof membrane is needed to assess its condition before considering retrofitting a green roof. At this point, any damage should be repaired before retrofitting a green roof (Wilkinson *et al.*, 2015). The age and estimated remaining life of the roof membrane is an important consideration. For example, if the roof membrane is in poor condition and is due to be replaced within 2 years or so, it could be worth either replacing the membrane prior to installing the green roof, or deferring installation until the membrane is replaced. Depending on the plant specification, and in consultation with the landscape architect or horticulturalist, a root barrier membrane may be required to protect the membrane from plant roots. This membrane is not required in extensive green roof systems.

Where provided, the existing roof insulation should be checked to ensure it has sufficient compressive strength to support the dead and live loads of the new green roof system. Sometimes insulation is provided on top of the structural slab, where in other cases it can be fixed below the slab. With flat roof construction there are cold decks (where the insulation is placed below the roof deck), warm decks (where insulation is placed over the deck and below the waterproof membrane), and finally an inverted roof (where insulation is placed over the roof deck and the membrane). Clearly, warm and inverted roofs are susceptible to damage to the insulation. A final consideration is that drainage must be designed to ensure water does not get trapped between the existing roof and the new green roof, as this will cause thermal cold spots, which will lead to building defects and a shorter lifespan.

2.6   Drainage

Overall, until the saturation point of the substrate is reached in the green roof, the flow of water entering the drainage system will be slower than if no green roof existed. Pitched roofs drain to gutters fixed to the eaves of the roof. The water is then discharged via drainpipes or downpipes, usually to a below-ground drainage system. In some instances, rainwater may be diverted to rainwater tanks for reuse. The aim is to prevent any materials, planting or substrate entering the drainage system as this may cause a blockage. Where water is able to accumulate, there may be problems with corrosion of metal gutters and downpipes or fixings, which may in turn lead to leaks and potential staining of the building façade if left unrepaired.

On flat roofs, the drainage can be external on the building façade or internal with downpipes located within the building envelope. There is similar potential for blockages of the gutters and downpipes as with the pitched roof design above. Where pipes are located internally, any building defects are often harder to see, especially where pipes are concealed within vertical ducting. By the time a defect, leak or stain is visible, considerable damage to the building structure and fabric may have occurred.

Roof drains are strongly recommended in all types of roof, since the existing domes in these types of drain provide efficient drainage of rainwater and also prevent debris from entering the drainage system.

2.7   Heritage

This needs careful consideration, as the visual impact of historic buildings is of primary importance. In summary, to satisfy the local authorities, heritage buildings must be able to accommodate a green roof without negatively altering the historic character of the building. All jurisdictions have slightly different classifications of heritage and historic buildings, and also allow different levels of intervention. Furthermore, guidelines are published by groups such as the Society for the Protection of Ancient Buildings (SPAB) in the UK, with similar guides existing in other countries. It may be that installations which can be removed easily, that are designed for disassembly or deconstruction, without damage to the original fabric of the building, will be preferable to some planning authorities. Finally, structural considerations are a key factor with heritage buildings that may have been structurally compromised – possibly by age, wear and tear, and/or previous adaptations.

2.8   Green Roof Access

Green roof access must be considered and included in any green roof design. Furthermore, the initial installation will be considerably cheaper if there is good, safe access. If a green roof is intended to be used as an amenity space, then how the space is accessed for this purpose (e.g., via lifts or stairs) needs to be considered. Accessible roof amenity spaces need to meet all relevant access and health and safety legislation, for example additional structures may need to be added to existing parapets. Additional certifications to prove compliance with building regulations and codes may be required in some cases. A chartered building surveyor, building control surveyor or other suitably qualified professional consultant will be able to advise on these aspects.

When considering green roof access, the following three green roof typologies are considered.

Terrace. This is defined as an external covered or uncovered garden space, typically housing vegetation, such as planter boxes that can be accessed internally by maintenance persons or externally by one of the following:
1. a building maintenance (BMU) system;
2. abseiling;
3. a cherry picker (depending on the height from the floor).

Multi-terrace. This is defined as an external covered or uncovered garden space, with a minimum double height, housing vegetation such as planter boxes and trees. Trees can be accessed internally via a monorail and platform system or externally by one of the following:
1. a BMU system;
2. abseiling;
3. a cherry picker (depending on the height from the floor).

Roof. This is defined as a typically uncovered rooftop space comprising a variety of vegetation such as lawns and trees. Access to trees on roof spaces is via a ladder or temporary scaffolding, depending on the height from the floor.

2.8.1   Access for Maintenance

Green roofs require regular monitoring and maintenance; this includes pruning and weed control, plant nutrition, plant installation/replacement, maintenance of supporting structure and waterproofing. As green roofs will likely increase the ongoing maintenance requirements of the roof, additional or improved access should be considered. Green roof access strategies should consider the current or proposed façade access plan and integrate where relevant.

2.8.2   Temporary or Permanent Access Strategies

During the construction or installation of a green roof, there are a number of considerations. For external access of a terrace or multi-terrace system, the maximum reach possible for a maintenance person is limited to 800 mm (via a cherry picker or BMU), whereas rope access enables full access. Where access is required to private property, it is advised that access is written into all tenancy agreements. The installation and removal of trees can be expensive, and the associated costs high, as these works typically require a crane to be hired. Depending on the project scope and design intention, avoiding the use of mature trees is preferred. Building code requirements may apply to the design of planter boxes and trees, particularly when located in close proximity to a balustrade. For example, in Australia AS1657 Fixed Platforms, walkways, stairways and ladders are relevant, and in AS1891 Fall, arrest systems. A minimum width of 600 mm is recommended between balustrade and internal planter boxes for sufficient access.

2.8.3   Maintenance Frequency

When specifying systems and horticulture, consideration of the frequency and costs of maintenance is crucial. For example, to minimise maintenance frequency, surveyors or consultants should identify and specify low-maintenance systems. To estimate the ongoing costs associated with the addition of a green roof system to a building lifecycle, it is recommended that a cost analysis based on data from previous projects is implemented where possible. Another consideration in some cases is the option of integrating green roof access strategies with the current or proposed façade access plan for cost-effective solutions. The planting selection can also impact the amount of maintenance required.

2.9   Other Issues

The orientation of the roof affects the amount of exposure to sun the roof will get, and this affects the type of plants that will flourish there (Wilkinson and Reed, 2009). Added to this, the surveyor also needs to consider any overshadowing from surrounding buildings as this affects access to sunlight for the plants. Finally, the height above ground will affect exposure levels to high winds in particular. Some rooftop environments can be hostile in different seasons, and planting specifications must take this into account (Williams *et al.*, 2010). A checklist for building surveyors to appraise the suitability for green roof retrofit is provided in Appendix 1.

2.10   How to Determine Which Green Roof Type is Best Suited to Different Structures

As previously mentioned, the choice of using either intensive or extensive green roofs will depend on the structural characteristics of the buildings. In most cases the use of extensive systems is imperative, since the existing buildings were not designed to support significant extra loads. Where structural designs consider such loads, intensive green roofs are recommended due to their adequacy for a wide variety of plants, including trees, and their better performance in thermal and runoff aspects. However, it is important to emphasise that this type of green roof is not preferred for pitched roofs.

In general, in terms of costs, setup, structural adequacy and maintenance, extensive green roofs are more indicated. As far as maintenance frequency is concerned, drought-tolerant plants are preferable. The choice of modular systems additionally improves the setup and maintenance aspects, being easily applied to any roof structure and covering. In addition, the need to use containers (trays for planting) is offset by the absence of an anti-root membrane. Table 2.3 summarises green roof types suitable for a range of different structures.

2.11   Illustrative Case Studies

This section uses four cases from different countries to illustrate how an existing building can be retrofitted successfully with a green roof for different purposes. However, it is important to highlight that the green roof design must meet the load-bearing capacity of the roof structure. In concrete structures, for example, such loads cannot be evaluated through a visual inspection, and thus a structural engineer must be consulted. As addressed in Section 2.4, it is expected that green roof soil depths lower than 10 cm will be acceptable for meeting the design loads of most of the roofs.

2.11.1   Australia – Surry Hills Library and Beare Park, Sydney

The City of Sydney intends to reintroduce greenery to homes as part of Sustainable Sydney 2030, where the mission is to make the local area as green as possible. The City of Sydney is committed to increasing the number of high-quality green roofs and walls, where, in April 2014, the city adopted its green roofs and walls policy (City of Sydney, 2013). The two case studies presented are the Surry Hills Library and Beare Park, Elizabeth Bay.

In the Surry Hills Library and Community Centre Building (Figure 2.5), it was intended to improve the air-quality system using the natural filtering properties of plants. The building was completed in 2009, comprises 2497 m², and is three storeys high. In this case, air is naturally cooled under the building, reducing by 50% the need for artificial cooling. The improvement in the air quality is provided when it is drawn in at the top of the atrium, passing through special plants that behave as passive filters. The building is also designed to minimise energy consumption, since the green roof reduces energy consumption due to its insulating properties (City of Sydney, 2013). The soil depth on the extensive green roof is 300 mm and the plant types are a mix of sedges and heath plants. Although it is a public building, the green roof is not accessible to the public. The key driver for sustainability features, including the green roof, was the objectives of Sustainable Sydney 2030 and the desires of the local community. Irrigation has been installed but is not routinely used for maintenance, and the water source is recycled rainwater stored on site. The building won the Best New

Table 2.3   Green roof type best suited to different structures

Characteristic	Notes	Intensive or extensive	Green roof types suited: amenity (A), biodiversity (B), stormwater (S), thermal (T)
Roof structure (flat)	Concrete (if able to support up to 225 kg/m²)	Extensive	B, S, T
Roof structure (flat)	Concrete (if able to support more than 225 kg/m²)	Intensive	A, B, S, T
Roof structure (flat)	Timber (if able to support up to 225 kg/m²)	Extensive	B, S, T
Roof structure (flat)	Timber (if able to support more than 225 kg/m²)	Intensive	A, B, S, T
Roof structure (pitched) 35° and lower	Timber (if able to support up to 225 kg/m²)	Extensive	B, S, T
Roof structure (pitched) 35° and lower	Metal (if able to support up to 225 kg/m²)	Extensive	B, S, T
Roof covering	Profiled metal sheeting (pitched or flat roofs)	Extensive	B, S, T
Roof covering	Roofing tiles (pitched)	N/A	N/A
Roof covering	Bituminous felt	Extensive/ intensive	A, B, S, T
Roof covering	Asphalt	Extensive/ intensive	A, B, S, T
Roof covering	Polymer	Extensive/ intensive	A, B, S, T
Available space	If good	Extensive/ intensive	A, B, S, T
Available space	If not good	Extensive/ intensive	B, S, T
Structural capacity	If good	Extensive/ intensive	A, B, S, T
Structural capacity	If not good	Extensive/ intensive	B, S, T
Waterproofing membranes	If poor condition, consider repair or replacing	N/A	N/A
Waterproofing membranes	If good condition	Extensive/ intensive	A, B, S, T
Drainage	If poor condition, consider repair or replacing	N/A	N/A
Drainage	If good condition	Extensive/ intensive	A, B, S, T
Accessibility	If poor, consider plant selection to avoid maintenance access	Extensive/ intensive	B, S, T
Accessibility	If good	Extensive/ intensive	A, B, S, T
Heritage	If local laws preclude green roof	N/A	N/A

Table 2.3 *(Cont'd)*

Characteristic	Notes	Intensive or extensive	Green roof types suited: amenity (A), biodiversity (B), stormwater (S), thermal (T)
Heritage	If local laws permit, depends on structure type, condition and load-bearing capacity	Extensive/ intensive	A, B, S, T
Access for maintenance	If good condition	Extensive/ intensive	A, B, S, T
Access for maintenance	If poor, consider plant selection to avoid maintenance access	Extensive/ intensive	B, S, T
Green roof access	If good, consider most economic option	Extensive/ intensive	A, B, S, T
Green roof access	If poor, consider plant selection to avoid maintenance access	Extensive/ intensive	B, S, T
Frequency of maintenance	If good	Extensive/ intensive	A, B, S, T
Frequency of maintenance	If poor, consider plant selection to avoid maintenance	Extensive/ intensive	B, S, T
Orientation	If good, consider plant selection	Extensive/ intensive	A, B, S, T
Orientation	If poor, consider plant selection carefully	Extensive/ intensive	A, B, S, T

Figure 2.5 Case study: Surry Hills Library and Community Centre Building, Sydney, Australia.
Source: Wilkinson, 2015.

Figure 2.6   Case study: Beare Park, Elizabeth Bay, Sydney, Australia.
Source: Wilkinson, 2015.

Global Design Award at the 2011 International Architecture Awards in Chicago for public and sustainable design (City of Sydney, 2016).

As shown in Figure 2.6, the second case study comprises a retrofit or an adaptive reuse of a single toilet in Beare Park, Elizabeth Bay, Sydney. The project aimed to refurbish an existing 1950s toilet block, upgrading the facility by making the building more sympathetic to the landscape using a green roof (40 m²) and a green wall (10 m²). The design aims were to make the building more sympathetic to the surrounding landscape through the green roof and walls, to upgrade the facility and improve access and public safety, and to retain as much of the original fabric as possible. The roof works cost $1625/m² when installed in 2007. There is irrigation, but it is rarely used and is sourced from recycled water. The roof was planted out with a variety of succulents and drought-resistant species suited to a shallow soil depth of 100 to 160 mm substrate. The total area covered is 40 m² and the roof has a 1° pitch (Figure 2.7). After 8 years, the green roof is thriving and has full coverage (City of Sydney, 2013).

2.11.2   Brazil

Two case studies are the Village Mall and Canal Saude Building (FioCruz Campus) in Rio de Janeiro. In both examples an extensive modular system was used. The green roof design in the Village Mall (Figure 2.8) comprised an area of 860 m², and had the main purpose of thermal and acoustic insulation. It was developed as a system to meet the load-bearing capacity

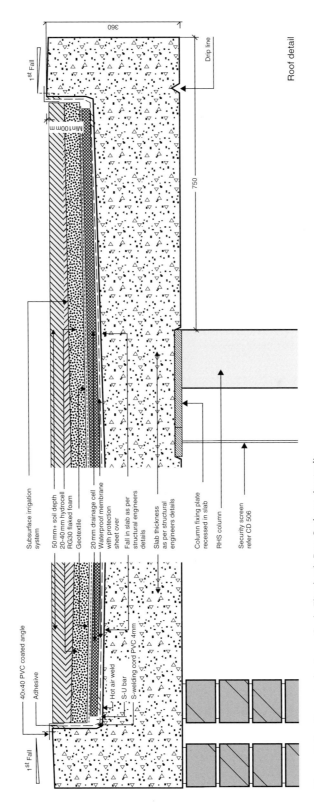

Figure 2.7 Case study: Beare Park, Elizabeth Bay, Sydney, Australia.
Source: City of Sydney (2013).

Roof detail

Drip line

1st Fall

Min 100 mm

360

750

Subsurface irrigation system

50 mm+ soil depth
20–40 mm hydrocell
RG30 flaked foam
Geotextile

20 mm drainage cell
Waterproof membrane with protection sheet over

Fall in slab as per structural engineers details

Slab thickness as per structural engineers details

Column fixing plate recessed in slab

RHS column

Security screen refer CD 506

40x40 PVC coated angle

Adhesive

1st Fall

Hot air weld

S-U bar

S-welding cord PVC 4mm

Figure 2.8   Case study: Village Mall, Rio de Janeiro, Brazil.
Source: Studio Cidade Jardim (2012).

Figure 2.9   Case study: Oswaldo Cruz Foundation (FioCruz), Rio de Janeiro, Brazil.

of the metallic roof underneath, so the load was not higher than 60 kg/m². Thus, the modules were designed with a drainage system that could allow a fast flow of rainwater.

In the Canal Saude Building, located at FioCruz (Oswaldo Cruz Foundation) Campus (Figure 2.9), a modular system composed of alveolar plastic boxes has been used to cover an existing metallic roof. The main reason for retrofitting is solar reflection towards the next building, which has windows facing the existing roof.

This is a pilot design of a low-cost green roof technology, where previously disposable vaccine boxes with 4 cm depth are reused as planting containers. Considering that the planting was carried out by FioCruz itself, this could be called a zero-cost project, where the main goal was to find alternatives to spread green roof use on a city-wide scale.

2.11.3   1214 Queen St West, Toronto, Ontario, Canada

In Toronto, a 540 m² extensive green roof was installed in 2009 at the Gladstone Hotel to reduce heating and cooling costs. The installation of the green roof (Figure 2.10) also remedied the hotel's flooding issues, with an estimated 264,585 litres per annum diverting much of the building's stormwater runoff. The Gladstone Hotel comprises 2787 m², built over four storeys, with a tower on the fifth storey. The hotel was built in 1889 in the Richardsonian Romanesque style and was refurbished in 1913, the 1950s, the late 1980s, and in 2004–2005 after a change in ownership. The new owners inherited many problems with the building, some of which were difficult to solve with conventional construction techniques.

The extensive green roof has a shallow, light growing medium with the landscaping designed to be self-sustaining, requiring minimal maintenance and structural support.

Figure 2.10   Case study: Gladstone Hotel, Toronto, Canada.
Source: Ecoroof (2011).

The total cost of the roof was C$54,845, however C$27,000 was paid as part of the Eco-Roof Incentive Programme (ERIP) funding to encourage greater uptake of green roof technology in the city. The City of Toronto's ERIP provides funds for green or cool roof retrofit projects on existing commercial, industrial and institutional buildings. The programme also provides funding for green roofs on new industrial buildings with a gross floor area of 2000 m² (21,528 sq. ft) or greater, and new institutional and commercial buildings of less than 2000 m². Eligible green roof projects receive $50/m² up to a maximum of C$100,000. Eligible cool roof projects receive $2–5/m² up to a maximum of C$50,000. The cost was C$101/m². The roof took 2 days to install, after a 2-month design and lead-in period. The annual gas saving, based on actual energy consumption, as indicated on pre- and post-installation energy records, is 31,131.5 GJ. This equates to GHG emission reductions of 59 kg of CO_2 equivalent.

2.11.4   107 Cheapside, London, UK

Unilever House is an office headquarters building located in the St Paul's area of the City of London (see Figure 2.11). It was constructed in 1929 prior to the implementation of the St Paul's height restrictions and, as a result, some parts of the roof exceed this. During the 2007 retrofit, the roof was rebuilt to create intensive roofs at Level 8 and Level 9, with a 200 mm deep planter substrate. Of the total roof area of 2614 m², 1825 m² (or 70% of the total area) was greened at a cost of £514,650, or £282/m² (City of

Figure 2.11   Case study: 107 Cheapside, London, UK.
Source: KPF.

London, 2011). The main aim was to provide an amenity space for users. Biodiverse plant species have been planted within the cradle cleaning zones, as these zones are less likely to be disturbed than in the general roof garden. Although no specific species have been targeted for this roof, it is hoped that with the variations in materials, substrate depths and plant species, the roof will support biodiversity (City of London, 2011).

The keys to success for the green roof retrofit were enthusiastic architects (KPF) with prior experience and a desire to return the roofscape to its original profile. The roof had been taken over by mechanical plant. The provision of amenity space was a key issue, and the green roof achieves this with views along the River Thames. The staff restaurant is co-located to provide a social green roof space. It was important to the client for the building to maintain importance and stature as the sustainable European headquarters for the Unilever company (City of London, 2011). The benefits are heavy use by the occupants as an amenity space, with accessibility from three access stairs, as well as opening out from the canteen and meeting rooms. Further, a sloping bed design allows for greater visibility of the planting and creates shelter from the wind.

A key barrier faced was that the existing roof was not as structurally sound as thought, and part of the roof had to be rebuilt to support the green roof. A further challenge was accommodating services around the roof garden plans, encouraging minimal plant on the roof and innovative design. Much of the plant was relocated to the basement level to keep the roof area as clear as possible. A small structure on the roof required planning permission, despite parts of the original roof being higher than the current height restrictions (City of London, 2011).

2.12   Conclusions

This chapter has examined the technical and engineering considerations that stakeholders need to take into account when evaluating green roof retrofit potential. This has included appraising the type and condition of the existing structure, the existing load-bearing capacity, access, power and water supply, orientation, exposure to sunlight and overshadowing, occupational health and safety. Table 2.3 has illustrated how to determine what type of green roof is suited to a given structure.

The illustrative case studies have shown how existing roofs have had sufficient load-bearing capacity to support a retrofitted green roof across a range of climate types and building types. The structural and waterproofing elements of green roofs, properly installed, require little maintenance. As with all aspects of building, good construction detailing reduces the risk of failures and facilitates access for repairs (e.g., in the unlikely event of leaks). Maintenance demands are reduced by integrated irrigation, but a small green wall needs no more tending than more conventional indoor plant arrangements. Larger installations may include programmable and automated watering systems. To date, there is a general preference to retrofit extensive green roofs due to their lighter loads.

References

City of London (2011) *City of London Green Roof Case Studies*. Available at: www.cityoflondon.gov.uk/services/environment-and-planning/planning/heritage-and-design/Documents/Green-roof-case-studies-28Nov11.pdf.

City of Sydney (2013) *Green Roofs and Walls*. Available at: www.cityofsydney.nsw.gov.au/vision/towards-2030/sustainability/greening-the-city/green-roofs-and-walls.

City of Sydney (2016) 'Surry Hills Library crowned a world leader', available at: www.sydneymedia.com.au/4647-surry-hills-library-crowned-a-world-leader/.

Douglas, J. (2013) *Understanding Building Failures*, 4th edn. Routledge: London.

Dunnett, N. and Kingsbury, N. (2008) *Planting Green and Living Walls*, 2nd edn. Timber Press: Portland, OR.

Ecoroof (2011) *Gladstone Hotel*. Available at: www1.toronto.ca/City%20Of%20Toronto/Environment%20and%20Energy/Programs%20for%20Residents/PDFs/Eco-Roof/ecoroof_gladstone.pdf.

Liu, K. (2011) 'Retrofitting existing buildings with green roofs,' in *Construction Canada*. Construction Specifications Canada: Toronto.

Peck, S. and Kuhn, M. (2003) *Design Guidelines for Green Roofs*. Ontario Association of Architects (OAA) and Canada Mortgage and Housing Corporation (CMHC): Ontario.

Riley, M. and Cotgrave, A. (2014) *Construction Technology 2: Industrial and Commercial Building*. Palgrave Macmillan: New York.

Studio Cidade Jardim (2012) *Village Mall – Rio de Janeiro*. Available at: www.studiocidadejardim.com.br/#!Village-Mall-Rio-de-Janeiro/cv53/RoomsListItem0_hvis0iyt667_0.

Williams, N. S., Rayner, J. P. and Raynor, K. J. (2010) 'Green roofs for a wide brown land: opportunities and barriers for rooftop greening in Australia', *Urban Forestry & Urban Greening*, 9(3), 245–251.

Wilkinson, S. J. and Reed, R. 2009. 'Green roof retrofit potential in the central business district', *Journal of Property Management*, 27(5), 284–301.

Wilkinson, S. J., Lamond, J., Proverbs, D., Sharman, L. and Manion, J. (2015) 'Technical considerations and stakeholder awareness in green roof retrofit for stormwater attenuation', *Structural Survey*, 33(1), 33–51.

Your Home (2013) *Green Roofs and Walls*. Available at: www.yourhome.gov.au/sites/prod.yourhome.gov.au/files/pdf/YOURHOME-3-Materials-14-GreenRoofsWalls-(4Dec13).pdf.

Zinco (2015) *Pitched Green Roofs*. Available at: www.zinco-greenroof.com/EN/downloads/pdfs/ZinCo_Pitched_Green_Roofs.pdf.

Green Roof Retrofit and the Urban Heat Island

Paul Osmond and Matthias Irger

UNSW, Sydney, Australia

3.0   Introduction

Global climate change and the UHI phenomenon – whereby cities absorb and release more heat than the surrounding countryside – carry growing potential to make urban life at particular times and places an exercise in low-grade misery (Chindapol *et al.*, 2014). The mitigating or temperature-moderating role of urban vegetation and green spaces (Bowler *et al.*, 2010), reflective materials (Santamouris, 2014) and strategies for reducing the release of heat from human activities like transport and air conditioning are increasingly well understood. Green roofs have also been widely recognised as playing a part in UHI mitigation (Rizwan *et al.*, 2008). This chapter reviews the literature around the microclimatic effects of green roof retrofitting and presents a model based on detailed remote-sensing data for metropolitan Sydney, Australia (Irger, 2014). This model is applied to explore the effects of installing extensive green roofs on 100% and 50% of rooftops across the variety of urban form typologies that characterise Sydney's built environment. The results suggest a modest but real reduction in heat island effects.

3.1   Defining the Urban Heat Island

The notion that there is 'something different' about city air versus country air has been understood since antiquity (e.g., Landsberg, 1981) – air *pollution* is nothing new. The idea that these differences could be extended to

Green Roof Retrofit: Building Urban Resilience, First Edition.
Edited by Sara Wilkinson and Tim Dixon.
© 2016 John Wiley & Sons, Ltd. Published 2016 by John Wiley & Sons, Ltd.

properties such as air *temperature* arguably originated with Luke Howard, Fellow of the British Royal Society, whose pioneering work on the climate of London opened the way for the new science of urban climatology. Howard was the first to document the UHI phenomenon, which in 1820 comprised a four-degree night-time difference in ambient temperature between London and its rural surrounds, and which he attributed to the heat generated by the burning of fuels (Howard, 1833).

Urban climates more generally are distinguished by the balance between the gain of incident shortwave solar radiation and heat losses from long-wave radiation re-radiated from walls, roofs and ground; by convective heat exchange between ground, buildings and atmosphere; and by heat genera-tion within the city itself (Givoni, 1998). The heat island phenomenon is undoubtedly the most intensively studied feature of the urban climate (Souch and Grimmond, 2006). Causative factors (Givoni, 1998; Coutts *et al.*, 2004; Grimmond, 2007) include:

- The lower albedo (reflectivity) and higher heat capacities and conduc-tivities of urban surfaces (roofs, walls, pavements) compared with those of rural surfaces (crops, trees), leading to increased absorption of incom-ing solar radiation, which is re-emitted, reflected and re-absorbed among buildings and pavements.
- The slower rate of radiant cooling (longwave radiation emission) at night as a result of the physical characteristics and configuration of urban form.
- Reduced evapotranspirative cooling from vegetation, soil and water bodies – less incoming solar radiation is dissipated as latent heat, so more goes into sensible heat.
- Nocturnal release of sensible heat stored in building mass during the daytime (night-time air temperature differences between city and coun-try are typically larger than during daylight hours).
- Anthropogenic heat release from urban activities, including industry, transport and space heating and cooling.
- Reduced overall wind speeds (hence reduced heat transport) due to increased friction.

The relative contribution of these causative factors varies between cities. For instance, solar gain will be the dominant influence on diurnal heat island formation during a cloudless day in the tropics, whereas anthropogenic heat release may be the main cause of a nocturnal UHI in a dense, high-rise city centre under a cloudy sky (Mirzaei and Haghighat, 2010).

Three types of heat island are recognised (Voogt, 2004): boundary layer, canopy layer (CLUHI) and surface (SUHI) heat islands. The first two refer to the warming of the urban atmosphere (see Figure 3.1); the last refers to the warming of urban surfaces. The urban canopy layer is the layer of air which extends from ground level to approximately the mean building height (Voogt, 2004). The boundary layer is that part of the atmosphere which interacts directly with the earth's surface – in this case, the 'rough' surface of the city.

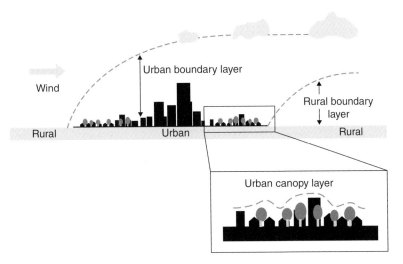

Figure 3.1   Urban boundary layer and canopy layer.
Source: Redrawn from Voogt (2004).

The annual average difference between the ambient temperature of a large city and that of the surrounding countryside, or canopy layer UHI *intensity*, typically averages about 1–3 °C (Oke, 1982), but can peak at 10–12 °C on still winter nights. The difference between urban and rural temperatures (ΔT_{u-r}) is generally greater at higher latitudes. However, the variation from the average may be considerable depending on synoptic conditions – for example, analysis of 19 years of Melbourne UHI data reveals a range from −3.16 °C to +6 °C (Morris and Simmonds, 2000).

3.1.1   UHI Impacts on Environment, Society and Economy

The effects of urban heat islands reach across the 'triple bottom line' – environment, society and economy. Impacts include heat-related deaths, illness and discomfort, worsened air pollution, greater electricity and water consumption and additional GHG emissions, as described below.

An anticipated effect of global warming is an increase in the frequency and intensity of heat waves and associated impacts on human health and wellbeing through thermal stress (Meehl *et al.*, 2001; Patz and Khaliq, 2002); the elevated temperatures associated with the UHI will only exacerbate the dangers to human health from climate change-induced heat waves. Higher night-time temperatures and a decrease in the difference between average minima and maxima – typical heat island phenomena – serve to prolong the stress and delay relief. Many studies have linked heat waves with increased morbidity and mortality, while others have modelled the persistent effects of the UHI and climate change (e.g., Dessai, 2002; Bi *et al.*, 2011). The elderly, the very young and the poor in the rapidly urbanising tropics and subtropics are particularly at risk (Chindapol *et al.*, 2014). One recent observational

project focused on a subtropical 'megacity' – Shanghai. Thirty years of meteorological records, together with mortality data, were analysed to ascertain
the relationship between UHI, heat waves and heat-related excess deaths
(Tan *et al.*, 2010). The results indicate heightened heat-related mortality in
built-up inner areas of the city compared with the suburbs, and the authors
conclude that the UHI is directly responsible, acting to worsen adverse
health effects from exposure to extreme thermal conditions. In Australia, it
has been estimated that heat waves have claimed more lives than any other
natural hazard (Nicholls *et al.*, 2008).

Hard, hot urban surfaces induce convection, which draws up city air
together with its burden of pollutants. Hence another distinctive feature of
the urban climate at city-wide scale, associated with the UHI, is what Piracha
and Marcotullio (2002) term the 'urban dust-dome', within which particulate and gaseous pollutants are trapped. Moreover, the increase in air temperature inherent to the UHI accelerates the rate of formation of secondary
pollutants such as ozone (Sarrat *et al.*, 2006; Fallmann *et al.*, 2014), which
can trigger and/or exacerbate a range of health problems. Finally, urban air
pollution can lead to greater cloud cover as pollutant particles provide
nuclei for condensation – which in turn helps to trap more heat.

Analysis of research from some 30 countries covering the world's main
climate zones showed that for each degree of temperature increase, the
growth in peak electricity load varies between 0.45% and 4.6% (Santamouris
et al., 2014). This rise in peak load both increases the prospect of power
outages and, being largely a consequence of air-conditioning use, generates
additional waste heat. Further, *total* electricity demand increases between 0.5%
and 8.5% per degree of temperature rise. Where fossil fuels are employed to
generate power, this will lead to a similar increment in electricity-related
greenhouse emissions.

Investigation of heat island influences on residential water use in Phoenix,
AZ found that a 1 °F (approximately 0.6 °C) rise in mean minimum temperature resulting from the city's UHI was associated with a 1.7% increase
in water use in single-family homes. A fall of 1 °F in the difference between
mean minimum and maximum temperatures, reflecting warmer nights, saw
a 4% rise in water consumption (Guhathakurta and Gober, 2007). In addition to the immediate financial expense to householders, longer-term economic implications include the cost of building and maintaining additional
water-supply infrastructure.

3.2   Microclimatic Effects of Rooftop Greening

Before examining the UHI mitigation and broader microclimatic effects
of green roofs, it is helpful to review some fundamental concepts of urban
climatology. The *urban canyon* (i.e., the street as defined by the buildings on
either side) is the key 'unit' of analysis, particularly at the micro (<10^2 m)
and local (10^2–10^3 m) scales. Urban canyons are characterised by four main
parameters: mean building height, canyon width, canyon length and orientation (Figure 3.2). The ratio of height to width is known as the aspect ratio.

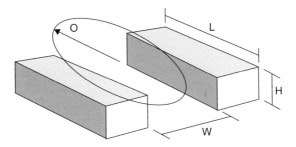

Figure 3.2   Properties of the urban canyon – length, width, height and orientation.

Together, these four geometric properties affect the solar exposure of buildings and open space, wind speed and direction, pollution dispersion and the intensity of heat island effects. In turn, these microclimatic factors affect building energy consumption for heating, cooling and lighting, and associated greenhouse emissions. They also influence outdoor comfort levels and thus physical activity and behaviour patterns, and ultimately the health and wellbeing of citizens.

As building density increases (either over time, or in space as we travel from countryside to city centre), the radiatively active surfaces move upwards from ground plane to rooftops. So in densely built urban environments, roofs are where a considerable amount of absorption, reflection and emission of solar radiation occurs (Bruse and Skinner, 1999). The corollary of urban densification is that there is less space for greening at ground level, although the UHI mitigation benefits of ground-level street trees, parks and gardens are well established (e.g., Bowler *et al.*, 2010). Hence, the option of retrofitting green roofs (and/or walls) becomes an increasingly logical response to moderating the effects of the UHI in densifying urban places.

So what degree of reduction in ambient and surface temperatures are we talking about? Research on UHI mitigation through rooftop greening falls into one or more of field measurement, simulation or remote sensing (Santamouris, 2014). It has expanded significantly since the initial studies of the late 1990s,[1] and the results in terms of projected temperature decreases are generally fairly consistent. Before discussing the numbers though, it is worth noting some general considerations (Alexandri and Jones, 2008), which underpin the effects of green roofs and/or walls on UHI mitigation across a variety of climate types:

- The more solar radiation a roof or wall receives, the greater the decrease in temperature when it is covered with vegetation.
- Where wind speeds inside an urban canyon are low, the wind direction has no significant effect on temperature decreases due to vegetation.
- The wider the canyon, the weaker the effect green roofs and walls have on temperatures.

---

[1] A Google Scholar search on the terms 'urban heat island' plus 'green roof' on 30 August 2015 gave 3020 hits.

- Green walls have a stronger effect than green roofs *within the canyon*.
- Green roofs have a greater effect at roof level and thus *at urban scale*, but predominantly with respect to the *surface* UHI.

Alexandri and Jones (2008) found that if applied to a single urban block, a combination of green roofs and green walls could create a small local 'cool island', or when applied at city scale, achieve more general UHI mitigation benefits. The city-wide UHI is the combined result of heat production and/ or retention at the micro and local scales (see Figure 3.1) (Norton *et al.*, 2014). This highlights an important difference between the extreme variability of urban ambient and surface temperatures when measured at the microscale, and the relative consistency of these properties when averaged across the local neighbourhood or city wide. Anecdotally, this dichotomy has led to misunderstandings among some end-users of urban climatology research, since it is not possible simply to 'scale up' green roof findings at building or block resolution to draw conclusions about UHI temperature reductions at the scale of the whole city. Perhaps unsurprisingly, Stewart (2011) points out that confusion of scales is also a common flaw in UHI research itself. The simplifying assumptions introduced to integrate scale-bound phenomena have been flagged as the main cause of discrepancies in UHI results (Mirzaei and Haghighat, 2010).

While an *individual* green roof can reduce roof surface temperature by 15–45 °C, near-surface air temperature by 2–5 °C and building energy consumption by up to 80% (Peng and Jim, 2013), credible research indicates quite modest city-wide UHI mitigation. For example, widely cited mesoscale (tens of kilometres) simulations identified city-wide cooling of 0.1–0.8 °C from retrofitting 50% of Toronto rooftops (Liu and Bass, 2005), and 0.4–1.1 °C for 100% roof greening in New York (Rosenzweig *et al.*, 2006b). This of course does not discount potentially important *local* cooling effects obtained through neighbourhood-scale green roof retrofitting (e.g., Peng and Jim, 2013; see also Section 3.5.2).

In relation to *vertical* scale, Section 3.1 notes the three main heat island types: surface, canopy layer and boundary layer. Norton *et al.* focus on the role of green infrastructure in mitigating the *surface* heat island, arguing that reduction of high urban surface temperatures represents a useful target because they are easier to measure (e.g., through aerial thermal photography) and compare accurately between areas (Norton *et al.*, 2014). The corresponding decrease in sensible heat flux to the atmosphere can contribute both to reducing ambient air temperature and to UHI mitigation overall. In contrast, a decrease in roof surface temperature, even with 100% rooftop greening, may not translate into a fall in ambient temperature where buildings are tall, as was discovered by Ng *et al.* (2012) in Hong Kong.

Figure 3.3 shows the surface thermal footprint of part of the Sydney suburb of Chatswood, taken at approximately 12 p.m. on 6 August 2012, from an aerial traverse of Sydney (Irger, 2014). Irger's model, explained in Section 3.6, informs the green roof UHI mitigation methodology and calculations presented in this chapter.

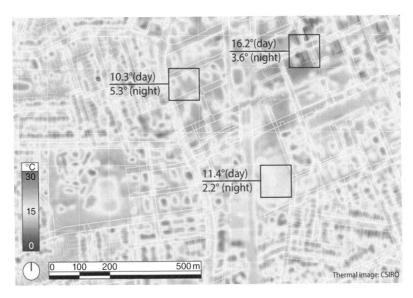

Figure 3.3   Airborne thermal image of the Sydney suburb of Chatswood (Irger, 2014). Indicated temperatures of grid cells show averages of night-time (approximately 12 a.m.) and daytime (approximately 12 p.m.) surface temperatures in degrees Celsius based on imagery obtained 5 August 2012.

3.3   Green Roof Cooling Mechanisms

The above-mentioned review by Santamouris (2014) compared the UHI reduction potential of 'cool' (i.e., reflective) and green roofs[2] (see also Chapter 11). The former are designed to reflect solar energy – their cooling capacity lies in their high albedo, or reflectivity. The mechanisms involved in the UHI mitigation capacity of green roofs are more complex (see Table 3.1 and Figure 3.4). One of the acknowledged benefits of green roofs is their ability to conserve building heating and cooling energy (Alexandri and Jones, 2008), and thereby reduce the amount of waste heat from air conditioning. This is attributable to a combination of insulation (U-value), which is determined by the thermal properties and thickness of the green roof, latent heat release through evapotranspiration and shading by vegetation. Plants also absorb solar energy to photosynthesise, which limits absorption of the radiation by the soil and the roof structure, as well as reflection and re-emission towards the sky and façades of taller buildings nearby. Perhaps counter-intuitively, the energy conservation benefit of green roofs is strongest in poorly insulated buildings, while in modern, well-insulated buildings the contribution is quite modest (Santamouris, 2014).

---

[2] His conclusion was that in sunny climates, reflective roofs are more effective, while in moderate and cold climates, green roofs can offer greater benefits. Of course, this relates to UHI mitigation only; green roofs provide a wider range of co-benefits compared with cool roofs.

Table 3.1   Key green roof properties which affect UHI mitigation

Property	Relationship to UHI mitigation
Ambient temperature	Determines the amount of sensible heat released by green roofs.
Wind speed and turbulence	Determine sensible heat flux – high wind speeds increase both the flux of sensible heat and evapotranspiration.
Solar radiation intensity	Largely determines the surface temperature of the roof, the amount of heat transmitted to the building and evaporation from the roof.
Relative humidity	Interacts with rooftop vegetation – high relative humidity suppresses evapotranspiration and reduces latent heat flux.
Precipitation and irrigation	Increase soil moisture and determine the latent heat flux.
Effective albedo	Determined by type and density of rooftop vegetation – high albedo decreases roof surface temperature and accumulation of heat, which means lower sensible heat fluxes and higher mitigation potential.
Emissivity	Defines ability of roofs to dissipate heat through emission of infrared radiation – higher emissivity means lower surface temperatures and higher mitigation potential.
Leaf area index	The key parameter defining evapotranspirative losses – vegetation must be dense to provide significant cooling.
Roof heat transfer coefficient	Determines the heat transferred to the building through the roof, which affects building cooling load.

Source: Based on Santamouris (2014).

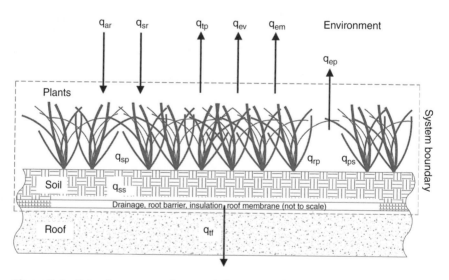

Figure 3.4   Extensive green roof energy balance model.
Source: Adapted from Feng *et al.* (2010).

Table 3.1, adapted from Santamouris (2014), summarises the key physical properties relating green roofs to UHI mitigation.

Fundamentally, the potential contribution of green roofs to UHI mitigation is defined by the gains, losses and storage of energy – the green roof energy balance. A variety of models of varying degrees of complexity have been advanced. Feng *et al.* (2010) propose a 'simple but practical' energy balance model[3] for extensive green roofs, which they have validated in the field. The model may be expressed in the following equation and is illustrated in Figure 3.4:

$$q_{sr} + q_{lr} + q_{cv} + q_{em} + q_{tp} + q_{ep} + q_{sp} + q_{ss} + q_{tf} + q_{ps} + q_{rp} = 0 \qquad (3.1)$$

where:

q_{sr} = heat gain from solar radiation
q_{lr} = heat gain from longwave radiation
q_{cv} = heat transferred by convection
q_{em} = heat loss by emission
q_{tp} = heat loss by transpiration
q_{ep} = heat loss by evaporation
q_{sp} = heat storage by plants
q_{ss} = heat storage by soil
q_{tf} = heat transferred into the building
q_{ps} = solar energy converted by photosynthesi
q_{rp} = heat generation by respiration.

The units are W/m² (Feng *et al.*, 2010).

3.4   Green Roof Retrofit for UHI Mitigation – Defining the Boundaries

As proposed in Section 3.3, the model applied to calculate green roof UHI mitigation potential (i.e., city cooling) is that which was developed through a combination of remote sensing and field measurement by Matthias Irger in his PhD thesis: 'The effect of urban form on urban microclimate' (Irger, 2014). However, the first task is to identify the extent, availability and suitability of roof space for retrofitting, focusing on our case study city, Sydney.

3.4.1   Roof Availability and Suitability

Urban cooling through green roof retrofitting is dependent on three[4] main factors: roof area as a proportion of a city's overall horizontal surface area; the proportion of rooftops available and suitable for greening; and the design of the green roofs themselves (design aspects are briefly canvassed in Section 3.5.2). Roof area as a percentage of urban surface area obviously

---

[3] Precipitation and irrigation inputs are excluded in this model.
[4] The role of building *height* in attenuating cooling effects is raised in Section 3.3 and should not be underestimated, especially in relation to city centres. However, height can be incorporated into building suitability analysis, discussed in this section, so is not considered here as a separate factor.

varies with building density. While rooftops comprise 45% of land surface for mid-Manhattan west, the figure for New York City as a whole is just 18% (Rosenzweig *et al.*, 2006a). Jacobson and Ten Hoeve (2012) have estimated that roofs make up 28% of urban land surface area globally. Using an adapted version of Stewart and Oke's (2012) local climate zone (LCZ) model, Irger (2014) found that in Sydney, roof area varied from more than 70% for the densest zone (**1e**: *compact high rise, mostly paved*) to near zero (**C**: *bush, scrub*). The most common LCZ (**6e**: *open low rise, mostly paved*), which takes in a sizeable part of Sydney suburbia, has a roof coverage of 34%.

An evaluation of buildings in the Melbourne CBD by Wilkinson and Reed (2009) established a set of benchmarks for assessing suitability for green roof retrofit. These criteria included roof pitch (those pitched above 30° and below 2% were rejected), structural criteria (concrete-framed construction was deemed most suitable because minimum structural alterations are required), presence of rooftop plant and equipment (retrofit was rejected where plant/equipment comprised ≥40% of roof area) and overshadowing by taller buildings. The authors found that 39.3% of CBD buildings were overshadowed and 36.3% were partially overshadowed, limiting suitability for green roof retrofit on the basis that there would be insufficient sunlight for planting to flourish. They concluded it was possible that greater potential for retrofitting existed in the suburbs or regional towns, where lower-rise buildings could reduce the amount of overshadowing found in city centres (Wilkinson and Reed, 2009). Wong and Lau, working in subtropical Hong Kong, took a more tolerant approach to overshadowing. Applying 3D modelling to the densely built Mongkok district, they identified that close to 94% of rooftops would receive at least three hours of direct sunlight per day, which they argued was adequate to support plant growth (Wong and Lau, 2013).

On the contrary, if the objective is to maximise UHI mitigation potential, it is those buildings that are more likely to overshadow than be overshadowed which may be less suitable for greening for purposes of lowering ambient temperature, as suggested by the conclusions in Ng *et al.* (2012), introduced in Section 3.3 above. Roof greening in the hot humid tropics may be effective with building heights of less than 10 m (Wong *et al.*, 2003), but an Australian study found that semi-intensive roof gardens modelled at 15 and 24 m height had little cooling influence beyond their immediate environs (Osmond, 2004). This suggests that the building height limit for useful mitigation of the urban canopy heat island (as distinct from the surface heat island) via roof greening may be as modest as three or four storeys. However, the pitfalls of generalising findings from building or block scale to precinct or city scale and vice versa, as mentioned in Section 3.3, are worth re-emphasising.

3.4.2   Design Considerations – Intensive Versus Extensive

Most research on UHI mitigation through roof greening has unsurprisingly focused on extensive green roofs, as building structural and financial considerations preclude broad-scale retrofitting of intensive roof gardens.

Analysis of the thermal insulation performance of an experimental 'sky woodland' in Hong Kong revealed that the 1 m deep substrate was acting as a heat sink; heat stored during the day was dissipated by transforming to sensible and convective heat at night (Jim and Tsang, 2011), suggesting minimal or even negative night-time UHI mitigation.

There has been very little research directly comparing the performance of the two green roof types. However, another Hong Kong project designed to investigate local-scale thermal comfort established that extensive green roofs reduced pedestrian-level air temperature by 0.4–0.7 °C, and intensive roofs by 0.5–1.7 °C, with maximum effects in more open low-rise sites (Peng and Jim, 2013). Building massing and heights reduced the movement of cool air generated by the green roofs. Significantly, the authors' research indicated a reduction in the diurnal duration of high heat stress of 6–9 hours for the extensive scenario, and 9–11 hours for the intensive scenario.

Research such as the above suggests that practical neighbourhood-scale retrofitting could perhaps combine a matrix of mainly extensive green roofs with a scattering of intensive roof gardens, where structural criteria and budgets permit. The latter could potentially even form useful nodes within a rooftop biodiversity network (see Chapter 8).

3.5   Green Roof Retrofit for UHI Mitigation – Developing the Model

As noted above, UHI research includes three distinct methods: fieldwork, numerical modelling and remote sensing. Each of these comes with strengths and weaknesses.

3.5.1   Overview of Methods

Field measurement typically involves assessment of the spatial distribution and intensity of the heat island using a combination of fixed and/or mobile stations. Usually this will require interpolations and approximations, given the inevitable limitations on the number of measurement locations, times and parameters measured (Mirzaei and Haghighat, 2010).

Field measurement is also employed to parameterise simulation models. Numerical modelling approaches can be classified according to scale. Mesoscale climate models applied in city-wide studies may extend over hundreds of square kilometres with a resolution (grid cell size) of 1 km – parameters such as building height and albedo are averaged for each cell (Burian et al., 2004; Masson, 2006). At the other extreme, microscale computational fluid dynamics (CFD) models can simulate flow processes in buildings or outdoor spaces to a resolution of centimetres. For urban climate applications the horizontal extent is usually of the order of a few hundred metres with a resolution of one or two metres. Whatever the scale, these models by definition simplify the complex processes of the UHI; at the microscale, there is the additional issue of establishing realistic boundary conditions to initialise the model (Mirzaei and Haghighat, 2010).

Satellite or aerial remote sensing involves acquisition of surface temperature data through thermal (infrared) imaging. Other sections of the electromagnetic spectrum may be employed to identify the spectral signatures of particular materials, vegetation, etc. Surface temperatures integrate the effects of several radiative and thermodynamic properties, including surface moisture, emissivity, albedo and interactions with the near-surface atmosphere. However, surface UHI differs from the canopy-layer UHI, where wind velocity and turbulence affect ambient air temperature (Mirzaei and Haghighat, 2010). Also, of course, vertical surfaces[5] as well as horizontal surfaces obscured by, for example, vegetation cannot be imaged.

The methodology discussed below combines remote sensing through aerial photogrammetry with mobile (vehicle transect) field measurement.

3.5.2   Modelling Roof Availability and Suitability

Three-dimensional information on buildings and their roof surface properties is a prerequisite for estimating the effect of rooftops on urban temperatures. While data on the height, roof area and slope of individual buildings is rarely readily accessible and is too time consuming to obtain manually for large areas, airborne remote sensing allows rapid morphological and radiative mapping at city-wide scale. Lidar, for instance, can obtain highly accurate 3D information on buildings and vegetation, while thermal and hyper- or multispectral sensors[6] can reveal detailed surface temperature, albedo and materiality data at the microscale.

A lidar system transmits a pulsed laser beam and records reflected signals as a set of points in space, often referred to as point clouds. The lidar point cloud data can be classified into vegetation, buildings and ground surface according to the signature of the return pulse. As lidar registers not only the geographic coordinates but also the altitude above sea level for each recorded point, the height of buildings and vegetation can be derived relative to the ground.

Lidar processing software such as LP360 (QCoherent, 2013) can trace outlines around clusters of similar points to generate building footprints. Roof heights relative to the ground can be derived by subtracting a digital *elevation* model created from points classified as buildings from a digital *terrain* model based on points identified as ground surface. A resolution of multiple points per square metre allows the calculation of individual roof slopes by triangulating the height information of individual points within each building's footprint.

---

[5] Walls may account for 47% of the total surface area in a city's 'urban core' (Ellefsen, 1990/91).

[6] Hyperspectral and multispectral imaging capture reflected electromagnetic radiation across a wide region of the electromagnetic spectrum. The main difference is the number and width of the wavelength bands – multispectral imaging involves fewer and wider bands vs more and narrower for hyperspectral imaging.

The spatial information derived from these remote-sensing techniques can be further analysed in a geographic information system (GIS) environment. This allows the researcher to estimate roof surface availability and suitability for a specific area or spatial unit, derive morphological parameters such as volumetric building density and urban canyon properties (see Figure 3.2), and facilitates automated urban classification into local climate zones (Irger, 2014).

3.5.3   Modelling Thermal Performance

The air and surface-temperature profile in a precinct or street is the result of a range of different interacting physical factors (see Section 3.3). To be able to estimate the mitigating potential of roof greening on canopy layer and surface heat island intensity, we need access to highly detailed spatial information and a comprehensive understanding of the complex interplay among the various factors that influence the urban microclimate in a given location.

With resolutions of up to 0.5 m/pixel, airborne remote thermal sensing is now able to provide surface-temperature mapping suitable for building-scale analysis. In combination with lidar-derived data, this level of detail allows broad-scale thermal assessment of rooftops across a variety of urban areas.

Multiple linear regression (MLR) analysis can quantify the contribution of individual urban form parameters such as roof area per LCZ or per hectare to the average air or surface temperature for the relevant spatial unit. An ordinary least squares MLR model estimates the best fit (correlation) between predicted and recorded variables for a number of observations within a data set. The resulting correlation coefficients approximate the effect of each independent variable on the dependent variable of interest – in this case, air or surface temperature. These coefficients can be expressed in an equation and used to predict the dependent variable for similar locations where the predictors are known.

When working with spatial data it is important to recognise that individual observations are generally affected by those in neighbouring areas (Tobler, 1970), a phenomenon known as spatial autocorrelation. One can imagine that clustering of similar LCZs in a given location could influence the thermal performance of a particular urban setting, for instance. Without controlling for spatial autocorrelation, a regression model becomes unstable and the correlation coefficients become inaccurate. The freely available software GeoDa, which can analyse GIS-based shape files, provides a number of statistical tests to identify the most appropriate model to deal with such spatial interdependencies (Anselin, 2013).

In Irger's research, the spatial error model (SEM) was successfully employed to manage this kind of autocorrelation between multiple variables and improve overall model performance. The SEM introduces the spatial error term λ in a global linear regression equation to improve the correctness of correlation coefficients by removing spatially related errors in individual variables (Anselin, 2003; Ward and Gleditsch, 2008). The model applied in this research can be expressed in the following equation:

$$y_i = \beta_0 + \sum\nolimits_p^{\square} \beta_p x_{ip} + \lambda w_i \xi_i + \varepsilon_i \qquad (3.2)$$

where:

y_i is the dependent variable for spatial units indexed by i
β_0 represents the model *constant* or *intercept*
β_p are the *parameter vectors* or *regression coefficients* for p independent variables
x_{ip} are the independent variables or *predictors*
λ is the *spatial error parameter* indicating the extent of the spatial correlation
w_i represents the *vector of connectivity* indicating the closeness of spatial units
ξ_i is the *spatial component* of the *error term*
ε_i is the *error term* of the regression (Ward and Gleditsch, 2008).

3.6   Model Implementation – Evaluating Sydney's Surface and Canopy-Layer Heat Islands

The above model was developed as part of Matthias Irger's (2014) PhD thesis and successfully applied in a case study of the Sydney metropolitan area. Irger's research analysed the morphology of different urban settings in relation to surface and urban canopy-layer heat island intensity at sub-precinct and street scale. The research centred on the question: How much do individual urban form parameters including volumetric building density, urban canyon geometry and orientation, vegetation content and structure and surface albedo modify overall air and surface temperatures?

High-resolution airborne remote sensing was used to record diurnal SUHI intensity and quantify the above-mentioned range of morphological parameters over an area of approximately $160\,km^2$, from the City of Sydney and Chatswood CBD in the east to the outer western suburbs. The airborne data collection was funded by the Climate Adaptation Research Flagship of the Commonwealth Scientific and Industrial Research Organisation (CSIRO), who commissioned two flights around midnight and noon in August 2012 to capture lidar, thermal and hyperspectral imagery under clear and calm conditions. Two simultaneous automobile transects recorded in-situ measurements of air temperature and relative humidity along the flight path.

Hyperspectral imagery with spectral range from visible light to shortwave infrared were used to derive albedo values for the urban surfaces by averaging the reflectivity of individual spectral bands. The same data were utilised to create a normalised difference vegetation index (NDVI)[7] image to

---

[7] NDVI is an index of vegetation 'greenness', representing photosynthetic activity.

help distinguish between impervious and vegetated ground surfaces. Lidar data were employed to generate roof outlines and building shapes, and to identify surfaces covered by low (<0.5 m), medium (0.5–2 m) and high (>2 m) vegetation.

The case study area was organised in a generic grid of 1 ha squares, which was found to be the smallest spatial unit able to represent distinctly recognisable urban settings. Averages of horizontal surface temperature and albedo were calculated for each grid cell, as well as the areas represented by roofs, trees, shrubs, low vegetation and impervious ground surfaces, the urban canyon aspect ratio and average building height. These parameters enabled the classification of each grid cell into LCZ subgroups as combinations of 'built' and 'natural' types via an automated GIS-based process.

Table 3.2 provides an overview of selected morphological parameters including averages of day and night-time air and surface temperatures for each LCZ (per hectare) as well as roof surface temperatures.

The overwhelming majority (more than 90%) of the case study area consisted of suburbs with low or very low urban densities, namely 'open low rise' (LCZ 6) and 'sparsely built' (LCZ 9) with roof surfaces covering 22–34% and around 7–10%/ha, respectively. These precincts featured largely uniform roof heights averaging 4.2 to 6.7 m (generally one to two storeys).

'Open midrise' (LCZ 5) was the third commonest LCZ, with 1.4% of the case study area and building heights of 11–14 m. 'Open high rise' (LCZ 4) areas with average building heights of more than 40 m were slightly less common and concentrated in city centres. While overall roof coverage is comparable across all 'open' LCZs, the variation of neighbouring roof levels or 'surface roughness' increases with average building height. 'Compact' low or high-rise urban settings with more than 50% roof coverage per hectare were very rare, just 0.1% of the study area.

Comparative analysis of thermal performance illustrated that SUHI intensity varies significantly within short distances even in winter with minimal solar radiation: the difference between average surface temperatures of individual LCZs reached up to 13.7 °C during the day and 7.7 °C at night.

The highest daytime average surface temperatures of around 19 °C were recorded in completely paved large low-rise developments with a high proportion of exposed rooftops (LCZ 8e), while densely forested areas (LCZs A and 9a) were up to 11.5 °C cooler. In general, SUHI intensity was greatest in low-rise suburban developments, and increased with the proportion of impervious ground and roof surfaces, and limited shade due to low building heights and distinct lack of trees.

At night, SUHI intensity is reversed, with the highest average surface temperatures recorded in compact urban settings and areas with dense vegetation, where closely set buildings and extensive tree canopies obstruct night-time cooling. Open and sparsely built low-rise developments with predominantly low plants (LCZ 6b and 9b) featured the coolest night-time surface temperatures.

As expected, roof surface temperatures appeared to be predominantly governed by material-specific thermal properties and the amount of

Table 3.2 LCZ subgroups, characteristic features and temperatures (surface and air)

LCZ subgroups	N	Area (% LCZ/ha)						Mean building height (m)	Mean surface temperature (°C)				Air temperature (°C)	
		Impervious ground (%)	Road (%)	Grass (%)	Shrubs (%)	Trees (%)	Rooftops (%)		LCZ @ night	Rooftops @ night	LCZ @ day	Rooftops @ day	LCZ @ night	LCZ @ day
LCZ 1e: Compact high rise, mostly paved	7	26.0	25.4	3.9	0.3	3.1	57.8	92.9	4.2	3.8	14.0	14.7	NA	NA
LCZ 2e: Compact midrise, mostly paved	9	25.1	21.8	3.0	0.6	7.5	56.5	18.7	4.4	4.1	12.1	12.6	12.3	18.3
LCZ 4e: Open high rise, mostly paved	25	34.1	26.5	11.3	2.0	4.4	35.4	41.5	4.0	3.4	13.0	13.8	12.1	18.4
LCZ 5b: Open midrise with scattered trees	7	11.1	25.5	28.7	2.0	28.7	24.7	11.4	4.5	4.0	12.0	14.5	NA	NA
LCZ 5e: Open midrise, mostly paved	120	32.1	25.6	11.9	1.6	6.3	36.7	14.0	3.8	3.1	13.1	14.0	9.2	18.9
LCZ 6a: Open low rise with dense trees	89	12.9	17.0	3.7	7.3	57.4	26.4	5.5	4.0	3.5	11.9	11.1	9.8	17.5
LCZ 6b: Open low rise with scattered trees	464	20.0	19.0	17.8	11.6	28.3	27.8	4.7	4.5	4.0	12.8	6.8	7.3	18.3
LCZ 6c: Open low rise with shrubs	12	24.8	19.7	32.0	13.9	8.7	22.5	4.2	5.5	5.3	14.4	15.1	4.2	20.1
LCZ 6d: Open low rise with low plants	15	20.6	17.3	42.9	4.6	6.9	22.9	4.6	3.1	2.7	13.1	14.7	NA	NA
LCZ 6e: Open low rise, mostly paved	3022	31.0	24.4	15.2	6.3	11.5	34.2	4.7	4.0	3.5	13.9	10.0	8.6	19.1
LCZ 8a: Large low rise with dense trees	2	12.9	9.5	14.3	8.4	52.5	27.1	5.8	4.7	4.5	12.1	16.1	NA	17.5

LCZ 8b:														
Large low rise with scattered trees	3	14.1	0.1	29.5	1.7	22.0	31.1	7.7	3.6	2.9	11.8	14.4	NA	NA
LCZ 8d:														
Large low rise with low plants	5	16.9	7.0	51.7	1.4	3.2	25.7	4.8	3.8	2.8	12.7	14.8	8.2	18.4
LCZ 8e:														
Large low rise, mostly paved	74	25.8	10.9	14.9	1.3	6.6	49.0	6.7	3.6	2.8	14.5	15.0	7.1	18.7
LCZ 9a:														
Sparsely built with dense trees	191	11.0	14.6	9.0	7.6	63.1	11.7	6.0	4.6	3.9	10.7	8.9	8.8	17.9
LCZ 9b:														
Sparsely built with scattered trees	1057	20.0	19.3	35.3	6.5	24.5	10.2	5.4	4.0	3.5	11.6	8.6	8.6	18.2
LCZ 9c:														
Sparsely built with shrubs	72	24.8	21.1	45.3	17.4	5.7	9.8	4.2	4.6	4.6	11.1	NA	5.0	18.1
LCZ 9d:														
Sparsely built with low plants	604	21.3	16.0	61.4	2.5	4.6	7.1	5.4	3.1	3.1	11.9	6.3	8.3	18.7
LCZ 9e:														
Sparsely built, mostly paved	1225	46.9	26.2	25.1	3.3	8.7	11.5	6.7	3.6	2.9	13.2	10.2	8.3	18.6
LCZ A:														
Dense trees	60	3.4	6.6	4.8	35.4	87.6	3.1	9.6	5.4	5.1	9.9	NA	NA	NA
LCZ B:														
Scattered trees	234	7.6	12.0	45.8	17.6	36.6	2.7	6.6	3.9	4.2	9.6	NA	5.8	18.4
LCZ C:														
Shrubs	13	1.7	11.2	70.8	16.6	6.2	0.9	5.1	2.6	3.7	9.4	9.7	NA	NA
LCZ D:														
Low plants	113	3.0	13.6	87.5	3.3	4.2	1.1	4.6	2.5	3.6	10.3	NA	NA	NA
LCZ E:														
Rock or paved	21	89.4	20.5	3.5	0.9	1.3	3.6	10.4	4.1	3.4	14.5	14.3	NA	NA

overshadowing by tall buildings and trees. As the proportion of roof area increases with rising compactness while vegetation content declines, the influence of roof characteristics on the average surface temperature of LCZs naturally becomes more pronounced.

The application of the above-mentioned SEM (equation (3.2)) allows us to go beyond descriptive trends and estimate the individual contribution of relevant urban form parameters on SUHI intensity, while controlling for situational factors such as the distance to the ocean and the average altitude of the location, as well as the effect of surrounding neighbours. The developed models predict average day and night-time surface temperatures as dependent variables (sT_{Day} and sT_{Night}) and can be expressed in the following equations:

$$sT_{Day} = \beta_0 + \beta_1 A_{VEG\_high} + \beta_2 A_{IMP\_ground} + \beta_3 A_{IMP\_roof} + \beta_4 \alpha_{IMP\_ground} + \beta_5 \alpha_{IMP\_roof}$$
$$+ \beta_6 HD + \beta_7 D_{coast} + \lambda + \varepsilon \qquad (3.3)$$

$$sT_{Night} = \beta_0 + \beta_1 A_{VEG\_high} + \beta_2 A_{IMP\_ground} + \beta_3 A_{IMP\_roof} + \beta_4 \alpha_{IMP\_ground} + \beta_5 \alpha_{IMP\_roof}$$
$$+ \beta_6 HD + \beta_7 ALT + \beta_8 D_{coast} + \beta_9 t_{Night} + \lambda + \varepsilon \qquad (3.4)$$

where:

sT_{Day} and sT_{Night} are the mean day and night-time surface temperatures of LCZs

β_0 represents the model constant

β_n are the correlation coefficients of significant independent variables

A_{VEG_high}, A_{IMP_ground} and A_{IMP_roof} are the percentage fractions of LCZ area covered by high vegetation, impervious ground and impervious roof surfaces, respectively

α_{IMP_ground} and α_{IMP_roof} are the mean albedo values of impervious ground and roof surfaces, respectively

HD is the height-to-distance ratio of buildings

ALT is the altitude in metres above sea level

D_{coast} is the distance to the coast in metres

t_{Night} represents the time since first measurement during the night in seconds

λ is the spatial error term

ε is the error term of the regression.

Based on the regression coefficients for the above equation, Table 3.3 illustrates the magnitude of change in average night and daytime surface temperatures of LCZs caused by the respective variable (°C) with all other factors held constant.

The statistical analysis confirmed that roof surfaces are indeed the most significant single contributor to overall SUHI intensity during the day. While their albedo appeared to be irrelevant, a 10% increase in the area of rooftops as a proportion of the overall surface area was responsible for an increase of almost 0.6 °C in the average daytime surface temperature of a given LCZ. The fact that this is nearly twice as high as the contribution of

Table 3.3 The effect of individual independent variables on night and daytime surface temperature of LCZs (°C)

Variable	Change	Effect on mean surface temperature	
		Night	Day
Area of high vegetation	+10%	↑ +0.13 °C	↓ −0.15 °C
Area of impervious ground surface	+10%	↑ +0.15 °C	↑ +0.32 °C
Area of roofs	**+10%**	↔ **−0.04 °C**	↑ **+0.57 °C**
Albedo of impervious ground surfaces	+0.1	↓ −0.22 °C	↑ +0.18 °C
Albedo of roofs	**+0.1**	↔ **+0.02 °C**	**Insignificant**
Building height to distance (*H/D*) ratio	+0.1	↔ +0.05 °C	↓ −0.15 °C
Altitude	+10 m	↑ +0.16 K	Insignificant
Distance to coast		Insignificant	

impervious ground surfaces indicates that the physical properties of surface materials, such as thermal inertia and emissivity,[8] in combination with the extent of solar exposure are the main drivers for SUHI intensity. Shading by trees and buildings appears to be largely responsible for lowering surface temperatures by 0.15 °C/10% increase in high vegetation and 0.1 in the height-to-distance ratio of buildings, respectively.

At night, roof surfaces had no influence on overall SUHI intensity, while a moderate effect of material-specific thermal properties was noticeable in the rate of surface warming of 0.15 °C/10% increase in impervious ground surfaces. The presence of trees had a similar warming effect due to sky-view reduction and heat trapping, but this was interestingly not the case for volumetric building density, the effect of which was insignificant at night.

3.7 Green Roof Retrofit for UHI Mitigation – Model Implementation

Apart from identifying and quantifying the factors responsible for local climate change, the main benefit of spatial regression modelling is its predictive capability. When the urban parameters for a given area are introduced into equation (3.2), we can simulate the average surface temperature of any urban setting with similar background climate. We can also model scenarios of potential green roof retrofit programmes, which can be compared with the baseline case. Table 3.4 illustrates by how much the average surface temperature of each LCZ would change if buildings were covered 50% and 100% by green roofs.

The above example demonstrates that it is possible to significantly reduce the average surface temperatures of a neighbourhood even in winter through green roof retrofits. As the main factor for SUHI intensity is the area of roofs

---

[8] The speed with which the temperature of an object approaches that of its surroundings, and the efficiency of a surface in emitting thermal energy, respectively.

Table 3.4 Observed versus predicted mean surface temperatures of LCZs (°C) modelled for mitigation scenarios with 50% and 100% extensive green roof retrofit, assuming 0% baseline green roof coverage in the case study area

	Predicted mean surface temperature (°C) of LCZ					
	0% green roofs		50% green roofs		100% green roofs	
LCZ subgroups	@ night	@ day	@ night	@ day	@ night	@ day
LCZ 1e:			+0.1	−1.7	+0.3	−3.3
Compact high rise, mostly paved	4.2	14.0	4.4	12.3	4.5	10.7
LCZ 2e:			+0.1	−1.6	+0.3	−3.2
Compact midrise, mostly paved	4.4	12.1	4.5	10.5	4.6	8.8
LCZ 4e:			+0.1	−1.0	+0.2	−2.0
Open high rise, mostly paved	4.0	13.0	4.1	12.0	4.1	11.0
LCZ 5b:			+0.1	−0.7	+0.1	−1.4
Open midrise with scattered trees	4.5	12.0	4.6	11.3	4.6	10.6
LCZ 5e:			+0.1	−1.0	+0.2	−2.1
Open midrise, mostly paved	3.8	13.1	3.9	12.0	4.0	11.0
LCZ 6a:			+0.1	−0.8	+0.1	−1.5
Open low rise with dense trees	4.0	11.9	4.1	11.2	4.2	10.4
LCZ 6b:			+0.1	−0.8	+0.1	−1.6
Open low rise with scattered trees	4.5	12.8	4.5	12.0	4.6	11.2
LCZ 6c:			+0.1	−0.6	+0.1	−1.3
Open low rise with shrubs	5.5	14.4	5.6	13.8	5.7	13.2
LCZ 6d:			+0.1	−0.7	+0.1	−1.3
Open low rise with low plants	3.1	13.1	3.2	12.4	3.2	11.8
LCZ 6e:			+0.1	−1.0	+0.2	−2.0
Open low rise, mostly paved	4.0	13.9	4.1	12.9	4.2	11.9
LCZ 8a:			0.1	−0.8	+0.1	−1.6
Large low rise with dense trees	4.7	12.1	4.7	11.3	4.8	10.5
LCZ 8b:			0.1	−0.9	+0.1	−1.8
Large low rise with scattered trees	3.6	11.8	3.7	10.9	3.7	10.0
LCZ 8d:			+0.1	−0.7	+0.1	−1.5
Large low rise with low plants	3.8	12.7	3.8	12.0	3.9	11.3
LCZ 8e:			+0.1	−1.4	+0.2	−2.8
Large low rise, mostly paved	3.6	14.5	3.7	13.1	3.8	11.7
LCZ 9a:			0.0	−0.3	0.1	−0.7
Sparsely built with dense trees	4.6	10.7	4.6	10.4	4.6	10.1
LCZ 9b:			0.0	−0.3	0.0	−0.6
Sparsely built with scattered trees	4.0	11.6	4.1	11.3	4.1	11.0
LCZ 9c:			0.0	−0.3	0.0	−0.6
Sparsely built with shrubs	4.6	11.1	4.6	10.8	4.6	10.5
LCZ 9d:			0.0	−0.2	0.0	−0.4
Sparsely built with low plants	3.1	11.9	3.1	11.7	3.1	11.5
LCZ 9e:			0.0	−0.3	0.1	−0.7
Sparsely built, mostly paved	3.6	13.2	3.6	12.8	3.6	12.5

as a proportion of LCZ, the mitigation potential is greatest during the day in compact high and midrise as well as large low-rise developments. With 100% extensive green roof coverage, daytime SUHI intensity in these LCZs would be reduced by about 3°C. Predominantly paved areas would benefit the most, with average surface cooling of 2°C or more, while the presence of trees appears to reduce this effect slightly.

In a scenario where half the conventional roof surfaces are greened, SUHI intensity during the day would still decline between 0.6 and 2°C in most urban settings. At night, however, both scenarios would have a marginal warming effect.

A preliminary street-scale statistical analysis of urban canyons revealed no significant correlation between surface and air temperatures, which could mean that green rooftop retrofits would not necessarily lead to substantial urban microclimate modification in winter, particularly if roof levels were more than 10 m above ground. This is consistent with a detailed analysis of existing simulation studies (Santamouris, 2014), which suggests that 100% green roof retrofitting applied on a city scale may reduce the average ambient temperature between 0.3 and 3°C.

This may be entirely different in summer, when surfaces frequently become more than 40°C hotter than ambient air and consequently contribute significantly more to local urban warming. Considering that the vast majority of urban development outside city centres is made up of buildings 4–7 m high with roof slopes generally less than 30°, the heat mitigation potential of green roof retrofits may be substantial during the warmer months of the year. However, it is important to note that the efficacy of mitigation is related to water availability for efficient photosynthesis and evapotranspiration to extract energy which otherwise would end up as sensible heat.

3.8   Conclusions – Where to from Here?

Thermal, lidar and hyperspectral data from aerial remote sensing were combined with mobile (vehicle transect) field measurements and analysed in a GIS environment using multiple linear regression to support the morphological classification, evaluation and prediction of the thermal performance of urban settings. Our research provides evidence that the specific morphological composition of precincts, in particular the proportion of roof surface per hectare, is responsible for significantly different SUHI intensities at local scale.

The automated LCZ classification comprehensively describes the composition of the actual urban fabric and provides insights into the availability of roof surfaces across the metropolitan region of Sydney.

By analysing observations of urban form indicators in relation to surface temperature, the spatial error regression model permits us to estimate the effect of rooftops on urban microclimate, while allowing for hidden, interdependent relationships between other contributing factors such as urban canyon geometry and orientation, the presence of vegetation and its structure, surface cover and albedo, volumetric building density of precincts, as well as geographical factors such as altitude or proximity to the ocean.

Detailed knowledge of these quantities is a prerequisite for this kind of microscale analysis. Airborne remote-sensing products can support efficient spatial and thermal analysis of rooftops in a city-wide application, while aggregation of manually collected data in individual locations is also possible but time consuming. Once evidence-based models have been developed for a given region, outcomes are transferable to other settlements with similar climate.

The combination of LCZ subgroup classification with spatial regression analysis allowed us to make assumptions about the effect of roof surfaces on overall surface temperature, albeit limited to winter conditions. The next obvious step is to expand this framework to include maximum summer temperatures and verify results in other cities across the country to develop a comprehensive understanding of the potential of green roof retrofit to mitigate local heat phenomena in all climate zones.

While the benefits of green roofs may be greatest in relation to aspects such as stormwater management, the potential for urban cooling may be significant when taking low plants and shrubs as indicator for surface temperatures of green roofs. Roof surface and road corridors are the main areas of interest for the implementation of effective mitigation strategies in existing suburbs most exposed to extreme temperatures.

3.8.1   Limitations of the Research and Opportunities for Further Work

In the absence of empirical data on rooftop vegetation, this study used low ground vegetation (<0.5 m) as a proxy. Given that the majority of roofs in the study area are less than 10 m high, this is not seen as a major source of error, but as with all models, this one is a simplification of reality. Factors such as plant species, substrate depth and seasonal water availability will have a significant impact on the diurnal thermal performance of green roofs and require thorough investigation.

The automobile collection of air temperature measurements was limited to streets and thus not considered representative of the complete LCZ. Further research is also needed to determine the temperature distribution across the air column within the urban canopy layer under maximum summer conditions in order to evaluate the mitigating effect of green roofs on CLUHI intensity, ideally also considering the effects of building façades (including green walls). Indeed, the effect of the *angle* of the greened surface from vertical to horizontal would seem a useful avenue to pursue.

Oke (1982) points out that the most significant meteorological variable governing heat island intensity is wind speed, followed by cloud cover. Hence, another aspect warranting investigation (e.g., via simulation) is the interaction between wind and surface temperature with and without green roofs for different LCZs.

The effect of building height on green roof UHI mitigation potential was flagged in Section 3.3 and remains an area of potential research interest, as does evaluation of the resilience and efficacy of green roofs during dry spells and heat waves. This latter issue raises the question of the relative performance of extensive versus intensive green roofs, including vegetation structure and water storage and retention capacities.

Finally, the *multi-functionality* of green roofs has been emphasised throughout this book, and opportunities for flora and fauna conservation, urban farming and other green roof retrofit benefits – which can co-exist with UHI mitigation – are addressed in other chapters.

References

Alexandri, E. and Jones, P. (2008) 'Temperature decreases in an urban canyon due to green walls and green roofs in diverse climates', *Building and Environment*, 43, 480–493.

Anselin, L. (2003) *GeoDa 0.9 User's Guide*. Spatial Analysis Laboratory, Center for Spatially Integrated Social Sciences, University of Illinois.

Anselin, L. (2013) *GeoDa*. Available at: geodacenter.asu.edu/software.

Bi, P., Pisaniello, D., Hansen, A., et al. (2011) 'The effects of extreme heat on human mortality and morbidity in Australia: implications for public health', *Asia-Pacific Journal of Public Health*, 23, 27S–36S.

Bowler, D. E., Buyung-Ali, L., Knight, T. M. and Pullin, A. S. (2010) 'Urban greening to cool towns and cities: a systematic review of the empirical evidence', *Landscape and Urban Planning*, 97, 147–155.

Bruse, M. and Skinner, C. J. (1999) 'Rooftop greening and local climate: a case study in Melbourne'. 15th International Congress of Biometeorology/International Conference on Urban Climatology, Sydney, pp. 21–25.

Burian, S. J., Brown, M. J., Ching, J., et al. (2004) 'Urban morphological analysis for mesoscale meteorological and dispersion modeling applications: current issues'. Fifth Symposium on the Urban Environment, Vancouver, Canada.

Chindapol, S., Blair, J., Osmond, P., King, S., and Prasad, D. (2014) 'Thermal stress and comfort in elderly people's housing in tropical climates: the need for policy'. World Sustainable Building Conference WSB14, Barcelona.

Coutts, A. M., Berlinger, J., Tapper, N. J. and Cleugh, H. (2004) 'The influence of housing density and urban design on the surface energy balance and local climates of Melbourne Australia and the impact on Melbourne's 2030 Vision'. Fifth Symposium on the Urban Environment, Vancouver, Canada.

Dessai, S. (2002) 'Heat stress and mortality in Lisbon. Part I. Model construction and validation', *International Journal of Biometeorology*, 47, 6–12.

Ellefsen, R. (1990/91) 'Mapping and measuring buildings in the urban canopy boundary layer in ten US cities', *Energy and Buildings*, 15/16, 1025–1049.

Fallmann, J., Emeis, S. and Suppan, P. (2014) 'Modeling of the urban heat island and its effect on air quality using WRF/WRF-Chem – assessment of mitigation strategies for a Central European city'. In Steyn, D. and Mathur, R. (eds), *Air Pollution Modeling and its Application XXIII*. Springer-Verlag: Berlin; pp. 373–377.

Feng, C., Meng, Q. and Zhang, Y. (2010) 'Theoretical and experimental analysis of the energy balance of extensive green roofs', *Energy and buildings*, 42, 959–965.

Givoni, B. (1998) *Climate Considerations in Building and Urban Design*. John Wiley & Sons: Chichester.

Grimmond, S. (2007) 'Urbanization and global environmental change: local effects of urban warming', *Geographical Journal*, 173, 83–88.

Guhathakurta, S. and Gober, P. (2007) 'The impact of the Phoenix urban heat island on residential water use', *Journal of the American Planning Association*, 73, 317–329.

Howard, L. (1833) *Climate of London Deduced from Meteorological Observations*. Harvey Darton: London.

Irger, M. (2014) 'The effect of urban form on urban microclimate'. Faculty of Built Environment, University of New South Wales.

Jacobson, M. Z. and Ten Hoeve, J. E. (2012) 'Effects of urban surfaces and white roofs on global and regional climate', *Journal of Climate*, 25, 1028–1044.

Jim, C. Y. and Tsang, S. W. (2011) 'Biophysical properties and thermal performance of an intensive green roof', *Building and Environment*, 46, 1263–1274.

Landsberg, H. E. (1981) *The Urban Climate*. Academic Press: New York.

Liu, K. and Bass, B. (2005) 'Performance of green roof systems'. National Research Council Canada Report, Toronto, Canada.

Masson, V. (2006) 'Urban surface modeling and the meso-scale impact of cities', *Theoretical and Applied Climatology*, 84, 35–46.

Meehl, G. A., Zwiers, F., Evans, J., Knutson, T., Mearns, L. and Whetton, P. (2001) 'Trends in extreme weather and climate events: issues related to modeling extremes in projections of future climate change', *Bulletin of the American Meteorological Society*, 81, 427–436.

Mirzaei, P. A. and Haghighat, F. (2010) 'Approaches to study urban heat island – abilities and limitations', *Building and Environment*, 45, 2192–2201.

Morris, C. J. G. and Simmonds, I. (2000) 'Associations between varying magnitudes of the urban heat island and the synoptic climatology in Melbourne, Australia', *International Journal of Climatology*, 20, 1931–1954.

Ng, E., Chen, L., Wang, Y. and Yuan, C. (2012) 'A study on the cooling effects of greening in a high-density city: an experience from Hong Kong', *Building and Environment*, 47, 256–271.

Nicholls, N., Skinner, C., Loughnan, M. and Tapper, N. (2008) 'A simple heat alert system for Melbourne', *International Journal of Biometeorology*, 52, 375–384.

Norton, B., Bosomworth, K., Coutts, A., *et al.* (2014) '*Planning for a cooler future: green infrastucture to reduce urban heat*'. Victorian Centre for Climate Change Adaptation Research (VCCCAR): Melbourne.

Oke, T. R. (1982) 'The energetic basis of the urban heat island', *Quarterly Journal of the Royal Meteorological Society*, 108, 1–24.

Osmond, P. (2004) 'Rooftop "greening" as an option for microclimatic amelioration in a high-density building complex'. American Meteorological Society, 5th Conference on the Urban Environment, Vancouver.

Patz, J. A. and Khaliq, M. (2002) 'Global climate change and health: challenges for future practitioners', *Journal of the American Medical Association*, 287, 2283–2284.

Peng, L. L. and Jim, C. Y. (2013) 'Green-roof effects on neighborhood microclimate and human thermal sensation', *Energies*, 6, 598–618.

Piracha, A. L. and Marcotullio, P. J. (2002) 'Urban ecosystem analysis: identifying tools and methods'. UNU/IAS Report, United Nations University Institute of Advanced Studies.

QCoherent (2013) LP360 for ArcGIS.

Rizwan, A. M., Dennis, L. Y. and Chunho, L. I. U. (2008) 'A review on the generation, determination and mitigation of Urban Heat Island', *Journal of Environmental Sciences*, 20, 120–128.

Rosenzweig, C., Solecki, W. and Slosberg, R. (2006a) Mitigating New York City's Heat Island with Urban Forestry, Living Roofs, and Light Surfaces: A Report to the New York State Energy Research and Development Authority.

Rosenzweig, C., Solecki, W. and Slosberg, R. (2006b) 'Mitigating New York City's heat island with urban forestry, living roofs and light surfaces'. American Meteorological Society, 6th Symposium on the Urban Environment, Atlanta, GA.

Santamouris, M. (2014) 'Cooling the cities – a review of reflective and green roof mitigation technologies to fight heat island and improve comfort in urban environments', *Solar Energy*, 103, 682–703.

Santamouris, M., Cartalis, C., Synnefa, A. and Kolokotsa, D. (2014) 'On the impact of urban heat island and global warming on the power demand and electricity consumption of buildings – a review', *Energy and Buildings*, 98, 119–124.

Sarrat, C., Lemonsu, A., Masson, V. and Guedalia, D. (2006) 'Impact of urban heat island on regional atmospheric pollution', *Atmospheric Environment*, 40, 1743–1758.

Souch, C. and Grimmond, S. (2006) 'Applied climatology: urban climate', *Progress in Physical Geography*, 30, 270–279.

Stewart, I. D. (2011) 'A systematic review and scientific critique of methodology in modern urban heat island literature', *International Journal of Climatology*, 31, 200–217.

Stewart, I. D. and Oke, T. R. (2012) 'Local climate zones for urban temperature studies', *Bulletin of the American Meteorological Society*, 93, 1879–1900.

Tan, J., Zheng, Y., Tang, X., *et al.* (2010) 'The urban heat island and its impact on heat waves and human health in Shanghai', *International Journal of Biometeorology*, 54, 75–84.

Tobler, W. (1970) 'A computer movie simulating urban growth in the Detroit region', *Economic Geography*, 46, 234–240.

Voogt, J. A. (2004) 'Urban heat islands: hotter cities', available at: www.actionbio science.org/environment/voogt.html?newwindow=true.

Ward, M. D. and Gleditsch, K. S. (2008) *Spatial Regression Models*. Sage Publications: London.

Wilkinson, S. J. and Reed, R. (2009) 'Green roof retrofit potential in the central business district', *Property Management*, 27, 284–301.

Wong, J. K. W. and Lau, L. S. K. (2013) 'From the "urban heat island" to the "green island"? A preliminary investigation into the potential of retrofitting green roofs in Mongkok district of Hong Kong', *Habitat International*, 39, 25–35.

Wong, N. H., Chen, Y., Ong, C. L. and Sia, A. (2003) 'Investigation of thermal benefits of rooftop garden in the tropical environment', *Building and Environment*, 38, 261–270.

Thermal Performance of Green Roof Retrofit

Sara Wilkinson[1] and Renato Castiglia Feitosa[2]
[1] UTS, Australia
[2] FioCruz, Rio de Janeiro, Brazil

4.0   Introduction

Green areas have decreased considerably in the urban environment due to uncontrolled growth of buildings and roads, resulting in an increase of air temperature and the worsening of air quality. As a result, urban areas have experienced an increase in air temperature, mostly by trapping thermal energy, which leads to much warmer temperatures compared with country areas (Lamond *et al.*, 2014). This is described as the UHI effect, and according to the EPA (2015), the annual mean air temperature of a city can be 1–3°C warmer than the surrounding areas. In the evening, the temperature difference can reach 12°C. Heat islands can increase GHG emissions, the cost of air conditioning, mortality and heat-related illness, and water quality. An alternative to reduce building-related GHG emissions, for cooling or heating environments, is to retrofit buildings with green roofs, which also have other social, economic and environmental benefits.

The social gain is the creation of spaces where people can have more contact with natural aspects. The 'biophilia' effect describes the phenomenon by which humans experience positive feelings due to a connection to the natural environment (Kellert and Wilkinson, 1993). Unfortunately, access to the natural environment is limited and diminishing for many city residents. For instance, it is estimated that there are less than 22 m^2 per resident in Sydney, and that the urban canopy coverage is only about 15.5% (City of Sydney, 2012). The city aims to increase this level of urban greenery, for the health and wellbeing of the community, by 20% before 2020 (Green, 2014), and the application of green roofs would be a way of contributing to this target. Owing to population growth and the lack of space in Rio de Janeiro, the amount of green areas has decreased substantially (Agência Brasil, 2014). No plans have been adopted yet to deal with this problem.

Economically, roof maintenance costs are reduced, since green roofs increase the lifespan of the waterproofing system (Castleton, 2010). There are erroneous perceptions, however, among the practitioner community that green roofs lead to higher maintenance costs – for example clearing blocked drainage outlets (Wilkinson *et al.*, 2013) – which is resulting in less application of green roof technology in buildings than could otherwise occur.

The environmental benefits comprise potential reductions in operational carbon emissions, attenuation in the urban heat island, increases in biodiversity, housing temperature attenuation and reductions in stormwater runoff (Castleton, 2010). An improvement in air quality is provided, since plants remove carbon dioxide and harmful pollutants from the atmosphere. In addition, green roofs provide habitats for insects, birds and reptiles, as shelter, a source of food and water (Williams *et al.*, 2010).

Thermally, green roofs improve the insulating qualities of the building by reducing heat gain or loss through inadequately insulated and poorly sealed roof structures. Some authors have evaluated the role of green roofs' cooling and warming potential in energy savings and the potential for retrofitting, based either on modelling or experimental data (Castleton, 2010; Langston, 2015).

This chapter reports an experiment on two small-scale profiled metal sheet roofs in Sydney (Australia) and Rio de Janeiro (Brazil) to assess thermal performance. Metal roof coverings are fairly common in Brazilian and Australian housing design and have less load-bearing capacity than other coverings. Thus, a lightweight, low-cost, easily installed module is tested. In each city, two identical roofs, one covered with modular lightweight trays planted with succulents and the other not, had their internal temperature recorded simultaneously and compared. Data collection was performed by using thermal data loggers over a summer and autumn season. In this chapter the findings for temperature attenuation and the potential for retrofitting residential stock with lightweight trays planted with succulents are discussed.

4.1   Green Roof Retrofit and Thermal Performance

Many cities have been experiencing rapid urban expansion and/or densification, which contributes to the creation of urban canyons, where heat is trapped between buildings, leading to negative human health impacts and even fatalities during excessively hot days (Oke, 1982; Harlan *et al.*, 2006). Recently, high temperatures have been observed. During February 2014, high-temperature records were registered in Rio de Janeiro (Portal G1, 2014). In the same year, Melbourne experienced four to five days in January with temperatures higher than 45°C, and more than twice the average rate of mortality was experienced. These deaths related to the extreme heat conditions, and were even more intense in the city centre, where heat was trapped between buildings and under tree cover in an urban canyon (ABC, 2014). In a scenario of predicted climate change impacts and an ageing population, these figures look likely to increase. On this basis, the focus for climate change mitigation is through adaptation and sustainable retrofitting of existing buildings based on viable solutions.

Green roofs can be classified as either extensive or intensive systems. According to Berndtsson (2010), in intensive systems soil depths are more than 10 cm, providing for the growth of small plants to trees. In contrast, extensive green roof systems comprise thinner soil layers and lighter vegetation, and thus can be retrofitted to most existing buildings without additional structural strengthening.

One of the points to be highlighted is that the majority of cities worldwide have buildings that can accommodate extra loads. In many countries there is little space available for planting, unless existing rooftops are considered. Stovin (2010) estimated that 40–50% of all horizontal surfaces in cities are rooftops. A viable solution for retrofitting housing must meet load-bearing capacity requirements, which tends to favour a lightweight green roof technology. The extra load applied per square metre to an existing structure is related to the soil depth. Under a conservative estimate, a typical saturated soil density of $2000 \, kg/m^3$ is expected so that a load limit of 100 and $2000 \, kg/m^2$ should be applied for green roof soil depths from 5 to 100 cm, respectively. As the design load of existing roofs varies between 50 and $200 \, kg/m^2$, it is anticipated that soil depths up to 10 cm do not require a structural upgrade (Liu, 2011). However, using lightweight substrate material with slightly greater depths, such as pumice and expanded clay, may reproduce the same loads as a single soil component. As cited by Peck and Kuhn (2003), the 36 cm depth green roof on the new library in Vancouver, B.C., Canada weighs $293 \, kg/m^2$ under saturated conditions, and based on the local building code does not require a structural upgrade. In comparison, the same depth of saturated sandy loam soil weighs $720 \, kg/m^2$.

Green roof applications have been observed worldwide. For instance, 260 green roofs have been created in Toronto from 1 February 2010 to 1 March 2015, comprising a total green roof area of $196,000 \, m^2$. In total, 444 green roofs exist in the City of Toronto (City of Toronto, 2015). Additionally, London, UK presents many examples of living roofs, including at Canary Wharf, Bishops Square, the Laban Centre, Deptford and Offord Street, Islington (Greater London Authority, 2008). In the USA, many communities have been taking action by encouraging or sponsoring green roof projects, and some cities such as Chicago, Portland and Seattle have developed more coordinated programmes and policies to promote green roofs (EPA, 2014). Although green roofs have become a topical subject nowadays, in Scandinavian countries such as Norway there are examples of buildings with green roofs that are hundreds of years old. According to Herman (2003), there were about $13.5 \, km^2$ of existing green roofs in Germany.

In the context of the urban environment as a whole, due to the lower temperatures observed in green roofs there is a lower heat transfer to the air above the roof, which helps to maintain the air at cooler temperatures compared with conventional roofs. According to EPA (2014), studies performed in Chicago (USA) compared summer-time surface temperatures on a green roof with a non-vegetated neighbouring building. The temperature of the conventional roof reached 76°C, whereas the green roof surface temperature ranged from 33°C to 48°C. A similar study performed in Florida observed a difference of 27°C comparing a green roof and an adjacent light-coloured roof surface.

A modelling approach performed for the City of Toronto (Canada) predicted that if green roofs were applied to 50% of the roof surfaces available, this would reduce the temperature of the city between 0.1°C and 0.8°C. Under well-irrigated conditions, these roofs could reduce the temperature further by about 2°C (Liu and Bass, 2005). A similar modelling study performed for New York City modelled a green roof application to all available roofs, and found for the whole city an air temperature reduction of 0.2°C, 2 m above the roof surface, was possible. However, it is important to highlight that temperature reduction is averaged over all times of the day. At three o'clock in the afternoon, the temperature would be 0.4°C cooler.

In addition, green roofs can reduce the energy used to cool and heat buildings. Under wet conditions, they reduce temperature fluctuations by absorbing and storing considerable amounts of heat. During dry periods, green roofs provide an insulating feature, attenuating the heat flux through the roof and reducing energy consumption for cooling or heating environments.

According to a modelling study carried out in Canada (Liu and Bass, 2005), a green roof provided an energy saving of 6% and 10%, respectively, for cooling and heating a one-storey commercial building in Toronto (2980 m^2). This study also pointed out that the energy savings for cooling would be even higher for lower latitudes (Lui and Bass, 2005). As an additional simulation example, considering a building location in Santa Barbara, CA, the cooling savings increased to 10% (Bass et al., 2003). A comparison between a green roof and an adjacent light-coloured roof performed in Florida (USA) showed that the heat flux through the former was more than 40% less than the latter. The reduction in heat flux is estimated to lower summer-time energy consumption of a 1000 m^2 building by 2.0 kWh/day (Cummings et al., 2007). Under winter conditions with external temperatures less than 13°C, the heat flux through the green roof is 50% less than the conventional roof (Sonne, 2006).

In non-insulated buildings, which are common in Rio de Janeiro, Brazil and Sydney, Australia, green roofs can improve the insulating properties and reduce annual energy consumption. According to Castleton (2010), several studies have shown that green roofs act, not only in summer cooling, but also in winter heating reduction. Niachou et al. (2001) showed an annual energy saving potential of green roofs on non-insulated buildings for heating of 45–46% and for cooling of 22–45%. Wong et al. (2003) found an annual energy saving of 10.5% comparing an uninsulated extensive green roof covered in turf with a non-greened uninsulated roof. However, the energy savings occur only on floors near to the roof. Alcazar and Bass (2005) state that, because of the tall nature of the buildings, roofs comprise around 16% of the total building envelope, and the largest reductions in energy consumption were seen in rooms directly below the green roof. Energy savings were found up to three floors below the roof (Alcazar and Bass, 2005).

Green roofs lead to numerous environmental benefits in urban settlements concerning enhanced thermal performance. The decision to retrofit a green roof has multiple variables and should not be evaluated on one variable alone, but on the multiple benefits that are delivered (Wilkinson *et al.*, 2013). For example, a thermal green roof will also attract biodiversity, improve air quality, reduce the urban heat island and attenuate stormwater flow to the drainage system. It may also provide an attractive view for adjoining and overlooking building occupants. Traditional air-conditioning systems can provide thermal comfort, reducing housing temperatures mechanically. However, these systems basically transfer the heat from internal to external environments. As a result, they contribute to an increase in external air temperature as a whole. In the case of thermal load attenuation, green roofs avoid the increase in temperature of internal environments and external surfaces.

Green roofs work in temperature attenuation by shading roof surfaces, increasing thermal insulation and promoting evapotranspiration. Plants reduce the surface temperature below by shading. These cooler surfaces decrease the heat transmission to the building or the re-emission to the atmosphere (EPA, 2014). Evapotranspiration absorbs heat from the air to evaporate water. Owing to shading, insulating properties and evapotranspiration processes, green roof surfaces remain cooler than conventional roofs during summer conditions.

However, barriers to the adoption of retrofitted green roofs include perceptions of structural adequacy, risk of water damage, high installation and maintenance costs, as well as access and security issues (Wilkinson and Reed, 2009). Some locations, such as London, will require thermal insulation against external low temperatures, whereas for other locations, such as Sydney and Rio de Janeiro, the intent will be to reduce heat gain. The ability to meet these demands will depend on the available budget and physical characteristics. Although the technology to design and retrofit green roofs exists, the uptake and demand have not been high because of the lack of governmental incentives and high commercial costs provided by green roof suppliers. Overall, the gains have not been deemed sufficient, and in both cities the existing numbers of residential and commercial green roofs confirm this observation. The City of Sydney adopted the first green roofs and walls policy for Australia in 2014, setting out a commitment to increase the number of high-quality green roofs and walls (City of Sydney, 2015). The policy includes a three-year implementation plan to ensure its understanding, adoption and integration. Sydney currently has 59 green roofs, which serve a variety of purposes, including enhancing thermal performance (City of Sydney, 2012). Rio de Janeiro has not adopted any policy to date.

Many Australian and Brazilian residential buildings have rooftop systems with little or no insulation to offset the high heat gains. Thus, green roofs may become an imperative solution to deal with the increasingly high temperatures experienced during the summer periods.

4.2   Research Methodology

The methodology adopted is based on the employment of simple technologies to mitigate the problems created by increasing urban densification, which exacerbates urban heat islands and contributes to uncomfortably high internal housing temperatures. Many technologies are available to conduct this research. However, in this case, the researchers aimed to use adaptive techniques to minimise initial costs and maintenance costs. Thus, this project used lightweight removable modules of vegetation (rectangular containers) of a low thickness, which enables planting, cultivation and maintenance off-site to be undertaken. This is an exploratory study to assess the thermal performance and feasibility of retrofitting with low-cost, lightweight roofing modules for any type of roof.

The authors evaluated the thermal performance of a green roof retrofit system, which could be widely used in metropolitan areas. At this point, there is a lack of empirical evidence on the performance of green roofs in Australia and South America, with most data coming from the USA and European countries, where climatic conditions are quite different (Mentens et al., 2006).

Succulent plants, such as variegated sedum, *Echeveria glauca* and *Kalanchoe quicksilver* were selected on the basis of their higher drought resistance qualities and a lower risk of fire. Furthermore, these species can develop easily in shallow soils and, therefore, no structural reinforcement of existing roofs is necessary. Additionally, due to the modular characteristics of the planting containers, the modules can be applied directly onto the roof covering, be it existing slabs, profiled metal sheeting or tiles. The modular systems comprise containers with a water storage system, which provides water to the soil through evaporation, enhancing the plants' survival, even during extended dry periods.

The soil is separated from the drainage system by a permeable fabric (Geotextile), which allows water flow but prevents soil passage into the water chamber. For the plant species used in this research, a soil with good drainage and low organic content was used. A composition of two parts of sand to one part of loam was employed.

Green roof performance in temperature attenuation is measured by the comparison between two small-scale housing prototypes with vegetated and non-vegetated roofs. Owing to financial limitations and because of the exploratory nature of the research, it was not possible to use full-scale housing for the experiment.

A simultaneous comparison between the records of temperature inside the vegetated and non-vegetated structures was made using data loggers that collect continuous temperature records over long periods of time. The temperature measurements were carried out every 30 minutes, using Extech TH10 temperature USB data loggers.

The data loggers were positioned at the same height inside each of the prototypes. Thus, the temperature differences observed are attributed only to the influence of heat incidence on the structures, given the identical weather conditions between the vegetated and non-vegetated prototypes.

4.3   Case study: Rio de Janeiro and Sydney

Two sets of experiments were performed in Brazil (Rio de Janeiro) and in Australia (Sydney). The Brazilian site is located on the roof of an existing building at the Oswaldo Cruz Foundation (FioCruz), and the Australian location is on the roof of a building at the University of Technology in Ultimo, Sydney.

Rio de Janeiro is geographically located at S 23°, W 43° and has a tropical wet and dry or savannah climate with dry winters (Aw); Sydney (S 33.9°, W 151.2°) has a humid subtropical climate (Cfa). The high and low annual average temperatures in Rio de Janeiro are 27.3°C and 21°C, respectively. In Sydney, these temperatures range from 21.7°C to 13.9°C. However, according to IPCC (2013), extreme higher temperatures are more commonly observed in Sydney (39.8–48.8°C) rather than in Rio de Janeiro (37.7–39°C).

Figure 4.1 shows the rectangular plastic containers or modular systems used on each site (Rio de Janeiro, 400 mm × 500 mm and Sydney, 190 mm × 330 mm).

The experimental setup for each site is illustrated in Figure 4.2. The Rio de Janeiro tests were carried out using small blockwork houses covered with metal sheeting, whereas in Sydney, metallic sheds were employed. In Australian housing, profiled metal sheet roofs are typically specified, and for this reason, the metal sheds were selected. The Rio de Janeiro data set comprised two different periods: 194 days, from 17 October 2012 to 29 April 2013 (spring to autumn, southern hemisphere); and 180 days, from 22 May 2014 to 18 November 2014 (autumn to spring). Sydney trial tests comprised a 134-day period from 11 December 2013 to 23 April 2014. The position of the temperature data loggers in Rio de Janeiro and Sydney housing prototypes is, respectively, 250 mm and 50 mm below the top of the roof structure.

(a)   (b)

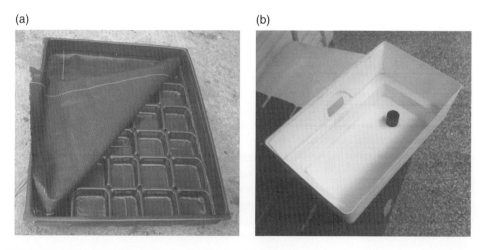

Figure 4.1   Rectangular plastic containers used in the temperature experiments. (a) Brazilian module, provided by Cidade Jardim Institute. (b) Australian module.

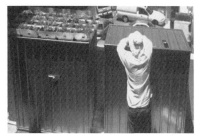

Figure 4.2   Housing thermal experiments. Left: Rio de Janeiro. Right: Sydney.

The results concerning the green roof cooling potential for the two experimental sites (Rio de Janeiro and Sydney) are shown in Figures 4.3–4.10. Notwithstanding some basic differences in the experimental setups (that is, block work in Rio de Janeiro and metal sheeting in Sydney), the tendency for temperature attenuation is evident. The measurements performed in both cities show that green roofs are able to attenuate daily variations of temperature.

4.3.1   Rio de Janeiro Case Study

Figure 4.3 presents a comparison between the non-green and green roofs' internal temperatures, during the 194-day data collection period, which comprises for the Brazilian site from the spring to the autumn period. Some of this work was partially reported in Feitosa (2012). Additional measurements from May to November 2014 (180 days) are presented in Figure 4.4. Besides, being collected in a different year, these complementary data cover part of autumn, winter and part of the spring period. In total, more than one year of data collection was performed for this site.

Based on daily variations of temperature, from the spring to the autumn period (2012–2013), the daytime temperatures for non-green and green roofs varied from 23.9°C to 41.4°C and from 23.2°C to 39.3°C, respectively. The minimum values that occurred during the night-time varied from 20.1°C to 31.8°C for the non-green roof and from 20.3°C to 31.8°C for the green roof. Considering the second set of data, comprising the autumn to spring (2014) period, the daytime temperatures ranged from 16.6°C to 29.7°C and from 15.9°C to 29.7°C for green and non-green roofs, respectively. The maximum, minimum and average temperatures for the entire two sets of data are presented in Table 4.1.

Comparing the simultaneous temperature differences between green and non-green roofs, these values varied from −1.7°C to 5.6°C. Positive values mean a higher non-green roof temperature and negative values indicate the opposite (a higher green roof temperature). From the first set of data, Figure 4.5 shows a typical detail of the temperature comparison between non-green and green roofs. It is evident that basically, positive differences occur during the daytime, while negative differences can be seen during the night-time and in the early morning. Additionally, from the same figure a delay is observed between the temperature peaks of non-green and green roofs.

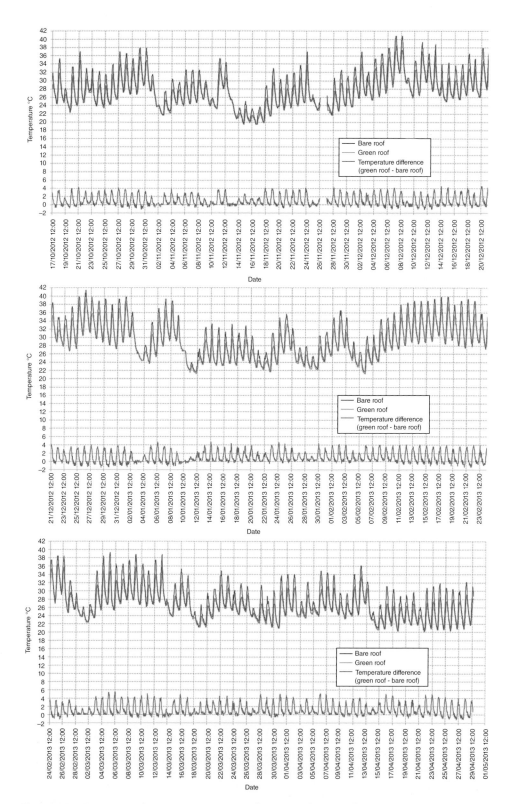

Figure 4.3 Comparison between non-green and green roofs' internal temperature, Rio de Janeiro, Brazil (first set of data: 17/10/2012–29/04/2013).

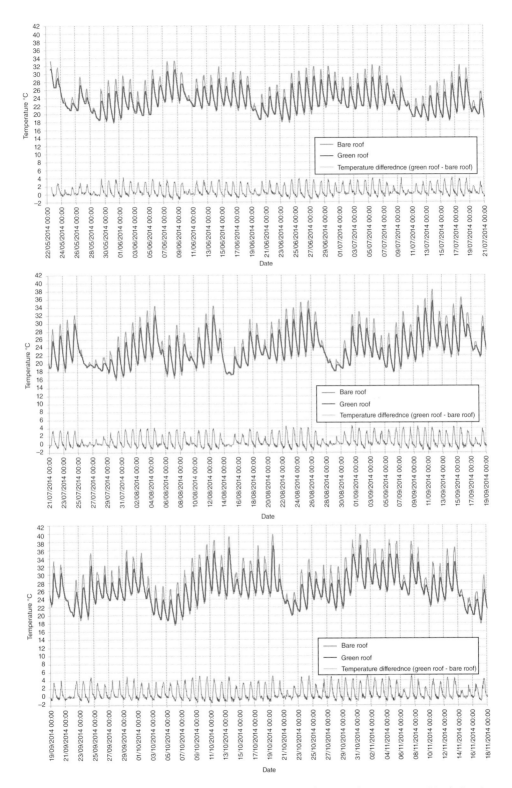

Figure 4.4 Comparison between non-green and green roofs' internal temperature, Rio de Janeiro, Brazil (second set of data: 22/05/2014–18/11/2014).

Table 4.1 Maximum, minimum and average temperatures for the two sets of data, Rio de Janeiro site

Period	Non-green roof temperatures (°C)			Green roof temperatures (°C)		
	Max.	Min.	Average	Max.	Min.	Average
17/10/2012–29/04/2013 spring to autumn	41.4	20.1	28.8	39.3	20.3	27.7
22/05/2014–18/11/2014 autumn to spring	39.8	15.9	25.3	37.0	16.6	24.5

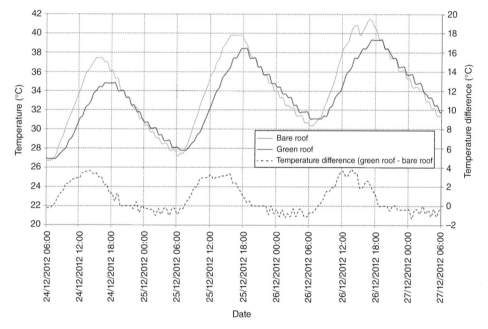

Figure 4.5 Typical detail of the temperature records between green and non-green (bare) roofs, Rio de Janeiro site.

In addition to this overall analysis of the temperature data, Figure 4.6 presents the maximum, minimum and average daily temperatures, as well as their differences, observed for non-green and green roofs. These values calculated for each of the 374 days (194 – first data set; 180 – second data set) are based on 48 records (30 minutes of sampling).

Compared with non-green roofs, the green roofs were capable of flattening the differences between maximum and minimum temperatures. Maximum temperatures were always higher for the non-green roof, whereas minimum temperatures were higher practically for all sets of data for the green roof. This fact is evidenced by the positive differences between maximum temperatures of non-green and green roofs and by the negative differences between their minimum temperatures. In all of 374 days, the average temperatures of the non-green roof were higher than those of the green roof.

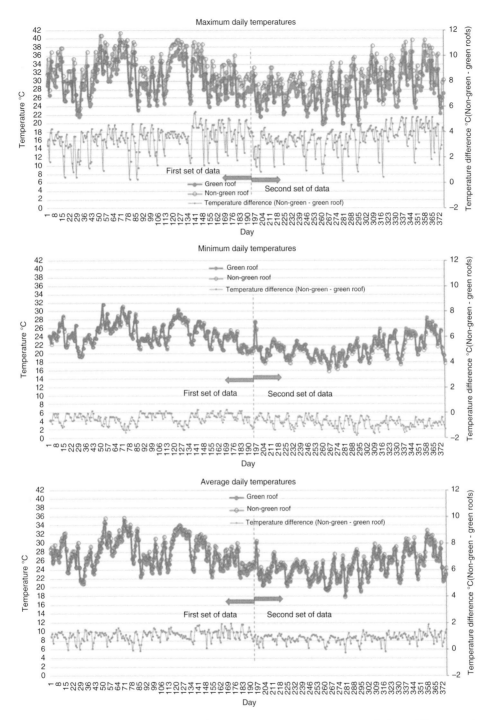

Figure 4.6 Maximum, minimum and average daily temperatures and their differences for non-green and green roofs, Rio de Janeiro.

Only five events occurred where the green roof's average temperatures were insignificantly higher than those of the non-green roof. In these cases, the differences observed between non-green and green roof temperatures were less than 0.2°C.

4.3.2   Sydney Case Study

Despite the shorter period of data compared with Rio de Janeiro, a significant temperature difference was observed in Sydney tests between non-green and green roof prototypes. However, based on the characteristics of the site where the experiments were performed, a particular pattern in temperature registers can be observed. As highlighted in Figure 4.7, a sudden reduction in temperature occurs both for non-green and green roofs around 3 p.m., due to the shading created by near buildings. This figure shows attenuation in temperature variation for green roofs, which is consistent with their insulating properties. The results are different compared with the Rio de Janeiro site, as a second set of data is not available due to technical problems in the data loggers.

Figure 4.8 presents a comparison between non-green and green roof inner temperatures, for 134 days from summer to the autumn period. For all sets of data, non-green roofs presented maximum, minimum and average temperatures equal to 50.3°C, 14.2°C and 25.4°C, respectively. The values observed for the green roof were 37.4°C, 14.8°C and 23.0°C.

Compared with the brick wall prototypes used in Rio de Janeiro experiments, as expected, the metal sheds used in Sydney show a faster response in terms of thermal exchange.

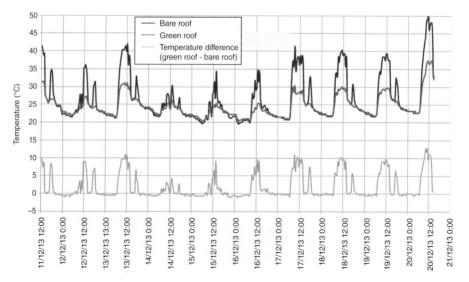

Figure 4.7   Influence of shadows on temperature caused by adjacent buildings for Sydney experimental roofs.

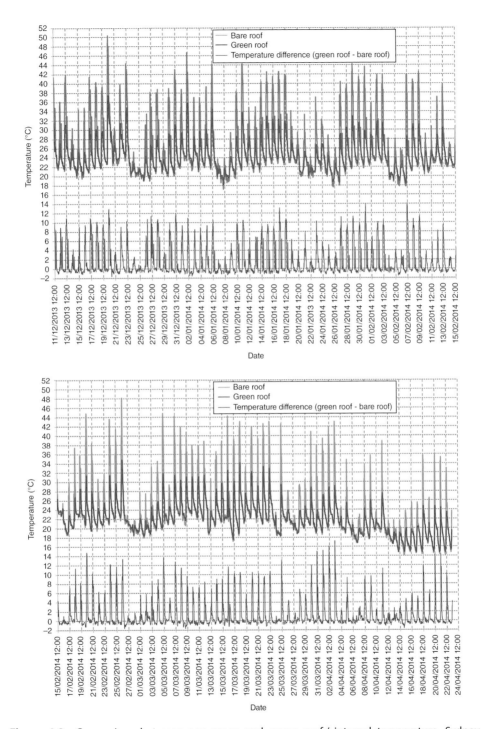

Figure 4.8 Comparison between non-green and green roofs' internal temperature, Sydney, Australia.

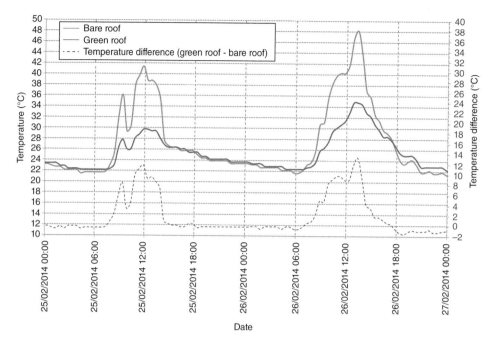

Figure 4.9 Typical detail of the temperature records between green and non-green roofs, Sydney, Australia.

Figure 4.9 depicts a two-day detail of the whole set of data presented in Figure 4.8. As at the Rio de Janeiro site, the highest differences in temperature between green and non-green roofs were also detected around noon. Negative differences were evident practically throughout the whole night and early morning periods, additionally corroborating the efficiency of the green roof in attenuating high and relatively low temperatures. Another point to be highlighted in Figure 4.9 is related to the observed delay between temperature peaks of non-green and green roofs. In comparison with the Rio de Janeiro experiments (Figure 4.5), a lower delay in the Sydney prototypes was observed, in all likelihood due to the poor insulating properties of the metal walls.

Analogous to the Rio de Janeiro experiments, Figure 4.10 presents the maximum, minimum and average daily temperatures, as well as their differences, observed for non-green and green roofs in Sydney. These values calculated for each of the 134 days are based on 48 records (30 minutes of sampling). Compared with the non-green roof, the green roof also showed attenuation of the differences between the maximum and minimum temperatures. Maximum temperatures were always higher for the non-green roof, and minimum temperatures were higher for all sets of data for green roofs. This fact is evidenced by the positive differences between non-green and green roof maximum temperatures (0.9°C to 17.2°C) and by the negative differences between their minimum temperatures (−1.6°C to −0.3°C). The average temperatures of non-green roofs were higher than those of green roofs, except for seven events where the green roof average temperatures were insignificantly higher (0.06–0.2°C).

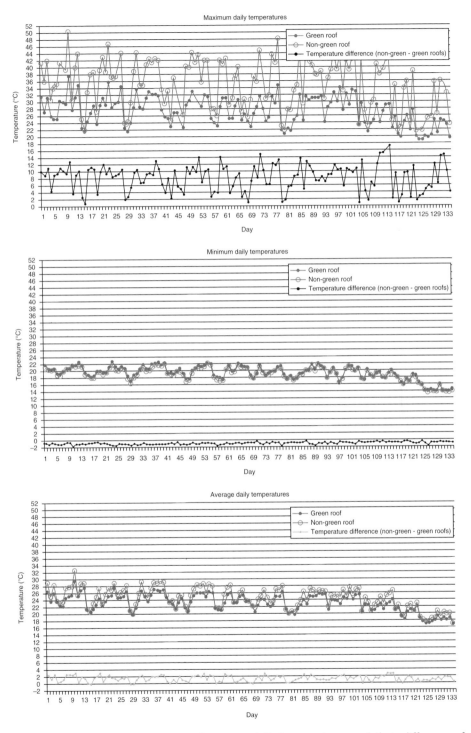

Figure 4.10 Maximum, minimum and average daily temperatures and their differences for non-green and green roofs, Sydney, Australia.

Table 4.2   Experimental temperature comparison between the Sydney and Rio de Janeiro sites

Temperatures (°C)	Rio de Janeiro			Sydney		
	Non-green roof	Green roof	Simultaneous temperature difference	Non-green roof	Green roof	Simultaneous temperature difference
Maximum	41.4	39.3	5.6	50.3	37.4	17.2
Minimum	15.9	16.6	−1.7	14.2	14.8	−1.6
Average	27.0	26.0	–	24.4	23.0	–

4.3.3   Evaluation of Rio de Janeiro and Sydney Cases

This section does not compare Sydney and Rio de Janeiro experiments, but rather evaluates the green roofs' potential to attenuate housing temperature.

Green roof tests performed in Rio de Janeiro and Sydney showed improvement in the insulating properties of the roof, due to heat influx reduction in the prototypes and, consequently, temperature attenuation compared with the non-green roof. That is to say, the vegetation increases the thermal performance of the roof quantified by the U-value, which indicates the heat gain or loss through a surface, and is also known as the overall heat transfer coefficient. A decrease in this parameter means an improvement in thermal performance due to the attenuation of heat transfer into the buildings. Wong *et al.* (2003) indicated that in a non-thermally insulating building, a green roof coverage with turf could reduce the U-value from 2.39 to 1.19 W/m²K.

Table 4.2 depicts, for the Rio de Janeiro and Sydney sites, the maximum, minimum and average temperatures of the non-green and green roofs, as well as their higher and lower differences. The green roof cooling potential in Sydney seemed to be greater than that in Rio de Janeiro, most likely due to the positioning of the temperature data loggers. These devices were placed 50 mm and 250 mm below the roof in Sydney and Rio de Janeiro, respectively. As already mentioned, the goal of this work is not direct comparison between the two sites. Surrounding buildings overshadowed the Sydney site for parts of the day, and the amount and duration of overshadowing changes with time as the sun's height increases or decreases. The study sought to evaluate the insulating properties of green roofs based on different scenarios. This can be corroborated at the Sydney site by the temperature differences (up to 17.2°C) taken close to the inner roof surface, composed of a good thermal conductor (metal sheet).

Compared with non-green roofs, besides insulation, green roofs also add thermal mass, which is the material capacity to absorb and store energy, and thus provide inertia against temperature fluctuation, resulting in a temperature peak delay (Castleton, 2010). However, analogous to Castleton (2010), in relation to non-green roofs, the green roof internal temperature peak delay observed is not much relevant. In the present work, Figures 4.5 and 4.9 show a slight time delay between green and non-green roof temperatures in both Rio de Janeiro and Sydney. The higher observed delays mostly ranged from 30 minutes (in Sydney) to 90 minutes (in Rio de Janeiro), showing more the insulating rather than the thermal mass property of the green roofs. Owing to its high heat capacity, water has a high thermal mass, since it gains and loses heat slowly. Thus, it is expected that the thermal mass will increase when the soil on the green roof is under well-watered conditions.

Besides the insulating properties, it is believed that neighbourhood shading conditions and different roof side conditions may affect green roofs' effects in temperature attenuation and, consequently, energy savings in urban environments.

Another aspect to consider is related to the amounts of water in the soil and storage systems. Owing to its high specific heat, water is supposed to provide inertia against temperature fluctuations. Although water levels have not been monitored in the current study, previous works have evaluated this effect (Del Barrio, 1998; Wong *et al.*, 2003; Alcazar and Bass, 2005; Lazzarin, 2005; Castleton, 2010). Alcazar and Bass (2005) revealed that the thermal performance decreases for wetter soils, since water is a better conductor than air, while oppositely, Del Barrio (1998) indicates that water promotes insulation. The results presented by Wong *et al.* (2003) concur with those of Niachou *et al.* (2001), Alcazar and Bass (2005) and Castleton (2010), where higher U-values (heat gain) are observed for higher water soil content.

Lazzarin *et al.* (2005) presented an evaluation of passive cooling and the role of evapotranspiration, under wet and dry soil conditions of the green roofs. According to these authors, compared with a traditional roof, green roofs reduce the incoming heat flux by 60%, even under dry conditions. However, in a wet green roof, the additional evapotranspiration acts as a heat sink in buildings. The water effect in the green roofs' cooling potential seems to be dependent simultaneously on the soil water content and the evapotranspiration process. According to Castleton (2010), the moisture levels in the soil influence the heat loss through evapotranspiration. Wet soils can promote heat removal from the building when evapotranspiration effects are considerable.

Different studies have assessed the evapotranspiration effect of succulents in extensive green roofs. According to Berghage *et al.* (2007), it has previously been hypothesised that, compared with evaporation from bare substrate, transpiration from succulents is not significant. However, these authors stated that the transpiration has a relevant role in the evapotranspiration process under well-watered soil conditions; during dry conditions, these plants stop transpiring, leading to similar levels of evapotranspiration and evaporation. Evapotranspiration processes are shown to be dependent on seasonal conditions. Planted plots with succulents transferred, for winter and summer, respectively, 34% and 51% more water to the atmosphere compared with bare soil (Rezaei *et al.*, 2005). The results from experiments performed by Voyde *et al.* (2010) challenge the hypothesis that succulent plants hold water all the time. In a lightweight modular system, their results indicated that when the water supply is not limited, transpiration contributes approximately 48% of the evapotranspiration.

Alcazar and Bass's (2005) studies revealed that water storage systems could improve the thermal performance of green roofs. Even without water level monitoring, their results showed a reduction in U-values compared with systems without water storage. Owing to water's thermal mass, it was expected in the Sydney and Rio de Janeiro results that there would be a delay between temperature peaks greater than those observed. The modular systems adopted in these studies were simply supported on top of the roof, and thus promote airflow, which is believed to enhance the thermal insulation. It is also important to highlight that solar radiation levels were not collected in the two exploratory studies presented. Thus, it is believed that the temperature attenuation provided by green roofs is directly related to solar radiation levels, and under cloudy conditions this effect tends to be less pronounced. It is considered that lightweight modules, similar to those adopted here, could easily be retrofitted to many existing houses with sheet metal roofs, increasing the thermal comfort of occupants, lowering energy bills and reducing GHG emissions.

4.4   Conclusions

Experimental setups in Rio de Janeiro and Sydney have demonstrated the potential of portable green roof modules for cooling buildings, reducing carbon emissions and contributing towards zero carbon targets. However, the exploratory experiments carried out in Sydney seem to have better green roof performance in temperature attenuation, most likely due to the closer positioning of the data loggers in relation to the roof.

Different types of green roof technology exist, from extensive to intensive systems. It is expected that different substrate composition, soil depths, soil moisture content, types of plant and water retention layer have a particular role in heat transmission, thermal inertia and evapotranspiration. The low cost, modular green roof systems adopted at both sites comprised an extensive system, where all the components are gathered in a single module. In this system, the existing space between modules and the underlying roof provides some air circulation and an extra insulating effect. However, considering the partial contact between the modules and the roof, some effect on inertia was observed, and the time shifts when the inner temperatures of the non-green and green roofs are compared. Similar results from experiments with modular systems (Lin and Lin, 2011) show the same trend observed in the present exploratory study.

The U-value parameter quantifies the heat exchange through a surface. In addition to Wong *et al.* (2003), who evaluated this parameter from exposed roofs to covered roofs with different types of vegetation and soil substrate, Niachou *et al.* (2001), Alcazar and Bass (2005) and Castleton (2010) evaluated this parameter, especially for extensive green roofs with depths from 50 to 100 mm. These authors, besides corroborating the role of the green roofs in reducing U-values compared with non-green roofs, revealed the effects of thermal inertia, evapotranspiration, soil moisture content and water storage. Besides insulation, green roofs add thermal mass and provide inertia against temperature fluctuation (Castleton, 2010). A green roof may work as a passive cooler. Under conditions of high external temperatures, not only is the heat influx cancelled, but a slight outflux is also produced due to the evapotranspiration cooling effect. The soil water content affects the extent of heat loss due to the evapotranspiration process, and also influences the thermal conductivity, since drier soils offer better thermal insulation.

As an alternative to green roofs, a common practice adopted in some Mediterranean countries is the cool roof, which consists of painting the roof surface white. This lowers the air and surface temperature, and the heat influx to the building. Cool roofs are covered in Chapter 11 of this book. According to Diep (2014), cool, or white, roofs have an extreme capacity to reflect sunlight and heat. Green roofs do not reflect as well as white roofs. However, both roofs manage to cool buildings on hot days. During summer periods, green roofs have a major role in energy savings, due to the cooling effect of evapotranspiration, while in the winter, they are able to reduce heat loss because of their more pronounced insulating properties. Green roofs have a major role in energy savings. In the summer, due to the cooling effect of evapotranspiration and in the winter, reducing the heat loss because of their more pronounced insulating properties. Despite the aforementioned benefits, white roofs may negatively affect neighbouring buildings, due to the solar radiation reflected towards windows facing these roofs.

Water levels were not monitored in this feasibility study. However, it is noted that due to the delay between the temperature peaks observed, the water levels do not seem to have a predominant role in green roof thermal performance. Furthermore, the passage of air is allowed in the modular system adopted, due to the existing space between the planted trays and the underside of the roof. This characteristic seems to enhance the insulating properties of the system and/or mitigate the effects of the water storage. Even though the present study did not monitor the water levels in the storage system, it could be seen, due to the delay between temperature peaks, that these levels do not seem to play a predominant role in the thermal performance of green roofs. In addition, the modular system adopted allows the air flux between the planted trays and the roof surface. This characteristic seems to enhance the insulating properties of the system and/or mitigate the effects of the water storage.

Even though no temperatures lower than 14°C have been measured, the negative differences observed (green roof temperature higher than non-green roof temperature) might indicate the green roofs' potential, due to their insulating properties, for attenuating extremes of temperature. It is probable that different substrate compositions will provide different results, and can be the object of further research.

Previous literature emphasises significant temperature differences between urban centres and green areas. Green roofs attenuate heat exchanges between the internal and external environments of buildings, and thus promote thermal comfort improvement. Additionally, according to a modelling study performed in Canada, if green roofs are adopted for new buildings and as retrofitting for existing buildings, it is expected that an attenuation of the urban heat islands will occur (see Chapter 3).

The research has demonstrated that roof structures planted with succulents are viable, as the plants survive well and could provide a low-cost, drought-tolerant, lightweight option to reduce heat gain and heat loss through roof structures. However, regarding the thermal aspect, the adoption of green roofs in urban centres is a partial solution only, due to the contribution of the building façades in the overall heating. Thus, a combination of green walls and green roofs could be an optimum solution for this problem. Furthermore, in terms of energy saving, considering that buildings comprise the most part of big cities, green roof adoption would only be relevant in top floors, which reinforces the combination of green roofs and green walls in urban environments.

Additional experiments with structures that more closely emulate typical Australian housing specifications in terms of wall construction would be very useful to consolidate the preliminary results found here. One of the limitations of this exploratory research is that the walls of the shed are profile metal sheeting, which is not typically specified in housing, although it does exist. In the Rio de Janeiro experiments, brick walls comprise a common type of solution adopted in the majority of housing. However, additional procedures, such as green walls, are the subject of current research to mitigate the rates of thermal transfer through walls.

The lightweight modular green roof system adopted in Rio de Janeiro prototypes has been subject to testing for approximately 2.5 years, during which time no maintenance has been required. The succulent plants have shown extreme resistance to intense heat, drought periods and atmospheric pollutants. The Sydney experiment has been underway for 1.5 years, and no maintenance of the plants has been required. The present study is based on new adaptive techniques, where the green roof setup costs have been substantially reduced using reusable materials. Currently, testing is underway in Rio de Janeiro at the FioCruz campus using cellular plastic boxes, which are commercially available at a low cost. This new modular system has been shown to be applicable to roofs and comprises a portable green patch solution that is intended for widespread use on a large scale in urban environments.

References

ABC (2014) 'Heatwave blamed for large spike in the number of deaths in Victoria last week', available at: www.abc.net.au/news/2014-01-23/heatwave-death-toll-expected-to-top-almost-400/5214496.

Agência Brasil (2014) 'Área verde por habitante cai 26% no Rio com avanço de favelas e especulação imobiliária', available at: memoria.ebc.com.br/agenciabrasil/noticia/2012-06-02/area-verde-por-habitante-cai-26-no-rio-com-avanco-de-favelas-e-especulacao-imobiliaria.

Alcazar, S. and Bass, B. (2005) 'Energy performance of green roofs in a multi storey residential building in Madrid'. *Greening Rooftops for Sustainable Communities*, Green Roofs for Healthy Cities Conference, Washington D.C.

Bass, B., Liu, K. K. Y. and Baskaran, B. A. (2003) 'Evaluating rooftop and vertical gardens as an adaptation strategy for urban areas', National Research Council, Canada.

Berghage, R. D., Jarrett, A. R., Beattie, D., *et al.* (2007) *Quantifying Evaporation and Transpirational Water Losses from Green Roofs and Green Roof Media Capacity for Neutralizing Acid Rain*. National Decentralized Water Resources Capacity Development Project, Penn State University, State College, PA.

Berndtsson, J. C. (2010) 'Green roof performance towards management of run-off water quantity and quality: a review', *Ecological Engineering*, 36, 351–360.

Castleton, H. (2010) 'Green roofs; building energy savings and the potential for retrofit', *Energy and Buildings*, 42, 1582–1591.

City of Sydney (2012) *Greening Sydney Plan*. Available at: www.cityofsydney.nsw. gov.au.

City of Sydney (2015) *Green Roofs and Walls Policy*. Available at: www.cityofsydney. nsw.gov.au/vision/towards-2030/sustainability/greening-the-city/green-roofs-and-walls.

City of Toronto (2015) *Green Roofs*. Available at: www1.toronto.ca/wps/portal/con tentonly?vgnextoid=3a7a036318061410VgnVCM10000071d60f89RCRD.

Cummings, J., Withers, C., Sonne, J., Parker, D. and Vieira, R. (2007) *UCF Recommissioning, Green Roofing Technology, and Building Science Training. Final Report*. Available at: www.fsec.ucf.edu/en/publications/pdf/FSEC-CR-1718-07.pdf.

Del Barrio, E. P. (1998) 'Analysis of the green roofs cooling potential in buildings', *Energy and Buildings*, 27, 179–193.

Diep, F. (2014) 'White roofs keep cities cooler than "green" ones, study finds', available at: www.popsci.com/article/science/white-roofs-keep-cities-cooler-green-ones-study-finds.

EPA (2014). *Reducing Urban Heat Islands: Compendium of Strategies. Green Roofs*. Available at: www.epa.gov/heatislands/resources/pdf/GreenRoofsCompendium. pdf.

EPA (2015) *Heat Island Effect*. Available at: www.epa.gov/heatisland/index.htm.

Feitosa, R. C. (2012) 'Telhados verdes reduzem temperatura interna de casas', available at: oglobo.globo.com/ciencia/telhados-verdes-reduzem-temperatura-interna-de-casas-5173467.

Greater London Authority (2008) *Living Roofs and Walls Technical Report*. Supporting London Plan Policy, London, UK.

Green (2014) *202020 Vision*. Available at: greenmagazine.com.au/202020-vision/.

Harlan, S., Brazer, A. J., Prashad, L., Stefanov, W. L. and Larsen, L. (2006) 'Neighbourhood microclimates and vulnerability to heat stress', *Social Science & Medicine*, 63, 2847–2863.

Herman, R. (2003) *Green Roofs in Germany: Yesterday, Today and Tomorrow*. Greening Rooftops for Sustainable Communities, Chicago, IL.

IPCC (2013) *Climate Change 2013: The Physical Science Basis*. Available at: www. ipcc.ch/report/ar5/wg1/.

Kellert, S. R. and Wilson, E. O. (1993) *The Biophilia Hypothesis*. Island Press: Washington D.C.

Lamond, J., Wilkinson, S. and Rose, C. (2014) 'Conceptualizing the benefits of green roof technology for commercial real estate owners and occupiers', Proceedings of Pacific Rim Real Estate Conference, Christchurch, New Zealand.

Langston, C. (2015) 'Green roof evaluation: a holistic "long life, loose fit, low energy" approach', *Construction Economics and Building*, 15(4), 76–94.

Lazzarin, R. M., Castellotti, F. and Busato, F. (2005) 'Experimental measurements and numerical modelling of a green roof', *Energy and Buildings*, 37, 1260–1267.

Lin, Y.-J. and Lin, H.-T. (2011) 'Thermal performance of different planting substrates and irrigation frequencies in extensive tropical rooftop greeneries', *Building and Environment*, 46, 345–355.

Liu, K. (2011) *Retrofitting Existing Buildings with Green Roofs*. Construction Canada: Toronto.

Liu, K. and Bass, B. (2005) *Performance of Green Roof Systems*. National Research Council Canada Report, Toronto.

Mentens, J., Raes, D. and Hermy, M. (2006) Green roofs as a tool for solving the rainwater runoff problem in the urbanized 21st century? *Landscape and Urban Planning*, 77, 217–226.

Niachou, A., Papakonstantinou, K., Santamouris, M., Tsangrassoulis, A. and Mihalakakou, G. (2001) 'Analysis of the green roof thermal properties and investigation of its energy performance', *Energy and Buildings*, 33, 719–729.

Oke, T. R. (1982) 'The energetic basis of the urban heat island', *Quarterly Journal of the Royal Meteorological Society*, 108, 1–24.

Peck, S. and Kuhn, M. (2003) *Design Guidelines for Green Roofs*. Ontario Association of Architects (OAA) and Canada Mortgage and Housing Corporation (CMHC), Ontario.

Portal G1 (2014) 'Rio tem novo recorde de calor e dia mais quente do ano chega a 41,4°C', available at: www.climatempo.com.br/destaques/tag/recorde-de-calor/.

Rezaei, F., Jarrett, A. R., Berghage, R. D. and Beattie, D. J. (2005) 'Evapotranspiration rates from extensive green roof plant species', Proceedings of the 2005 ASAE Annual International Meeting, Tampa, FL.

Sonne, J. (2006) 'Energy performance aspects of a Florida green roof', Fifteenth Symposium on Improving Building Systems in Hot and Humid Climates, Orlando, FL.

Stovin, V. (2010) The potential of green roofs to manage Urban Stormwater. Water and Environment Journal 24, 192–199.

Voyde, E., Fassman, E., Simcock, R. and Wells, J. (2010) 'Quantifying evapotranspiration rates for New Zealand green roofs', *Journal of Hydrologic Engineering*, 15, 395–403.

Wilkinson, S. J. and Reed, R. (2009) 'Green roof retrofit potential in the central business district', *Journal of Property Management*, 27, 284–301.

Wilkinson, S. J., Ghosh, S. and Page, L. (2013) 'Options for green roof retrofit and urban food production in the Sydney CBD', Proceedings of RICS COBRA Conference, New Delhi.

Williams, N., Raynor, J. and Raynor, K. (2010) 'Green roofs for a wide brown land: opportunities and barriers for rooftop greening in Australia', *Urban Forestry & Urban Greening*, 9, 169–272.

Wong, N. H., Cheong, D. K. W., Yan, H., Soh, J., Ong, C. L. and Sia, A. (2003) 'The effects of rooftop garden on energy consumption of a commercial building in Singapore', *Energy and Buildings*, 35, 353–364.

Stormwater Attenuation and Green Roof Retrofit

Jessica Lamond[1], Sara Wilkinson[2] and David Proverbs[3]

[1] University of the West of England, UK
[2] University of Technology, Sydney
[3] Birmingham City University, UK

This chapter describes research demonstrating how to make an assessment of whether to retrofit with green roofs as a way of attenuating stormwater runoff. The problem of pluvial flooding in terms of financial costs and the impact on our urban settlements is the starting point for a discussion on the potential of retrofitted green roofs as a mitigation measure. A range of technical specifications for stormwater roofs and critical issues to consider in retrofitting existing buildings are evaluated.

Theoretical frameworks of the distributed benefits of green roofs are presented, and a methodology to estimate the potential for stormwater attenuation of green roof retrofit at city-scale level is described in detail. The chapter reports on recent empirical research undertaken in two cities with very different climatic conditions: Melbourne, Australia and Newcastle, UK, at city-scale level. Having examined the city-scale level, a second illustrative case study at an individual building scale outlines stormwater performance and the assessment process in Portland, OR. The chapter concludes by describing how the stormwater effectiveness of green roofs may be limited in certain conditions by the availability of suitable buildings and the source of floodwater. A summary of the potential benefits of green roof retrofit for stormwater attenuation is made.

5.1   The Problem of Pluvial Flooding

Flooding in all forms causes severe problems for urban areas worldwide. For example, in 2010 alone, 178 million people were affected by floods. The total losses in exceptional years, such as 1998 and 2010, exceeded US$40bn. Many of these disasters are caused by extreme weather events at a large scale, rainfall events that cause rivers to swell and burst their banks (fluvial flooding), and storm events that result in coastal surge and flooding. Pluvial flooding, also called surface water flooding, or flooding from intense rainfall events is caused directly by rainfall that has not yet reached watercourses or drainage systems, particularly in dense urban areas with low permeability, and results in overland flows of water that can often be characterised by sudden onset and high velocity. Among the predicted changes in weather patterns consistent with a warming global climate (Met Office Hadley Centre for Climate Research, 2007; Solomon and Qin, 2007), consensus exists that the frequency of intense rainfall events is rising even where average rainfall is decreasing.

Pluvial flooding can be one of the most unpredictable forms of urban flooding, and this adds to the problems associated with preparing for and protecting against it. In some circumstances, pluvial flooding can be the most dangerous due to rapid onset and velocity of water taking communities by surprise. Equally, some pluvial flooding can be seen as nuisance flooding, affecting properties on a regular basis with shallow flood characteristics for a relatively brief period of time. Nevertheless, for those communities affected, the effect of frequent inundation can be very corrosive in the long term, affecting their ability to repair and insure their assets. For example, in the UK, 3.8 million properties in England are estimated to be at risk from surface water flooding alone (Environment Agency, 2013). Disruption associated with pluvial flooding can also be very detrimental to the functioning of businesses and the wider infrastructure network, even if the damage in terms of individual properties is limited due to low depths. Within the CBD of cities, arguably, the impact of disruption and long-term impacts due to recovery time are at least as important as the direct damages caused to property and contents during the flood (Bhattacharya-Mis et al., 2015). Floods in city centres are disruptive to all who live, work and pass through them, particularly if transport networks are involved, resulting in long-lasting cost to local economies if businesses fail to recover (BMG research, 2011; Ingirige and Wedawatta, 2011; Wedawatta et al., 2011).

Causes of increased pluvial flooding are not limited to changes in weather, but also driven by increased development pressures and urbanisation (Jha et al., 2011). Urban densification policies and practice in the UK and Australia have increased the concentration of impermeable surfaces in cities (White and Howe, 2002). Stormwater runs swiftly off these surfaces and in many business districts, piped drainage systems have not been updated to accommodate the increased runoff (French et al., 2011). As an alternative to the expensive and disruptive business of retrofitting extra capacity into the piped drainage, measures designed to increase infiltration and evapotranspiration within urban areas have been suggested. Within existing business

Figure 5.1 Overviews of the building styles in Newcastle-upon-Tyne's CBD (left) and Melbourne (right).
Source: J. Lamond and S. Wilkinson.

districts, this approach could include the widespread retrofit of green roofs according to many authors including Charlesworth and Warwick (2011). However, the viability of such a retrofit from a structural and functional point of view, and the associated reduction of flood risk and delivery of other multiple benefits, is yet to be fully explored (Wilkinson and Reed, 2009; Lawson *et al.*, 2014).

The cities selected for the research described here (Newcastle, UK and Melbourne, Australia – shown in Figure 5.1) represent historic cities that have expanded and densified over time. Furthermore, the cities are on the banks of major watercourses and contain streets that have been built over culverted watercourses, further reducing the permeability and flow potential within them. It is not surprising, then, that pluvial flood risk exists in both cities and, in fact, they have both recently been subject to severe pluvial flood events.

In 2012, Newcastle experienced a severe rainfall event in which the whole of the expected total rainfall for June fell within a two-hour period (Environment Agency – Yorkshire & North East Region, 2012). In their survey, Newcastle City Council determined that temporary closure was experienced by around 40% of non-residential properties in the CBD. This included the Central Railway Station (Total Research and Technical Services Newcastle City Council, 2013).

Similarly, the Melbourne area experienced a severe storm in 2010, during which almost a month's rain fell in a single 24-hour period (Bureau of Meteorology (Australia), undated). Massive disruption included a number of roads in the CBD rendered impassable for several hours, flooding of Flinders Street railway station and disruption of the trams. An even more intense storm occurred in February 2011 when, during a 20-minute cloudburst, 17 mm fell in the CBD (News.com, 2011). A further flood occurred in June 2015, causing extensive damage to the city (City of Melbourne, 2015).

The City of Portland in the USA, also the subject of research referred to in Section 5.4.1, has been subject to nuisance flooding over many decades and instituted a green infrastructure policy that included the encouragement of green roof installation. Many acres of green roofs have been installed under the programme; a roof garden is visible in Figure 5.2(a), including one on

(a)   (b)

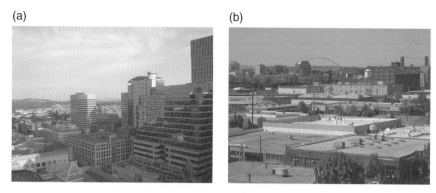

Figure 5.2   Roofscapes of Portland, OR taken from two vantage points: (a) the heart of the city with views of green roofs; (b) across the Williamette from the green roof of the Multnomah building.

what is now the Apple building opposite Pioneer Place, which has a brand new green roof. However, it is clear that there is still considerable untapped potential in the rooftops of Portland.

5.2   Specifications for Stormwater Roofs and Issues for Retrofit

Modelling of the impact of green roofs on stormwater and other benefits is carried out at different spatial scales and for different purposes. This chapter describes modelling at two different spatial scales contextualised within the perspectives of stakeholders involved in the decision-making process.

For new developments and retrofit installations there are software resources available to aid in calculating the impact of sustainable drainage on runoff. Some have a green roof feature, for example 'SWMM' software (US EPA) and 'xpdrainage' (XP Solutions). These software packages require or assume design features, climate and rainfall patterns. At a feasibility and design stage, more detailed local monitoring and detailed structural calculations can be made at an individual building scale. However, at a larger spatial scale, and for the formulation of policy and incentive schemes to encourage uptake, a less detailed methodology is needed. At whatever spatial scale, it is contended that two critical factors are the criteria for assessment of the suitability of buildings for green roof retrofit and the estimate of runoff reduction assumed or modelled.

5.2.1   Technical and Physical Issues in Retrofit

When retrofitting a green roof it is useful to undertake a survey of the roof space to determine the available space for vegetation. Many rooftops accommodate mechanical equipment (such as air-handling units). Before designing a green roof it is vital to undertake an investigation to determine the building's existing structural load-bearing capacity and to check for damage, and this may be undertaken by a surveyor. The building's structural capacity determines the type of vegetation that can be grown. An inspection of the existing roof membrane determines its condition, and any damage should be repaired. Green roofs require regular maintenance, therefore safe access must be provided. If a green roof is to be used as an amenity space, then how the space is accessed for this purpose (e.g., via lifts/stairs) needs to be considered. Accessible roof amenity spaces need to meet access and health and safety legislation; additional structures may need to be added to existing parapets. Considering the visual impact of historic buildings is of primary importance. Heritage buildings must be able to accommodate a green roof without negatively altering the historic character of the building. Green roofs require regular monitoring and maintenance; this includes pruning and weed control, plant nutrition, plant installation/replacement, maintenance of supporting structure and waterproofing. The orientation of the roof affects the amount of exposure to sun the roof will get, and this affects the type of plants that will flourish there (Wilkinson and Reed, 2009). Added to this, the surveyor needs to consider any overshadowing from surrounding buildings as this affects access to sunlight for the plants. Finally, the height above ground will affect exposure levels to high winds in particular. Some rooftop environments can be hostile in different seasons, and planting specifications must take this into account (Williams *et al.*, 2010).

5.2.2   Estimating Runoff Reduction

In designing or planning for green roof retrofit, a sensible choice of runoff performance is needed and this can be gained from theory and modelling or from analysis and monitoring of other similar roofs. Using the data from previous measurement of the retention or runoff reduction from green roofs is complicated by the variety of performance measures used by researchers. Researchers may measure the percentage of annual rainfall retained, the average percentage retained during a given storm size or the reduction in peak flow during a storm. In their meta-analysis, Rose and Lamond (2013) note that reported performance ranged from 42–90% of annual rainfall, whilst average retention during storm events varied from 30–100%.

According to Mentens *et al.* (2006), the stormwater performance of green roofs relies on three actions: absorption by the substrate delays runoff from the roof during a storm event until it is saturated; storage of this water throughout the storm reduces total flow and is likely to reduce peak flow; water stored by the roof is released back into the atmosphere through evapotranspiration, thereby reducing the total load on the ground-level drainage and treatment systems. There are therefore several factors that can impact on the performance by influencing the quantity of water stored and the speed with which it is released. For example, design features like the growing medium, presence and size of reservoir storage (Wilkinson and Reed, 2009) and choice of vegetation can each affect interception rates by 50–60% (Nagase and Dunnett, 2012). Slope, or roof pitch, is also a factor (Wilkinson and Reed, 2009).

Non-design factors that can potentially have an impact include regional climatic variation and expected rainfall patterns. For example, subtropical Mediterranean climates (Fioretti *et al.*, 2010) place different demands on vegetation, including roofs, with the result that the performance of roofs varies from that in temperate maritime climates (MacIvor and Lundholm, 2011). Most measurements have been taken under northern US climate conditions with very little data available for subtropical Mediterranean-type climates. In a retrofit scenario, roof characteristics such as overshadowing (which can inhibit vegetation growth) and the degree of pitch of the roof (Wilkinson *et al.*, 2009) may also be fixed characteristics of the urban environment that can impact on runoff reduction.

Advice previously given for 'rule of thumb' estimates for the design and installation of vegetated roofs include the San Francisco toolbox, which gives figures of 50–65% of annual rainfall and 50% of peak events (Sanfran, 2010) and Groundwork Sheffield (2011) citing, for the UK, 50–70% in summer and 25–40% in winter. However, it should be noted that relying on measured performance limits the technical considerations to a small range of installations, often designed for a specified storm event. This runs the risk of underestimating the potential to design roofs to a higher specification if peak attenuation is a major goal for the roof.

5.3   Modelling for City-Scale Stormwater Attenuation

Estimation of reduced runoff (that is, the reduction in the quantity of surface water that flows off a surface), which results from the retrofitting of SuDS features, is useful for a number of different purposes and at different scales. For example, on an individual building basis the reduction in runoff from a green roof could result in savings in wastewater disposal or it could be used to determine the appropriate size for ground-level SuDS (Ma *et al.*, 2012). At a city-wide level it could be used to determine the reduction in flood hazard and the resultant decrease in expected flood damage (Gordon-Walker *et al.*, 2007). This type of assessment may be carried out by city or local authorities (among others) while formulating policy or during the planning cycle. Roofs can represent a high proportion of impermeable surfaces in urban areas, for example Stovin (2010) estimated 40–50% of the impermeable surfaces in urban locations were roofs. These surfaces offer mitigation potential without the need for land-take, however the area and location of suitable roofs will have a large influence on the quantity and pattern or attenuation and therefore hazard reduction. The perspective of different agencies or authorities in determining the benefits of retrofit has been discussed by Abbott *et al.* (2013) in the UK context. As adapted for green roof benefits, the match between investment and benefit is shown in Figure 5.3. In the UK, where lead local flood authorities bear a large part of the responsibility for the management of surface water flooding and also much of the cost of clearing up after a flood, runoff for flood reduction purposes is strongly within the remit of the local authority. However, in other contexts the responsibility may fall on other bodies, for example in

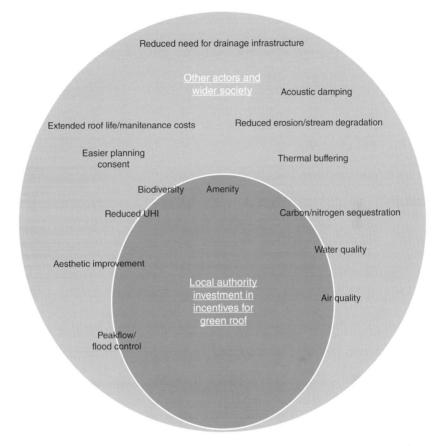

Figure 5.3 Distribution of benefits from local authority investment in green roofs. *Source*: After Abbott *et al.* (2013).

Australia, responsibilities are shared between local authorities, State and Federal authorities. In this framework, flood prevention is one of the key quantifications that a public body may focus on.

On a city-wide scale, any assessment of retrofit potential will need to make generalised assumptions about the type and design of green roofs to be retrofitted. Of the two main types of green roof, the extensive roof (incorporating shallow-rooted species in a relatively thin substrate) is regarded as more suitable for retrofit because there will be a lower load superimposed on existing structures. Therefore, it was assumed in this study that an extensive roof would be the preferred option in modelling runoff. Choosing a runoff percentage is still challenging given that the cities were in different climate zones and that the percentage rates of runoff retention vary for different storm scales. The view that green roofs are unlikely to prevent flooding in the most severe events led to the decision to look at average annual retention as this is the most measured and is relevant for stormwater management and nuisance flooding. Based on the meta-analysis described in Section 5.2.2, an estimate of 60% was chosen.

Databases of buildings suitable for green roof retrofit were established for Melbourne and Newcastle using a desk-based approach that drew on evidence from the literature as summarised in Section 5.2.1. This was used to determine criteria for whether a building could be deemed suitable for retrofit. Information from existing databases of building characteristics was first accessed. The next stage involved a visual inspection of each identified roof using the Google Earth and Google Map software (Google Earth 6.0, 2008). An evaluation of the potential of each roof for retrofitting with green roof technology was undertaken, resulting in one of three classifications, namely (a) 'yes', (b) 'no' or (c) 'don't know' with regards to retrofitting. The evaluation was based on roof pitch (i.e., those pitched above 30° and below 2% were deemed unsuitable). The amount of rooftop plant, especially equipment which vents air from the building, and the provision of rooftop window-cleaning equipment, safety handrails and PV units was taken into account; where coverage exceeded 40% of the roof area, the roof was deemed unsuitable for retrofit. Roofs with listed or conservation status, overshadowing or lightweight construction were deemed unsuitable.

5.3.1   Melbourne, Australia

Using this approach, 526 buildings in the Melbourne CBD database were evaluated in terms of suitability for green roof retrofit. The analysis also considered other characteristics that might affect the ease and likelihood of retrofit in the near future, and the type of planting suitable.

An age profile analysis of the buildings gave an average property age of 61 years, with a range of construction dating from 1853 to 2005 (although some buildings have been completed since 2005 they were not in the database, which covered the time period from 1850 to 2005). The data reflects considerable post-war construction in the Melbourne CBD with 302 (or 60.4%) new commercial CBD buildings built during this era. 237 Melbourne CBD buildings date from the 1960s, therefore a large amount of stock is due for adaptation and retrofitting green roofs could be considered.

The site and the location of the building were also considered (Kincaid, 2003) and within the CBD, locations were categorised as 'prime' (the best location), 'low prime', 'high secondary', 'secondary' and the lowest grade 'fringe'. 7.6% of all buildings were located in the prime zone, 15.2% in the low prime area, and 7% in the high secondary area – thus 29.8% of all properties were located in the higher-grade location zones. The highest proportion (43.2%) was in the low secondary area and nearly a quarter (24.7%) was located in the fringe area at the periphery of the CBD grid. Wilkinson (2014) has examined attributes which make Melbourne offices more or less likely to be retrofitted and found that higher-grade stock typically has more activity.

Building height and overshadowing are important considerations in green roof retrofit, and most buildings are low rise (three storeys) and often partially or totally overshadowed. Overall, 68.1% of the stock is 10 storeys high or less, 24.5% between 10 and 20 storeys, while only 7.4% is above 20 storeys high. A definition of a high-rise building refers to metres in height

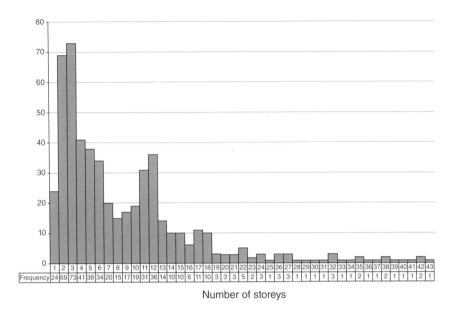

Number of storeys	1	2	3	4	5	6	7	8	9	10	11	12	13	14	15	16	17	18	19	20	21	22	23	24	25	26	27	28	29	30	31	32	33	34	35	36	37	38	39	40	41	42	43
Frequency	24	69	73	41	38	34	20	15	17	19	31	36	14	10	10	6	11	10	3	3	3	5	2	3	1	3	3	1	1	1	1	3	1	1	2	1	1	2	1	1	1	2	1

Figure 5.4   Number of storeys in Melbourne CBD buildings.
Source: Wilkinson and Reed (2009).

rather than number of storeys. According to some definitions, buildings over approximately 7 storeys (or 23 m high) are in the high-rise category and those over 80 m (approximately 20 storeys) are deemed skyscrapers. Figure 5.4 shows that a minority of all buildings are high rise or skyscrapers, which cast shadows over adjoining lower buildings as the sun moves across the sky during the day. Such an arrangement of buildings could mean that existing buildings with adequate structural strength to accommodate green roof retrofit may be unsuitable due to overshadowing adversely affecting planting.

Orientation also has an influence on how much exposure to sunlight a roof may benefit from. In the southern hemisphere, exposure to sunlight will be greatest for north-facing properties and this will affect the type of plants specified and/or whether green roof retrofitting is viable. Analysis of a sample of 72 buildings in the database revealed that the highest number (41.17%) faced east followed by west-facing (30.88%), south-facing (16.17%) and finally north-facing buildings, which comprised 11.76% of the sample (see Figure 5.5). Therefore, it appears that a large proportion of CBD buildings will only have partial exposure to sunlight, even before overshadowing is considered.

Ease of access for construction and attachment to neighbours was considered, because cost/disruption and the need to interface with neighbouring property can be a further constraint in the uptake of green roof retrofitting. In the Melbourne CBD sample, the highest number of properties were bounded on two sides (47.4%), 21.9% were bounded on one side only and 18% bounded on three sides. Only 12.1% were free-standing. This shows that access is not an issue for the majority of properties, however, most properties in the sample might need to consider the views and/or co-operation of their neighbours.

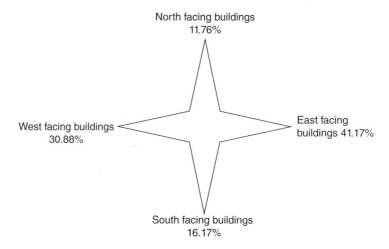

Figure 5.5   Building orientation in Melbourne CBD.
Source: Adapted from Wilkinson and Reed (2009).

Table 5.1   Green roof option

		Frequency	Valid (%)
Valid	Yes	78	15.0
	No	418	80.2
	Don't know	25	4.8
	Total	521	100.0
Missing	System	5	
Total		526	

Source: Adapted from Wilkinson and Reed (2009).

The structural capacity of a building affects the feasibility and ease of retrofit of a green roof. The majority (60.6%) of commercial buildings in the Melbourne CBD sample have framed structures, with concrete framing preferred over steel. The remaining 39.4% of properties are of traditional load-bearing brickwork and/or stone construction. Using remote visual inspection and information from the database, this analysis concluded there was good potential for retrofit (on the basis of structural strength), with minimal structural changes required for most of the CBD buildings. It should be noted that a full structural appraisal (noted above) would be required on an individual building basis to determine structural suitability for retrofit.

The results in Table 5.1 show that, using this approach, 15% of the buildings were judged suitable for retrofit with green roof technology. A relatively low 4.8% of buildings were classed as 'don't know', and a significant percentage (80.2%) were not considered suitable for retrofit based on the criteria above – such as having pitched roofs, being overshadowed substantially or with no access and so on.

5.3.2   Newcastle-upon-Tyne, UK CBD Database

An analysis of the 507 commercially rateable buildings in three postcodes in the Newcastle CBD was undertaken using similar characteristics as for Melbourne. Slight differences in the availability of information within UK databases and a different type of building stock meant the analysis emphasised different limitations.

The precise age of buildings was not available for all buildings in the Newcastle database. However, a general picture emerges of a preponderance of historic buildings, for example many are listed, with 30 grade 1 and 189 grade 2 listings. The centre of Newcastle is also designated with multiple conservation areas. For the sample this encompassed 386 (76%) of the buildings. Clearly the potential to retrofit listed buildings may be limited, but it will be important to establish the feasibility of retrofitting on non-listed buildings within the conservation area. Although the conservation areas contain historic buildings, there is also significant amounts of more modern development that is not listed, some constructed as recently as 2012.

There is very little potential for massive overshadowing from skyscrapers in Newcastle as the tallest building in the database has 18 storeys. The average number of storeys for the Newcastle sample is 4, and 98% of the buildings would be regarded as low rise with only 2% of buildings identified as having 10 storeys or more. In Figure 5.6, buildings over 10 storeys are grouped together.

When considering access and the need for disruption during retrofit and maintenance, it was seen that nearly half of the buildings (47.3%) have street access only, raising concerns about any extra disruption required when retrofitting and maintaining the roofs. The properties in the Newcastle CBD were predominantly bounded on two sides or more. This comprised 37.7% bounded on two sides, 30.8% bounded on three sides and 14% bounded on four.

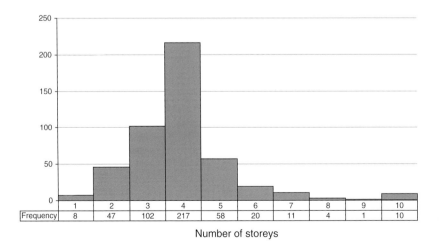

Figure 5.6   Histogram of building heights in storeys for Newcastle study area.

Construction type, as might be expected, was significantly related to the age of buildings, with a shift over time from load-bearing masonry to framed buildings. The visual inspection estimated that most buildings in the study area are load-bearing brick or stone (80.7%), with 13.4% steel or concrete frame construction, the rest indeterminate. There was also a strong correlation between construction type, listing and conservation area (see Table 5.2). This means that the majority of the steel or concrete-framed buildings are outside the conservation area and not listed.

From visual inspection of roof pitch it appears that only 99 buildings have the slight pitch most suitable for green roof retrofitting (see Table 5.3). Among those with a slight pitch, about half are steel or concrete with the other half load-bearing brick or stone. It is also apparent that roof pitch is highly associated with the age of buildings. The majority of older buildings have been constructed with a steep pitch considered unsuitable for green roof retrofitting. Given the high correlation between historic listing and pitch, it is not necessary to include historic listing separately in the assessment of retrofit suitability for this sample in Newcastle.

Car parking is at a premium in the centre of Newcastle, and several large roofs have parking on them. Examining the coverage of the roof by plant or

Table 5.2 Cross tabulation of conservation area, construction type and historic listing

| | | Historic listing status | | | |
		Grade 1	Grade 2	Not listed	Total
Inside conservation area	Load-bearing brick or stone	26	176	136	338
	Steel or concrete frame	0	6	20	26
	Unknown/other	4	4	14	22
	Total	30	186	170	386
Outside conservation area	Load-bearing brick or stone		3	68	71
	Steel or concrete frame		0	42	42
	Unknown/other		0	5	5
	Total		3	115	118
Total	Load-bearing brick or stone	26	179	204	409
	Steel or concrete frame	0	6	62	68
	Unknown/other	4	4	19	27
	Total	30	189	285	504

Table 5.3 Cross tabulation of pitch and construction type for Newcastle study area

| | | Construction type | | | |
		Load-bearing brick or stone	Steel or concrete frame	Unknown/ other	Total
Pitch of roof okay;	Yes	49	45	5	99
and building not	No	359	22	8	389
listed	Unknown	1	1	17	19
Total		409	68	30	507

car-parking spaces further reduces the potential space available for a green roof retrofit, as shown in Table 5.4. Plant was naturally more common on rooftops with low pitch (see Table 5.4), and using a cut-off point of 40% plant reduces the number of suitable rooftops to 76, representing 15% of the CBD buildings.

If construction type is also considered, there are 30 potential retrofit rooftops that could take extra heavy loading; including access and site boundaries brings the number judged suitable down to only 20, as shown in Table 5.5. Therefore, if intensive roofs were considered, the potential for retrofit would be less than 4%.

5.3.3   Melbourne and Newcastle Runoff Estimation

526 office buildings were examined in the Melbourne CBD for their potential for green roof retrofit, compared with 507 buildings in Newcastle. The Melbourne stock ranged from 9 years to 161 years, with an average age of 61 years, whereas no age data was available for the Newcastle stock. 76.13% was located in conservation areas, with 43.19% listed, which suggests the Newcastle stock is older than the Melbourne stock. Melbourne is a new city compared with Newcastle, and the CBD was laid out in a grid formation by the military surveyor Robert Hoddle in 1837. Table 5.6 summarises the main similarities and differences for the two databases.

For both cities, the majority of buildings were low rise; on average, three storeys in Melbourne and four storeys in Newcastle. However, the distribution of taller buildings across the two locations was much more contrasted. Melbourne had more potential for overshadowing from high-rise stock than Newcastle, with buildings up to 66 storeys. The highest Newcastle building was 18 storeys high. Melbourne stock was more likely to be concrete framed, whereas load-bearing masonry construction predominated in the Newcastle

Table 5.4   Roofs judged suitable for extensive green roof retrofit based on pitch, historic listing and percentage coverage by plant in the Newcastle study area

	Frequency	Percentage
Suitable	76	15.0
Not suitable	410	80.9
Unknown	21	4.1
Total	507	100.0

Table 5.5   Roofs potentially suitable for intensive green roof retrofit in the Newcastle study area

		Frequency	Percentage	Valid (%)
Valid	Yes	20	3.9	3.9
	No	479	94.5	94.5
	Unknown	8	1.6	1.6
	Total	507	100.0	100.0

database. As reflects the grid-planned layout of Melbourne, the buildings here were less likely to be attached to others compared with Newcastle, where most buildings were attached to others on more than one side. The degree of attachment of other buildings affects the ease of retrofit and access for contractors and maintenance.

In summary, Melbourne buildings are more likely to be overshadowed but are structurally more suited to green roof retrofitting. The Newcastle stock is likely to have good exposure to sunlight but is less structurally suited to retrofitting, especially with the heavier types of green roof design. Despite these differences, both cities had 15% of their stock found suitable for green roof retrofitting. To calculate the total potential average runoff performance, the assumption is that 15% of rooftops will be suitable.

Runoff calculations were made based on three assumptions, as shown in Table 5.7. The calculation takes into account the percentage of the CBD

Table 5.6   Melbourne and Newcastle stock compared for green roof retrofit

Green roof criterion	Melbourne stock	Newcastle stock
Age	Newer	More listed and older stock
Height	Low rise	Low rise
Overshadowing	Higher levels	Lower levels
Construction type	More suited – more flat concrete roofs	Less suited – more pitched roof construction
Adjoining buildings and accessibility for retrofit	Fewer attached to other buildings	Most attached to other buildings
Percentage of roofs suited	15	15

Table 5.7   Runoff calculations for Melbourne and Newcastle showing estimated percentage of total rainfall falling on the CBD managed by potential retrofit under three scenarios

	Assume all roof retrofit		Assume suitable roof retrofit		Assume half of suitable roof retrofit	
	Melbourne	Newcastle	Melbourne	Newcastle	Melbourne	Newcastle
Total study area (1000 m²)	2150.0	853.0	2150.0	853.0	2150.0	853.0
Area of selected roof (1000 m²)	1150.0 (100%)	388.0	172.5 (15%)	58.2 (15%)	86.3 (7.5%)	29.1 (7.5%)
Percentage of CBD covered by selected roofs	53%	45%	8%	7%	4%	3.5%
Runoff reduction roof (% of total rainfall)[1]	32.1%	27.3%	4.8%	4.1%	2.4%	2.0%

[1] Assume 60% runoff reduction over the area of the green roof.

area covered by roofs to estimate the reduction in total CBD rainfall that may be intercepted by roofs. In the case of these two cities, the coverage by roofs is 53% for Melbourne and 45% for Newcastle, slightly high in comparison with the 40–50% average mentioned by Stovin (2010), but within expectations. It also assumes a runoff percentage reduction of 60% to represent the average capture by a retrofit extensive green roof to those rooftop spaces. The maximum runoff reduction achievable if all roofs are considered suitable for retrofit is the first scenario. The second scenario assumes that all of the roofs deemed suitable are retrofitted with green roofs and the third scenario recognises that other constraints may prevent retrofit and that only half of suitable roofs are retrofit.

According to the research findings, a 10% reduction in runoff to the sewer system has the potential to prevent 90% of flood incidents (Gordon-Walker *et al.*, 2007). The analysis of retrofit potential summarised in Table 5.7 indicates that the retrofitting of roofs to intercept stormwater could be a significant mitigation factor for both Newcastle and Melbourne, but that limitations on the availability of roofs deemed suitable for retrofit has reduced the estimates significantly from the all-roof retrofit scenario. Despite the limitations of the analysis in terms of simplifying assumptions to deal with the city-wide spatial scale, the findings are revealing in that they demonstrate the importance of the assessment of rooftop suitability because it can make a sizeable difference to the estimates of potential. Without building-characteristic assessment, cities may overestimate the benefits of a green roof incentive programme. However, if assumptions for roof suitability are relaxed, for example retrofitting roofs with higher pitch or specifying plants that are tolerant of overshadowing, the potential for runoff reduction changes. Therefore, the databases can be used in sensitivity analysis as a basis for informed discussion to determine the parameters for any policy drivers or technical improvements that may increase the potential for green roof retrofit in a city. For the specific case studies of Newcastle and Melbourne, these findings imply that further detailed feasibility studies and modelling are warranted.

5.4   Assessment of Retrofit at a Building Scale

When considering retrofit at a building scale, different stakeholders become involved, namely the building owners and occupiers. Lamond *et al.* (2014) considered the motivation for building owners and occupiers to install green roofs, deriving a conceptual model for distributed benefits (Figure 5.7). This model reveals that, as for the local authority, the distribution of benefits is much wider than the investor and, in this case, few of them affect the investor directly. In particular, the stormwater management benefits accrue to the neighbourhood and perhaps beyond rather than to the property owner or occupier. The cost of installing a green roof is, however, likely to be incurred by the owner or occupier of the building (unless specific incentive schemes exist). It follows that unless regulation is in place, or specific charges are made for runoff, or discounts offered for a reduction of discharge into

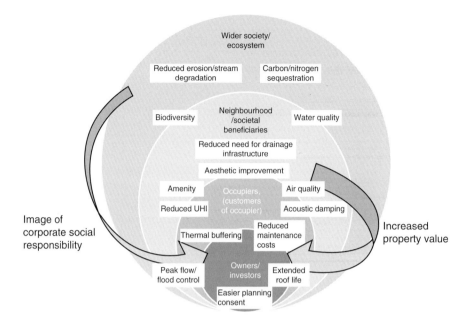

Figure 5.7   Conceptual model of distributed benefits of green roof technology from the perspective of owners and occupiers of commercial buildings.
Source: Lamond *et al.* (2014).

drainage networks, the stormwater features of green roofs do not benefit the installer. For example, in Australia, green roofs are not recognised as a feature that can be used in complying with development requirements for runoff reduction.

The model posits that there are, however, additional reputational and operational factors that affect the value of a commercial site to owners and occupiers. The perceived wider societal benefits have the potential to feed back into the value of a building and affect the owners or investors. The installation of a green roof may, for example, be seen as socially responsible, as it contributes to stormwater management. The benefit of this corporate social responsibility may accrue to the owner and investor and also the occupier in terms of reputational benefit, regardless of the actual performance of the roof. It may be enhanced or reduced by accessibility, publicity and visibility of the roof, as well as any status applied through labelling and marketing.

In some instances, measureable direct benefits (such as reduced heating and cooling costs) can offset the cost of green roof installation over time. Therefore, at a building level it is highly important to estimate the multiple benefits that may be offset against the cost of retrofit. This model suggests that the business case for retrofit of green roofs must be predicated on the consideration of multiple direct benefits, as well as recognising feedback from wider societal and ecological beneficiaries. This kind of approach is exemplified below by considering the work of the Bureau of Environmental Services (BES) and others in Portland when developing and implementing the Portland Ecoroof programme.

5.4.1   Portland Ecoroof Programme

The Portland Ecoroof programme is one example of a city's effort to increase the uptake of green infrastructure in order to manage stormwater. In Portland, the incentive to improve stormwater management has been driven by the level of nuisance flooding and the need to avoid overextending the municipal drainage and water treatment facilities while improving water quality in the Williamette River through greater infiltration. In their 2008 study (Bureau of Environmental Services – City of Portland, 2008), the BES evaluated the city-wide benefits of extensive green roof retrofit but also recognised the difference between private and public benefits of stormwater and other multiple benefits of vegetated roofs.

Using estimates of the cost to the city of managing stormwater, the study estimated that a discount of 35% on stormwater fees could be offered to owners that effectively reduced the impervious area on their site via installation of an Ecoroof. At 2008 rates this would generate a saving of $2.77/ sq. ft of roof. For a 40,000 sq. ft roof this could result in a monthly saving of $110.74 (Bureau of Environmental Services – City of Portland, 2008). Monitoring of two specific buildings that had been retrofitted with green roofs was also carried out by Bureau staff (Kurtz, 2010), finding higher average performances than predicted by benefits transfer estimates, with precipitation retention being calculated at 69% on average and almost 100% during dry-period storm events.

Recognising the need to understand the multiple benefits, the Bureau also estimated other owner benefits such as those identified in the conceptual model above. Reduced heating and cooling costs were calculated based on an average R-valued building being converted to a rye grass green roof. The resulting improvement in thermal efficiency could save 0.156 kWh annually per square foot, making the 40,000 sq. ft roof amass a saving of 6240 kWh.

Studies suggest that a green roof can extend the life of the roof membrane from 20 to 40 years, saving the cost of one replacement out of two. The Bureau estimated this as a saving of $600,000 and a saving of $21,000 on HVAC equipment over 20 years. The findings from the study are summarised in Table 5.8, and show that over 40 years the private owner has a net benefit from the factors considered but that over a 5-year timeframe the installation is not cost beneficial.

Amenity/aesthetics of green roofs was assessed by a follow-up study (Entrix, 2010) and found to depend on the level of access or visibility of the green roof. The well-publicised green roof atop the Multnomah building, for example, provides public access for visitors, educative displays and is visible to several neighbouring buildings. However, for the property owner the most relevant question may relate to increased rental potential. Rental uplift from green roof installation has not been widely measured in the commercial property market, but many authors suggest that the recreational amenity value of a green roof can be extrapolated from values for landscaping or parks and could represent massive capital uplifts on large CBD offices if predicated on a 7% increase in rental value (Clements *et al.*, 2013). However, if a city-wide programme is successful, it may be argued that the differential benefit of

Table 5.8   Summary of Ecoroof costs and benefits for private owner/investor

Focus area	Costs		Benefits		Summary	
	One-time ($)	Annual ($)	One-time ($)	Annual ($)	5-year (2008$)	40-year (2008$)
Stormwater management volume reduction				1,330	6,992	45,866
Cooling energy reduction				680	3,424	19,983
Heating energy reduction				800	4,028	23,509
Construction cost	230,000				(230,000)	(230,000)
Avoided stormwater costs			69,000		69,000	69,000
Increased operation/ maintenance costs		600			(3,077)	(20,677)
Roof longevity			600,000			474,951
HVAC sizing			21,000		21,000	21,000
Total	230,000	600	690,000	2,810	(128,803)	403,632

Source: Adapted from BES (2008).

having a green roof would be much lower than 7%. More research into this is warranted, because of the potential incentive such benefits could provide.

5.5   Conclusions – Where to Next?

This chapter has described recent research towards assessing the contribution of green roof retrofit to attenuating stormwater runoff as a means of mitigating pluvial flooding within the CBD. The challenges posed by pluvial or surface-water flooding have been identified and characterised by their unpredictability, sudden onset and high velocity; the frequency of pluvial flooding is likely to increase in the future due to changes in weather patterns caused by a warming climate and the concentration of impermeable surfaces in cities caused by urban densification. The disruption and damage caused by pluvial flooding in the CBD have been highlighted, including the direct damage to buildings and contents caused by floodwater as well as the long-term impact on local communities and economies.

One study reported the development of a novel methodology to estimate the potential benefits of green roof retrofit. The methodology developed uses a desk-based approach to the development of a database of buildings, Google maps to gauge the suitability of existing buildings for green roof retrofit and the latest green roof stormwater attenuation modelling to establish the potential impacts and benefits of a green roof retrofit at a city scale. The methodology is not without its limitations, but this study has demonstrated the benefits of such an approach.

The two contrasting cities selected for this research (Newcastle, UK and Melbourne, Australia) have been described, and their vulnerability to severe pluvial flood events has been observed. The two cities have contrasting building stocks in the CBD, with Newcastle being characterised by generally older, low-rise buildings, many of historic importance within conservation areas, albeit with some more modern developments. By contrast, the building stock in Melbourne is more modern, with an average age of 61 years and being of frame construction. Other considerations – such as the orientation of buildings, roof pitch, access for installation and maintenance purposes and the shadowing caused by neighbouring buildings – have also been highlighted as factors that might make buildings unsuitable for green roof retrofit. Despite these contrasts, it was observed that approximately 15% of the existing building stock in both Melbourne and Newcastle was regarded as suitable for green roof retrofit.

A conceptual model of the distributed benefits of green roof technology has highlighted the direct and indirect benefits to owners and occupiers of commercial buildings. The model recognises that the measurable direct benefits may not be sufficiently attractive (i.e., in financial terms) to convince property owners to commit to green roof retrofit. However, the multiple direct benefits – including those to wider societal and ecological beneficiaries – are likely to provide a compelling case. Further research into the impact on property values in response to pro-environmental behaviour and company reputation is needed, so that suitable incentives and other interventions that would support such adaptations can be called for.

The findings indicate that retrofit could be a significant mitigating factor for both Newcastle and Melbourne if high levels of retrofit could be achieved. However, achieving this high level will be challenging unless ways can be found to render more buildings suitable for retrofit – for example, careful choice of planting that can survive overshadowing.

The chapter draws on lessons from the Portland Ecoroof programme in the USA, as a good-practice example of how a city's efforts to increase the uptake of green infrastructure can be effectively implemented. The Portland Ecoroof programme highlighted the multiple benefits afforded by green roof retrofit, including reduced heating and cooling costs and the savings provided by extending the life of the roof membrane from 20 to 40 years.

The work discussed in this chapter highlights that the benefits of retrofit at the individual building scale are unlikely to be suitably attractive to convince building owners and occupiers to invest in green roof retrofit, unless specific incentive schemes exist or more compelling evidence of indirect benefits is generated. It is posited here that there exist perceived wider social benefits (such as corporate social responsibility and potential reputational gains) that could be attractive to owners and occupiers. That is, the model suggests that the business case for retrofit of green roofs must be predicated on the consideration of multiple direct benefits, as well as recognising the wider societal and ecological benefits.

References

Abbott, J., Davies, P., Simkins, P., Morgan, C., Levin, D. and Robinson, P. (2013) *Creating Water Sensitive Places – Scoping the Potential for Water Sensitive Urban Design in the UK*. CIRIA: London.

Bhattacharya-Mis, N., Joseph, R., Proverbs, D. and Lamond, J. (2015) 'Grass-root preparedness against potential flood risk among residential and commercial property holders', *International Journal of Disaster Resilience in the Built Environment*, 6, 44–56.

BMG Research (2011) *Cumbria Business Survey 2010*. Cumbria Intelligence Observatory.

Bureau of Environmental Services – City of Portland (2008) *Cost Benefit Evaluation of Ecoroofs 2008*. City of Portland, Portland, OR.

Bureau of Meteorology (Australia) (undated) *Melbourne Metropolitan Area and Environs in March 2010*. Available at: www.bom.gov.au/climate/current/month/vic/archive/201003.melbourne.shtml#records RainTtlRecenthigh.

Charlesworth, S. M. and Warwick, F. (2011) 'Adapting to and mitigating floods using sustainable urban drainage systems'. In Lamond, J., Booth, C., Hammond, F. and Proverbs, D. (eds), *Flood Hazards: Impacts and Responses for the Built Environment*. CRC/Taylor & Francis: Boca Raton, FL; pp. 207–234.

City of Melbourne (2015) http://www.melbourne.vic.gov.au/about-council/vision-goals/eco-city/pages/adapting-to-climate-change.aspx.

City of San Francisco (2010) *San Francisco Stormwater Design Guidelines: Appendix A: BMP Factsheets*. San Francisco: City of San Francisco, Public Utilities Commission, Port of San Francisco.

Clements, J., St. Juliana, A., Davis, P. and Levine, L. (2013) *The Green Edge: How Commercial Property Investment in Green Infrastructure Creates Value*. Natural Resources Defense Council: New York.

Entrix (2010) *Portland's Green Infrastructure: Quantifying the Health, Energy, and Community Livability Benefits*. City of Portland, Bureau of Environmental Services, Portland, OR.

Environment Agency – Yorkshire & North East Region (2012) *Hydrology of the Tyneside*, June 2012 Flood Environment Agency.

Environment Agency (2013) *Flooding in England – A National Assessment of Flood Risk* Environment Agency: Bristol.

Fioretti, R., Palla, A., Lanza, L. G. and Principi, P. (2010) 'Green roof energy and water related performance in the Mediterranean climate', *Building and Environment*, 45, 1890–1904.

French, L., Samwinga, V. and Proverbs, D. (2011) 'The UK sewer network: perceptions of its condition and role in flood risk'. In Lamond, J. E., Proverbs, D. G., Booth, C. A. and Hammond, F. N. (eds), *Flood Hazards, Impacts and Responses for the Built Environment*. CRC/Taylor & Francis: Boca Raton, FL.

Gordon-Walker, S., Harle, T. and Naismith, I. (2007) *Cost–Benefit of SUDS Retrofit in Urban Areas*. Science Report No. SC060024. Environment Agency: Bristol.

Groundwork (2011) *Green Roof Developer's Guide*. Groundwork: Sheffield.

Ingirige, B. and Wedawatta, G. (2011) 'Impacts of flood hazard on small and medium sized companies strategies for property level protection and business continuity'. In Lamond, J. E., Proverbs, D. G., Booth, C. A. and Hammond, F. N. (eds), *Flood Hazards, Impacts and Responses for the Built Environment*. CRC/Taylor & Francis: Boca Raton, FL.

Jha, A., Lamond, J., Bloch, R., *et al.* (2011) *'Five feet high and rising – cities and flooding in the 21st century'*. Policy Research Working Paper No. 5648. The World Bank: Washington, D.C.

Kincaid, D. (2003) *Adapting Buildings for Changing Uses: Guidelines for change of use refurbishment*. Routledge: London.

Kurtz, T. (2010) 'Ecoroof performance monitoring in Portland, Oregon', 2010 International Low Impact Development Conference – Redefining Water in the City, 11–14 April. American Society of Civil Engineers: San Francisco, CA; pp. 1234–1246.

Lamond, J. E., Wilkinson, S. and Rose, C. (2014) 'Conceptualising the benefits of green roof technology for commercial real estate owners and occupiers'. *Resilient Communities: Providing for the Future. 20th Annual Pacific Rim Real Estate Conference (PRRES)*: Christchurch, New Zealand.

Lawson, E., Thorne, C., Ahilan, S., *et al.* (2014) *Delivering and Evaluating the Multiple Flood Risk Benefits in Blue–Green Cities: An Interdisciplinary Approach.* Flood Recovery Innovation and Response IV. WIT Press: Southampton.

Ma, L., Qin, B. and Zuo, C. (2012) 'Performance of urban rainwater retention by green roof: a case study of Jinan', 2nd International Conference on Civil Engineering, Architecture and Building Materials (CEABM 2012), 25–27 May. Trans Tech Publications: Yantai, China; pp. 295–299.

MacIvor, J. S. and Lundholm, J. (2011) 'Performance evaluation of native plants suited to extensive green roof conditions in a maritime climate', *Ecological Engineering*, 37, 407–417.

Mentens, J., Raes, D. and Hermy, M. (2006) 'Green roofs as a tool for solving the rainwater runoff problem in the urbanized 21st century?', *Landscape and Urban Planning*, 77, 217–226.

Met Office Hadley Centre for Climate Research (2007) *Climate Research at the Met Office Hadley Centre – Informing Government Policy into the Future.* Available at: www.metoffice.gov.uk/research/hadleycentre/pubs/brochures/clim_res_had_fut_pol.pdf.

Nagase, A. and Dunnett, N. (2012) 'Amount of water runoff from different vegetation types on extensive green roofs: effects of plant species, diversity and plant structure', *Landscape and Urban Planning*, 104, 356–363.

News.com (2011) 'Severe storms, flash floods hit Melbourne and parts of Victoria'. Available at: www.news.com.au/national/storm-to-move-south-and-soak-victoria/storye6frfkvr-1226000442820.

Rose, C. and Lamond, J. (2013) 'Performance of sustainable drainage for urban flood control, lessons from Europe and Asia', International Conference on Flood Resilience: Experiences in Asia and Europe, 5–7 September, Exeter, UK.

Solomon, S. and Qin, D. (2007) *Climate Change 2007: The Physical Science Basis.* Contribution of Working Group 1 to the Fourth Assessment Report of the Intergovernmental Panel on Climate Change. Cambridge University Press: Cambridge.

Stovin, V. (2010) 'The potential of green roofs to manage urban stormwater', *Water and Environment Journal*, 24, 192–199.

Total Research and Technical Services Newcastle City Council (2013) *Summer 2012 Flooding in Newcastle-upon-Tyne.* A report on the experiences of residents and non-residential property managers. Newcastle City Council: Newcastle-upon-Tyne.

Wedawatta, G., Ingirige, B., Jones, K. and Proverbs, D. (2011) 'Extreme weather events and construction SMEs: vulnerability, impacts and responses', *Structural Survey*, 29, 106–119.

White, I. and Howe, J. (2002) 'Flooding and the role of planning in England and Wales: a critical review', *Journal of Environmental Planning and Management*, 45, 735–745.

Wilkinson, S. J. (2014) 'The preliminary assessment of adaptation potential in existing office buildings', *International Journal of Strategic Property Management*, 18(1), 77–87.

Wilkinson, S. J. and Reed, R. (2009) 'Green roof retrofit potential in the central business district', *Property Management*, 27, 284–301.

Wilkinson, S. J., Reed, R. and James, K. (2009) 'Using building adaptation to deliver sustainability in Australia', *Structural Survey*, 27, 46–61.

Williams, N. S., Raynor, J. P. and Raynor, K. J. (2010) 'Green roofs for a wide brown land: opportunities and barriers for rooftop greening in Australia', *Urban Forestry and Urban Greening*, 9, 245–251.

Biodiversity and Green Roof Retrofit

Tanya Latty
University of Sydney, Australia

Tanya Latty
University of Sydney, Australia

6.0   Introduction

The conversion of pristine habitat and agricultural lands into urbanised landscapes is increasing. By 2030, 60% of the population is expected to be living within a city (Ksiazek *et al.*, 2014). It is clear that the explosive growth of cities has had tremendous effects on animal life; indeed, urbanisation is recognised as a leading threatening process to global biodiversity (deGroot *et al.*, 2010). Although there are many indirect effects (e.g., the heat island effect, introduction of non-native species, changes to soils and biogeochemical cycles; Kowarik, 2011), the major consequence of urbanisation is the conversion of continuous native vegetation into a patchwork of habitats interspersed with a matrix of impervious surfaces (pavement and buildings) and grassy lawns (McGuire *et al.*, 2013). As the urbanisation process progresses, some habitats are lost entirely, while the remaining habitats are fragmented. Habitat fragmentation acts to isolate individual habitat patches, thereby isolating organisms with limited mobility and eliminating species that require large patches of habitat. Urbanisation also decreases the structural complexity of vegetation, since landscaping typically involves the removal of shrubs and woody debris. The formerly complex vegetation is then replaced with simpler grasses and forbs. Since the biodiversity of many animal groups is positively correlated with vegetation complexity (e.g., see Langellotto and Denno, 2004), habitat simplification can lead to declines in biodiversity.

Although urbanisation generally leads to declines in biodiversity, cities are also able to support high numbers of particular species. These animals ('urban adaptors') possess behaviours or physiological adaptations that allow them to thrive in urban environments; pigeons, the Australian white

Green Roof Retrofit: Building Urban Resilience, First Edition.
Edited by Sara Wilkinson and Tim Dixon.
© 2016 John Wiley & Sons, Ltd. Published 2016 by John Wiley & Sons, Ltd.

Ibis and some cockroach species are excellent examples. The role of urban green spaces in protecting and conserving biodiversity is increasingly being recognised by ecologists and urban planners (Ishimatsu and Ito, 2013). For example, the City of Sydney has an Urban Ecology Action Plan designed to enhance and protect biodiversity within its heavily urbanised city core (Sydney, 2014b). In many developed countries, there are initiatives aimed at increasing biodiversity in urban gardens (Goddard *et al.*, 2010). In the USA, for example, the National Wildlife Federation (www.nwf.org/) grants 'Certified Wildlife Habitat' status to homeowners who can demonstrate that their yard provides five key habitat elements: the provision of food, the provision of water, the provision of cover, places to raise young, and the use of no or low-chemical sustainable gardening techniques, including the use of native plants.

Arguably, the most effective way to mitigate habitat loss and fragmentation is to increase the number of native vegetation patches within cities. In most cases this is logistically infeasible, as competing land uses often preclude the conversion of commercial or residential spaces into parklands. The urbanisation process is therefore difficult to reverse; for example, due to land values and ownership patterns, apartment blocks are rarely replaced with parks, and shopping centres rarely give way to native meadows. Green roofs, and retrofitted green roofs, offer a potential solution to the dilemma of urban biodiversity by converting otherwise unused roof space into habitat for native species. At the same time, these habitat patches can increase habitat connectivity, thus providing a potential antidote to habitat fragmentation. Finally, the relative inaccessibility of green roofs might create havens where species can grow and multiply undisturbed by human activity. The exciting potential of green roofs has already led some municipal governments to include them in their biodiversity plans. For example, the cities of Toronto (Canada) and Basel (Switzerland) have published guidelines for enhancing biodiversity on green roofs (Toronto, 2013; Gunnarsson and Federsel, 2014).

Although the potential biodiversity benefits of green roofs are exciting, some scepticism is warranted because there are several important factors which might make green roofs unsuitable for the conservation of biodiversity. First, green roofs are generally small, so they are unable to support animals that have larger range requirements (most mammals). As such, the habitat provision benefit of green roofs is probably limited to small animals like insects and other arthropods. Second, green roofs tend to be spatially isolated and are inaccessible to all but the most mobile of animals. Third, green roofs provide a very harsh environment, with higher temperatures and higher wind velocities than ground-level habitats. Thus, they are unsuited for many species. Given these potential difficulties, what role can retrofitted and new green roofs play in the conservation of animal biodiversity? This chapter will review current literature on the effectiveness of green roofs as tools for supporting urban biodiversity, starting with a brief introduction to the concept and measurement of biodiversity. The chapter will discuss research focused on the impact of green roofs on vertebrate and invertebrate biodiversity, and will conclude with recommendations for supporting biodiversity on green roofs.

6.1   What is Biodiversity?

Enhancing or creating biodiversity is often cited as an objective of building a green roof retrofit: but what does 'biodiversity' actually mean? How is it measured? Biologists generally describe three kinds of biodiversity (Box 6.1), of which 'species diversity' is the type most applicable to green roofs. When designing a biodiverse green roof, it is worth considering exactly what kind

Box 6.1   Biological Diversity

Biologists delineate three distinct types of biodiversity: species diversity, genetic diversity and ecological diversity. *Species diversity* is the most relevant for green roofs, as it refers to the species within an area. It is commonly assessed as 'species richness', which is simply the total number of species within a given area. Species richness does not take into account the number of representatives of each species; thus, a region with 1000 individuals of species A and only 1 representative of species B would have the same richness (2) as would a site that had 50 individuals of species A and 50 individuals of species B. Ecologists use a measure called '*species evenness*' to account for the different sizes of species populations. Communities where the number of individuals in each species is similar (our second example) are scored as being more 'even' than communities in which there is a big difference in the population sizes of the species present. Other indices, such as the Shannon index, take into account both the number of species and the evenness of the sample.

Genetic diversity refers to the amount of genetic variation within a particular species. Species with low genetic diversity often suffer from an inability to adapt to changing environments. Other effects, such as reduced reproduction due to inbreeding depression, can also have serious negative consequences for populations. Habitat fragmentation tends to decrease genetic diversity by isolating populations, which then have no choice but to mate amongst themselves. This can be mitigated to some extent by providing corridors that allow individuals to move from one fragment to another. The potential of green roofs to increase genetic diversity has not been explored directly, although a recent study (which will be discussed in detail later in this chapter) found that green roofs can act as 'corridors in the sky', effectively linking otherwise isolated populations (Dunnett, 2006).

Ecosystem diversity refers to the number of ecosystems in an area, and at first appears to be irrelevant to the study of green roofs. However, green roofs tend to have higher temperature and lower rainfall than ground-level sites; as a consequence, green roofs might support ecosystems quite different from the ecosystems present at ground level. For example, the presence of green roofs could result in the co-existence of Mediterranean-type ecosystems on roofs and temperate ecosystems at ground level. Green roofs could therefore have the potential to increase ecosystem diversity.

of biodiversity we are hoping to enhance or increase. It is also important to clearly define a reference habitat, so that the success of the green roof can be assessed. For example, one might build a green roof with the goal of increasing the total number of species ('species richness') that live on the roof, relative to the surrounding area. Alternatively, we may wish to target species of particular conservation concern, such as an endangered bird. In that case, the appropriate measure of biodiversity might be the number of chicks that successfully fledge from the green roof relative to the fledging success of birds nesting on the ground.

A second consideration, often overlooked, is to determine the taxonomic level of biodiversity that is being targeted. Are we interested only in bird species? Soil-dwelling species? Bee species? While many green roof strategies aim towards 'biodiversity', in practise, collecting and identifying all the species present in a given area is a massive and logistically infeasible task. Different groups, for example, require very different sampling regimes. Identifying bird and mammal species can usually be done by non-specialists, while identifying invertebrates such as insects generally requires extensive training. Indeed, some species of insect are indistinguishable from one another without the use of microscopes or even dissections. Finally, as we will discuss below, different animal groups have different requirements, and so the techniques used to encourage biodiversity need to reflect the target group.

6.2   Green Roofs for Vertebrate Conservation

Attempts to increase vertebrate biodiversity typically target birds and/or bats (with birds reviewed in Fernandez-Canero and Gonzalez-Redondo, 2010). This makes sense, since the inaccessibility of rooftops suggests that only highly mobile winged species will be able to access them. Vertebrates are relatively large, and it is unlikely that a single green roof can provide all necessary resources for them. For example, a bat needs not only food resources, but also adequate nest sites and access to water; all of these resources must be within the animal's flight range. Thus, green roofs usually support vertebrates by providing one or a few critical resources.

One of the simplest ways a green roof can support vertebrate fauna is by providing food. As we will see later in this chapter, green roofs can serve as a habitat for invertebrates, which may in turn attract predatory birds and bats. Seeds, berries, nectar and other plant matter can also provide food resources for birds (Fernandez-Canero and Gonzalez-Redondo, 2010). Pearce and Walters (2012) investigated the value of conventional roofs and two types of green roofs (biodiverse and sedum based) on the feeding behaviour of bats in Greater London (UK). Three bat species were recorded feeding over biodiverse roofs, and their feeding activity was significantly greater than over conventional or sedum roofs. While there are reports of birds feeding on or around green roofs (Fernandez-Canero and Gonzalez-Redondo, 2010), surprisingly few peer-reviewed studies have explicitly tested the hypothesis that green roofs can provide valuable food resources for vertebrates.

The idea that green roofs might provide nesting sites for birds has been investigated by Baumann (2006), who found that Northern Lapwings, an endangered species, used rooftop gardens as nesting sites. They found evidence of old nesting sites, suggesting that the lapwings had been using the rooftops over multiple seasons. However, in 2005 and 2006, not one of the broods was successful. In most cases chicks hatched, but later died. Improvements to the roof's vegetation improved chick life expectancy, although no chicks survived to adulthood. This study raises the important point that simply observing the presence of a species on a green roof does not mean that the green roof is necessarily benefiting the animal in question. In some cases green roofs may act as 'ecological traps', diverting wildlife away from appropriate habitat into habitat that cannot support it. It is absolutely crucial that studies investigating the biodiversity value of green roofs do not stop at simply observing the presence of key species, but that they also investigate the eventual reproductive success of individuals using the habitat relative to those using other urban habitats.

To date, the available evidence on the conservation value of green roofs to vertebrates is mixed at best. At least some literature suggests we should be cautious about assuming that the creation of habitat will necessarily have a positive influence on species. In addition, none of the studies to date have actually assessed biodiversity per se; in all cases, the authors were interested in measuring the abundance of only one or a few vertebrate species, with no real attempt to quantify species richness. One could argue that, since each free-living vertebrate probably harbours a multitude of parasites – both internal and external – anything that benefits a single species necessarily benefits a veritable universe of species. However, the fact that we have not yet quantified vertebrate species richness on green roofs means that we still know very little about the actual role green roofs play in conserving biodiversity. The studies above focus primarily on birds, but there has been at least one effort to create green roofs for reptiles. For example, deGroot *et al.* (2010) investigated the potential of green roofs as habitat for an endemic New Zealand skink species. While they found that the roofs would likely meet the skinks' habitat requirements, no experiments that test the survivorship and reproduction of skinks on rooftop habitats have yet been reported.

6.3   Green Roofs for Invertebrate Conservation

Invertebrate animals such as insects are generally much smaller than vertebrates; as such, it is possible for all of their habitat needs to be met on a single green roof. In addition, many invertebrate taxa are highly mobile and so can access spatially isolated roofs. Insects, for example, often have wings, which allow them to travel large distances. Despite lacking wings, spiderlings can 'fly' by ballooning along on a fine piece of silk. Green roofs therefore have great potential in the conservation of invertebrate taxa. Several studies have reported the presence of large numbers of invertebrates on green roofs. Nagase and Nomura (2014) reported 46 invertebrate species representing 11 different orders on a green roof in Japan, while other research identified 26 bee species on 7 green roofs in Chicago (Ksiazek *et al.*, 2014). Kadas (2006) found that 10% of the species captured on green roofs had received the designation 'nationally rare or scarce', suggesting that green roofs can serve as refuges for threatened invertebrate taxa. Interestingly, a large proportion (50%) of the invertebrates captured were snails; this is surprising, as snails are not particularly mobile and would not be amongst the taxa normally expected to rapidly colonise rooftops. However, Kadas (2006) points out that snails are abundant on the farms where green roof plants are grown, and so they may have 'hitch hiked' in on the vegetation. Once established, it is likely that snail populations expanded due to the absence of mammalian predators. Thus, it is worth remembering that the ecosystems which emerge on green roofs can include not only high-mobility animals, but also those capable of 'hitch hiking' on plants or other animals.

It is clear that green roofs are capable of supporting large numbers of invertebrates. But how does the biodiversity of green roofs compare with similarly sized ground-level sites? MacIvor (2011) found no difference between the number of species or the number of individual insects found on green roofs compared with ground-level sites. Tonietto *et al.* (2011), however, found that while many native bee species were present on green roofs, the number of individuals and the number of bee species was lower than observed in traditional parks, or in areas of remnant tall grass prairie. Similarly, Ksiazek *et al.* (2014) found fewer individuals and species on green roofs compared with ground-level sites. Based on this small number of studies, it appears that green roofs usually contain less biodiversity than ground-level sites, although there are exceptions. Care must therefore be taken when assuming that rooftop sites can simply replace equivalent ground-level sites.

The specific composition of green roofs has a strong effect on invertebrate biodiversity. In general, invertebrate diversity increases with increasing veg-etation complexity; the same appears to be true on green roofs. Madre *et al.* (2013) found that green roofs with the most structurally complex vegetation had the highest arthropod abundance. Similarly, Schindler *et al.* (2011) found a positive relationship between arthropod abundance and vegetation cover; indeed, vegetation cover was more important than plant diversity. Planting a variety of structurally complex plants is therefore a good strategy for maximising biodiversity on green roofs.

There is evidence that the hot, dry environment on green roofs favours species that are pre-adapted to similarly arid conditions. It has been suggested that urban environments favour cliff-dwelling species, which are already adapted to life on hot, rocky surfaces (Lundholm, 2006). For example, Madre (2013) noted an abundance of dry, heat-loving species on green roofs, while Rumble and Gange (2013) noted that the soil microarthropod community of green roofs was dominated by heat and drought-tolerant species. Moisture-sensitive species such as annelids and millipedes were completely absent.

In addition to increasing the number of species in the urban environment, green roofs can act as 'stepping stones' connecting distant areas together and increasing the 'permeability' of the city (Braaker *et al.*, 2013). Small-bodied bee species, for example, are typically restricted to flight ranges of less than 500 m. Both the nesting site and all flower resources must be located within this 500 m radius. If areas of habitat are isolated, then the offspring of our hypothetical small bee will not disperse across the landscape; they will be limited to the 500 m radius of their forefathers, leading to inbreeding. However, if habitat patches are connected, perhaps by green roofs, then dispersing offspring can hop to a new patch. Over time, this allows for increasing ranges and, more importantly, connects isolated populations. This connectivity is crucial for conservation as well-connected populations are thought to be more resilient to disturbance, since areas can be recolonised after local extinction events (Braaker *et al.*, 2013). The benefits of better connectivity extend to the plants pollinated by insects, as these will now have access to a pollinator whose range may have previously been restricted by lack of connectivity.

6.4   Conclusions

The study of green roofs as habitat is in its infancy, and as yet there are too few studies from which to draw strong conclusions. As Williams *et al.* (2014) point out in their excellent review, there is still a tremendous paucity of data about the impact of green roofs on biodiversity. In particular, more studies that compare green roofs to ground sites are needed. It is not enough to simply observe that certain species are present on green roofs; we need to know the extent to which green roofs contribute to urban biodiversity compared with other types of urban green space. There seems to be little evidence that green roofs outperform ground-level sites in terms of biodiversity (Williams *et al.*, 2014). This is not surprising, given that the harsh conditions and general inaccessibility of green roofs probably act as a 'filter', screening for species that are capable of colonising and surviving in these novel environments. Future research would do well to study the filter effect in greater detail. Few studies have examined the dynamics of green roof communities, so we have little understanding of how green roof ecosystems change over time. Some work in this direction has already occurred. For example, Schrader and Böning (2006) found slightly higher collembolan (small soil-dwelling arthropods) diversity on older green roofs than on younger green roofs, and observed that older roofs had more stable environments due to the formation of mature soils.

Although vertebrate conservation is typically better funded than invertebrate conservation, the evidence for a strong role of green roofs in increasing vertebrate biodiversity is weak. While green roofs can provide some resources (i.e., insects as food for bats and birds), there is currently no evidence that they provide high-quality breeding habitats. Indeed, studies which show breeding failure in roof-breeding birds serve as a strong caution against assuming that the provision of habitat will necessarily increase abundance or biodiversity. Future research will need to determine if roofs purposely built to fulfil the needs of particular vertebrate species are capable of supporting appreciable populations, and importantly, whether these sites are equivalent or superior to ground-level conservation efforts. Given the aridity of roof-top gardens, a useful approach might be to focus on vertebrates from similar habitats.

Invertebrates are typically overlooked in conservation efforts, despite the fact that they make up 98% of animal life and are absolutely crucial in the provision of many ecosystem services such as pollination. In addition, building green roofs that have greater invertebrate biodiversity can increase the amount of food available for vertebrates. Supporting insect pollinators can in turn have positive effects on plant diversity. Indeed, it is suggested that in terms of maximising conservation value, green roof designers would do well to focus on providing pollinator habitat. Pollinators are ecologically important, well loved by the public and highly mobile. Studies that have investigated bees and insects on rooftops suggest that many species are able to use green roofs as habitat, and their ability to fly might allow green roofs to serve as ecological corridors in the sky, connecting otherwise disconnected pieces of habitat together.

At present, the study of green roof biodiversity suffers from a lack of methodological consistency. Studies use vastly different trapping regimes (from pitfall traps, to intercept traps, to pan traps, to direct observations). This has a tremendous impact on the results and makes comparisons between studies difficult. It is therefore important that green roof researchers adopt some of the standard assessment protocols that have been developed for particular groups. For example, there is an established, widely used protocol for sampling bees (Bee Inventory Protocol; Droege *et al.*, 2003). Invertebrate-focused studies vary tremendously in their degree of taxonomic resolution, with some studies identifying insects to species, several only identifying to order, and others simply using 'morpho-species' to refer to groups of individuals that look different from one another and are thought to be members of the same species. This is hugely problematic, as each insect order, for example, can contain upwards of 100,000 species, each with differing ecology. In none of the papers referenced here did the authors mention the existence of a reference collection. The deposition of a reference collection, which contains examples of all the insects collected during a project, is a standard practice in insect ecology. Reference collections ensure that identifications can be double-checked by other researchers. Invertebrates are notoriously difficult to identify, with specialist help often being required. Since the number of trained insect taxonomists is declining rapidly, it is not surprising that most studies struggled with their identifications. Nevertheless, correct identification is absolutely crucial to understanding how green roofs effect invertebrate diversity. Therefore, future researchers need to collaborate with university or museum-based taxonomists who can help ensure that identifications are correct.

6.4.1   Designing Biodiverse Green Roofs

How do we go about increasing the biodiversity value of green roofs (Appendix 2)? As we have seen throughout this chapter, greater vegetative complexity equals more species in greater abundance. This is unsurprising, given that research from ground-level sites consistently shows a strong positive relationship between vegetation complexity and biodiversity. Greater complexity means more niches, and this leads to greater diversity. For pollinators, ensuring a diversity of floral resources with differing flowering times is likely key to increasing diversity. Different plants provide different insects with different resources. For example, some flowering plants serve as excellent nectar sources; many animals – including wasps, beetles, bees, butterflies and some birds – use nectar as a source of carbohydrates. Other plants provide nutritious pollen, which is a source of protein for animals including bees, beetles, flies and butterflies. Planting a mixture of nectar and pollen-producing plants helps to ensure that the food requirements of a larger variety of animals are met. Along similar lines, planting flowers that have different flowering periods ensures a continuous supply of pollen and nectar throughout the season.

In addition to vegetative complexity, we should also consider diversity in both the substrate and the topology of green roofs. Large rocks can provide shelter for a variety of invertebrates, while altering stone sizes can create an array of different microclimates for soil-dwelling microarthropods. Small piles of sticks, wood and pine cones can add structural complexity and provide homes for more invertebrate species. In addition, adding small slopes, hills and piles can change the microhydrology of the site, creating areas of varying moisture. Recently, many ground-level gardens have started using 'insect hotels' to boost invertebrate diversity by providing nesting sites, primarily for bees and wasps. Insect hotels typically consist of combinations of drilled wood blocks, hollow reeds and clay blocks. The ability of insect hotels to attract and maintain insect populations has been noted by several authors (Gathmann et al., 1994; Tscharntke et al., 1998; Steffan-Dewenter, 2002). However, a recent study of more than 300 insect hotels found that they housed a high number of invasive species, and that they tended to act as accumulators for parasitoid species (MacIvor and Packer, 2015). Therefore, the use of insect hotels as a conservation tool should proceed with caution, as they may have a negative impact on overall bee populations. This study highlights the importance of careful, well-replicated studies to assess the impacts of various habitat modifications on conservation.

While all the studies referenced here have focused on measures of 'species diversity', there is tremendous scope for green roofs to increase genetic diversity by acting collectively as stepping stones connecting otherwise isolated animal communities. Increasing habitat connectivity through green roofs requires a city-wide approach to green roof management. The City of Toronto, for example, provides an excellent case study for developing city-wide guidelines for increasing biodiversity (Box 6.2). If designers follow the guidelines set out by the City of Toronto, then green roofs no longer act in isolation; rather, they become part of an interconnected habitat corridor. In addition, taking a landscape view that incorporates not just the green roof but also the surrounding habitat can lead to more successful attempts to increase or enhance biodiversity. For example, if a roof is within flying distance of a pond (or other water source), a roof aiming to increase bird biodiversity may not need to provide a water source. In contrast, a roof that provides nesting spaces for solitary bees, but which is surrounded by a concrete jungle, will need to provide flowers if the bees are to survive and prosper.

Box 6.2   Case study: City of Toronto guidelines for biodiverse green roofs.

The City of Toronto, Canada was the first city in North America to require the construction of green roofs on new developments (Toronto, 2013). By law, new developments must include green roofs that cover between 20% and 60% of the roof area. As part of the green roof programme, the City of Toronto also publishes a set of guidelines which lay out best practices for the creation of roofs that increase biodiversity through the creation of habitat. A positive feature of the City of Toronto's guidelines is their clear distinction between creating generally biodiverse habitats and creating habitat for specific target specimens. They aim to increase biodiversity using several design strategies:

- Varying the composition of the substrate to promote diverse arthropod communities.
- Providing topographic variety using slopes, different heights of edging, planter boxes and modules.
- Providing shady microclimates using rocks, plants and building elements.
- Maximising the diversity of plants.
- Providing a variety of nesting opportunities such as bird houses, logs and branches, open soil areas and bee hotels.
- Providing water sources such as basins, bird baths, pitted rocks and water features.
- Providing perching habitats such as branches, rocks, shrubs and logs.

The city's guidelines also incorporate a landscape perspective by providing specific design strategies for rooftops adjacent to particular habitats. For example, it is suggested that rooftops adjacent to lakeside habitat be planted with seed-producing plants, which can provide food for early spring migratory birds.

The city also encourages the planting of diverse flowers, which bloom at different times of the year. The guidelines provide a list of plants that support caterpillars and butterflies.

In summary, carefully designed green roofs have the potential to alleviate some of the biodiversity loss associated with urbanisation. We are, however, in dire need of more well-designed studies to assess and monitor the novel ecosystems created atop green roofs.

References

Baumann, N. (2006) 'Ground-nesting birds on green roofs in Switzerland: preliminary observations', *Urban Habitats*, 4(1), 37–50.

Braaker, S., Ghazoul, J., Obrist, M. K. and Moretti, M. (2013) 'Habitat connectivity shapes urban arthropod communities: the key role of green roofs', *Ecology*, 95, 1010–1021.

deGroot, C., Boult, M., Ussher, G., Toft, R., Simcock, R. and Davies, R. (2010) 'Elevated enclaves – living roof biodiversity enhancement through prosthetic habitats'.

Droege, S., Griswold, T., Minckley, R. and LeBuhn, G. (2003) A Standardized Method for Monitoring Bee Populations – The Bee Inventory (BI) Plot. Available at: online.sfsu.edu/~beeplot/pdfs/Bee%20Plot%202003.pdf.

Dunnett, N. (2006) 'Green roofs for biodiversity: reconciling aesthetics with ecology'. Fourth Annual Greening Rooftops for Sustainable Communities Conference, Boston.

Fernandez-Canero, R. and Gonzalez-Redondo, P. (2010) 'Green roofs as a habitat for birds: a review', *Journal of Animal and Veterinary Advances*, 9, 2041–2052.

Gathmann, A., Greiler, H.-J. and Tscharntke, T. (1994) 'Trap-nesting bees and wasps colonizing set-aside fields: succession and body size, management by cutting and sowing', *Oecologia*, 98, 8–14.

Goddard, M. A., Dougill, A. J. and Benton, T. G. (2010) 'Scaling up from gardens: biodiversity conservation in urban environments', *Trends in Ecology & Evolution*, 25, 90–98.

Gunnarsson, B. and Federsel, L. M. (2014) 'Bumblebees in the city: abundance, species richness and diversity in two urban habitats', *Journal of Insect Conservation*, 18, 1185–1191.

Ishimatsu, K. and Ito, K. (2013) 'Brown/biodiverse roofs: a conservation action for threatened brownfields to support urban biodiversity', *Landscape and Ecological Engineering*, 9, 299–304.

Kadas, G. (2006) 'Rare invertebrates colonizing green roofs in London', *Urban Habitats*, 4, 66–86.

Kowarik, I. (2011) 'Novel urban ecosystems, biodiversity, and conservation', *Environmental Pollution*, 159, 1974–1983.

Ksiazek, K., Tonietto, R. and Ascher, J. S. (2014) 'Ten bee species new to green roofs in the Chicago area', Michigan Entomological Society 47: 87.

Langellotto, G. A. and Denno, R. F. (2004) 'Responses of invertebrate natural enemies to complex-structured habitats: a meta-analytical synthesis', *Oecologia*, 139, 1–10.

Lundholm, J. T. (2006) 'Green roofs and facades: a habitat template approach', *Urban Habitats*, 4(1), 87–101.

MacIvor, J. S. and Packer, L. (2015) '"Bee hotels" as tools for native pollinator conservation: a premature verdict?', *PloS ONE*, 10(3), e0122126.

Madre, F., Vergnes, A., Machon, N. and Clergeau, P. (2014) 'Green roofs as habitats for wild plant species in urban landscapes: first insights from a large-scale sampling', *Landscape and Urban Planning*, 122, 100–107.

McGuire, K. L., Payne, S. G., Palmer, M. I., *et al.* (2013) 'Digging the New York City skyline: soil fungal communities in green roofs and city parks', *PLoS ONE*, 8(3), e58020.

Pearce, H. and Walters, C. L. (2012) 'Do green roofs provide habitat for bats in urban areas?', *Acta chiropterologica*, 14(2), 469–478.

Rumble, H. and Gange, A. C. (2013) 'Soil microarthropod community dynamics in extensive green roofs', *Ecological Engineering*, 57, 197–204.

Schindler, B. Y., Griffith, A. B. and Jones, K. N. (2011) 'Factors influencing arthropod diversity on green roofs', *Cities and the Environment (CATE)*, 4(1), 5.

Schrader, S. and Böning, M. (2006) 'Soil formation on green roofs and its contribution to urban biodiversity with emphasis on Collembolans', *Pedobiologia*, 50, 347–356.

Steffan-Dewenter, I. (2002) 'Landscape context affects trap-nesting bees, wasps, and their natural enemies', *Ecological Entomology*, 27, 631–637.

Sydney (2014a) Green Roofs and Walls Implementation Plan. City of Sydney.

Sydney (2014b) Urban Ecology Strategic Action Plan. City of Sydney.

Tonietto, R., Fant, J., Ascher, J., Ellis, K. and Larkin, D. (2011) 'A comparison of bee communities of Chicago green roofs, parks and prairies', *Landscape and Urban Planning*, 103(1), 102–108.

Toronto (2013) City of Toronto Guidelines for Biodiverse Roofs.

Tscharntke, T., Gathmann, A. and Steffan-Dewenter, I. (1998) 'Bioindication using trap-nesting bees and wasps and their natural enemies: community structure and interactions', *Journal of Applied Ecology*, 35, 708–719.

Vitiello, D., Nairn, M. and Planning, P. (2009) Community Gardening in Philadelphia: 2008 Harvest Report. Penn Planning and Urban Studies, University of Pennsylvania.

Williams, N. S., Lundholm, J. and MacIvor, J. S. (2014) 'Do green roofs help urban biodiversity conservation?', *Journal of Applied Ecology*, 51, 1643–1649.

Planting Choices for Retrofitted Green Roofs

Tijana Blanusa[1,2], Madalena Vaz Monteiro[2], Sarah Kemp[2] and Ross Cameron[3]
[1] RHS Wisley, Woking, UK
[2] School of Agriculture, Policy and Development, University of Reading, UK
[3] Department of Landscape, University of Sheffield, UK

7.0   Introduction

Several parameters currently determine which plant species are chosen for a particular green roof type and location. These include the ability of plants to survive and grow on a given roof depth, in given substrate and climatic conditions, the cost of plant installation and maintenance and, to a degree, the aesthetic appeal of chosen species. Designing a green roof with the delivery of the ecosystem services in mind is still not a mainstream consideration. Irrespective of the local climate, currently most widely used species on shallower (extensive/semi-extensive) green roofs, which have a tendency to quickly dry out, are various *Sedum* (e.g., *S. album*, *S. acre*, *S. sexangulare*, *S. spurium*, etc.) (Kolb and Schwarz, 1999; Monterusso *et al.*, 2005; Köhler, 2006; Dunnett and Kingsbury, 2008). *Sedum* establish rapidly, provide good surface coverage, survive in a range of environmental conditions and require low maintenance. Bulbs and grasses are also frequent choices (Pahlke, 1989; Liesecke, 2001) as well as the perennial forbs (Lundholm *et al.*, 2010; Nagase and Dunnett, 2010). In the last few years, however, in scientific research (if not so widely in practice), a wider range of species is being considered due to their potential to provide more environmental benefits/

Green Roof Retrofit: Building Urban Resilience, First Edition.
Edited by Sara Wilkinson and Tim Dixon.
© 2016 John Wiley & Sons, Ltd. Published 2016 by John Wiley & Sons, Ltd.

(a)

(b)

Figure 7.1 Conventional plant species choice on green roofs could include (a) *Sedum* mixes, grasses and bulbs, while a wider range can be considered to include (b) herbaceous perennials and sub-shrubs where additional irrigation is possible.

ecosystem services (Figure 7.1). Consequently, a broader choice of substrate depths (Savi *et al.*, 2013) and compositions (Molineux *et al.*, 2009; Mickovski *et al.*, 2013; Graceson *et al.*, 2014) are also being considered in order to support this wider range of plant species.

7.1   Ecosystem Services Delivery By Green Roofs: The Importance of Plant Choice

Ecosystem services have been defined as the benefits that humans derive, either directly or indirectly, from the functioning of (healthy) ecosystems (Costanza *et al.*, 1997). Green roofs are increasingly being considered as one such ecosystem, with the ability to contribute to regulating ecosystem services (such as water cycling, pollutant trapping, temperature moderation and carbon storage) as well as provisioning (e.g., rooftop food production) and cultural/social ecosystem services (e.g., recreation areas) (Oberndorfer *et al.*, 2007; Rowe, 2011). The contribution of green roofs to ecosystem services delivery had been studied particularly in the urban environment context; the turn of the 21st century saw a surge in green roof (and ecosystem services) research, focusing on describing green roofs' support of urban biodiversity (Brenneisen, 2006; Kadas, 2006), their ability to contribute to stormwater retention and circulation (Stovin, 2010), air temperature regulation and thermal comfort of urban residents (Wong *et al.*, 2003) and air pollution (Speak *et al.*, 2012). With the increasing number of published studies covering a range of ecosystem services (Ascione *et al.*, 2013; Speak *et al.*, 2014; Volder and Dvorak, 2014; Poë *et al.*, 2015), it is becoming increasingly clear that plant species choice will significantly affect the extent of ecosystem services provision of green roofs.

In this chapter we present a case for considering a wider range of herbaceous plants for semi-extensive green roofs to enhance the roofs' ability to support a number of ecosystem services, using examples from our own research on (1) plants' cooling and building insulation capacity and (2) water sequestration. We will also highlight some more recent studies on the contribution of green roofs to biodiversity support and air pollution mitigation, and explore the significance of widening planting choices to improve the delivery of these services.

7.2   Plant Species Choice and Building Cooling/Insulation

7.2.1   Plants and Cooling – Basic Principles

Urban landscapes are typically warmer than the adjacent rural areas (Oke, 1987; Grimmond, 2007); this leads to a reduction of residents' (thermal) comfort and the need for buildings cooling (Grimmond, 2007). It has been suggested that when maximum daily temperatures are above a threshold of 15°C, a further rise of 1°C in the air temperature will increase the peak air-conditioning energy consumption by 2–4% (Akbari *et al.*, 1997, 2001). Thus, strategically positioned vegetation on/around a building's envelope, which can reduce the energy load on the building during summer, decreasing reliance on artificial air conditioning and saving energy (McPherson *et al.*, 1988; Akbari *et al.*, 2001; Saiz *et al.*, 2006), can be part of the solution. Energy exchange processes within a green roof have been summarised in Figure 7.2. Energy inputs include long and shortwave radiation, which may be immediately (a) reflected away from the building and (b) transmitted into the building. The remaining radiation is absorbed and dissipated as:

1. emitted longwave radiation;
2. sensible heat though convection (when plants are cooler than the surrounding environment);
3. latent heat through evapotranspiration (Figure 7.2).

Additionally, a small proportion (3–6% of the photosynthetically active radiation, i.e., radiation in the visible spectrum) of incoming irradiance is converted to chemical energy through the process of photosynthesis, and this can be subject to further energy losses through chlorophyll fluorescence and non-photochemical quenching (Taiz and Zeiger, 2010). The cooling benefits of plants are thus provided via three main mechanisms:

1. reflecting the incoming light energy;
2. shading the surface;
3. evapotranspiration (i.e., controlled water loss through leaf stomata) (Akbari *et al.*, 2001; Lazzarin *et al.*, 2005).

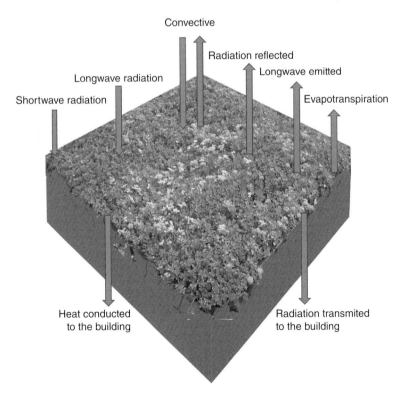

Figure 7.2 Representation of energy exchange processes on a green roof. *Source*: Vaz Monteiro (2015).

Cooling by energy reflection is not plant-specific and can be achieved using a range of materials and structures. So-called 'cool roofs' (light-coloured, unvegetated roofs, where albedo can be increased to 0.4 compared with conventional roofs with albedo of 0.1; Saiz et al., 2006) are also able to provide effective surface and building cooling by energy reflection (Coutts et al., 2013) (see also Chapter 10). However, compared with dark urban materials such as roof felt, bitumen and asphalt, plants can also absorb less heat, due to canopies' higher albedo (e.g., in the range of 0.15–0.30) (Taha et al., 1988). Although cooling by shading is not plant-specific either, plants (in addition to structures such as pergolas) can intercept some of the solar irradiance, thus reducing the radiation load to the building fabric (McPherson et al., 1988; Shashua-Bar et al., 2009). For example, a 500 W/m² reduction in the summer solar radiation reaching a concrete building façade located in Athens was observed in areas where the wall was shaded by deciduous trees and thus contributed to less heat reaching the buildings; areas of wall protected by the trees had temperatures up to 8°C lower than those measured on areas where the wall was unshaded (Papadakis et al., 2001). Another, UK, summer-time study showed that the leaves of *Prunus laurocerasus* shrubs screening a brick wall were up to 6.3°C cooler than bare, exposed wall when temperatures were assessed around 15:00 h on a sunny summer day (Cameron et al., 2014).

However, it is the cooling through evapotranspiration that is particularly important, as it is an effective way of *consuming* heat, without warming up the surrounding surfaces (Gates, 1966). Transpiration is specific to plants and thus puts them in a unique position compared with other, artificial materials. The physical process involved in the change of liquid water to vapour absorbs 585 calories per gram (i.e., ml) of water (Monteith, 1965). Therefore, this process of latent heat loss reduces the energy available to be dissipated as sensible heat. A reduction in the ratio of local sensible heat to latent heat fluxes during the daytime (described as the Bowen ratio) will lead to an 'oasis' effect, lowering air temperatures overall (Taha et al., 1988), with higher plant evapotranspiration rates potentially leading to greater cooling. The range of inherent transpiration rates in various plant taxa under optimal substrate moisture conditions varies several-fold: from, for example, 110 mol/m²/s in succulent species such as *Sedum* to 320 mol/m²/s in *Salvia* (Vaz Monteiro, 2015). This, therefore, suggests that the extent of cooling that different plant species can provide is likely to vary too.

For example, the most widely used *Sedum* (and similar succulent species in the *Crassulaceae* family) are unlikely to offer substantial evapotranspira-tional cooling and a reduction in air temperature when the weather is hot and the substrate is dry. This is because their metabolism under water defi-ciency switches from daytime CO_2 uptake and fixation to night-time (the so-called CAM pathway), when water is limiting. Consequently, the stomata close during the light period, thus conserving water (Kluge and Ting, 1978). This encourages survival of such species in harsh environmental conditions (including those of dry and exposed rooftops), but it does not allow plants to exploit daytime transpirational cooling as a key strategy, and restricts cooling the surrounding environment (Vaz Monteiro, 2015).

7.2.2   Plant Species Choice and Summer-Time Surface Cooling

The focus of our research was therefore on understanding which species exhibit sufficient evapotranspiration to provide measurable (roof) surface and aerial cooling, but are also robust enough to tolerate the adverse conditions associated with roofs and façades, and have acceptable ecological properties (e.g., promotion of urban biodiversity and ability to capture particle air pollutants while being low emitters of biogenic volatile organic compounds, reducing the likelihood of negative interaction with gaseous air pollutants such as nitrogen dioxide, NO_2 and ozone, O_3, etc.). More broadly, we were interested in establishing basic principles on which leaf/plant structural and functional traits should be considered when designing green roofs to provide maximal cooling and building insulation. The research was set in the context of the mild temperate climate of southeast England, where the annual rainfall averages around 600 mm (and >40 mm per month in the period June–August) (www.met office.gov.uk/climate/uk/regional-climates/so). Our initial hypothesis was that broad-leaved, relatively vigorous perennial plants would likely provide better transpirational cooling, substrate insulation and shading than small-leaved succulents, due to higher evapo-transpiration (ETp) rates and larger leaf area indices (LAI). However, as a degree of water-saving strategies in chosen plants would be required even on UK green roofs, we focused on species with relatively large leaf diameters, but which are known to have effective water use efficiency indices (Cameron et al., 2006) and a high degree of drought tolerance (Cameron et al., 2008). These may be appropriate for green roofs, especially if semi-extensive systems (20 cm substrate depth) are employed to improve anchorage for root systems and increase the water storage of the green roof.

In a series of glasshouse and field experiments, an industrial standard *Sedum* species mix ('Enviromat' matting system, Q Lawns, Hockwold, Norfolk, UK; a random mix of *S. album, S. spurium, S. acre* and *S. sexangulare)* was compared with a number of other potential planting options (*Bergenia cordifolia, Stachys byzantina, Hedera hibernica*) and bare substrate (Blanusa et al., 2013) (Figure 7.3).

Plants were chosen on the basis of differences in canopy leaf areas, transpiration rates and presence or absence of leaf hairs and grown in substrate depths of 20 cm initially, but then reducing the depth to 10 cm for final outdoor experiments. We examined how *Sedums'* ability to cool their own leaves as well as the surrounding spaces (i.e., substrate 10 mm below surface and air 10 cm above bare or vegetated surface) compared with that of other broad-leaf species. This was complemented by a range of detailed biological measurements of leaf stomatal conductance and transpiration, leaf temperature and LAI (Blanusa et al., 2013).

In this study, *Stachys byzantina* outperformed the other tested species in terms of leaf surface cooling, cooling the substrate beneath its canopy and even – during short intervals over the hottest still periods – the air above the canopy, when the soil moisture was not limited (Blanusa et al., 2013). For example, we found on one of the hottest days of the experiment

(a)

(b)

Figure 7.3 Images of plant species used in the experiment: (a) *Sedum*; (b) *Bergenia*; (c) *Stachys*; (d) *Hedera*.

(c)

(d)

Figure 7.3   (Continued)

(maximum air temperature 28°C), on the outdoor plots, that the temperature of the substrate below *Stachys* was 12°C cooler than under *Sedum* and 15°C cooler than for bare, uncovered ground. This could have significant implications for the temperature of the building, as well as a reduced need for summer-time air-conditioning use, if these plants were installed on the roof. *Stachys* is unlikely to be as resilient as *Sedum* in terms of survival in the most droughty, extensive green roofs (e.g., ≤10 cm deep), but is a drought-adapted species in its own right, capable of survival and persistence in semi-extensive systems.

This research confirmed our hypothesis about plants differing in their ability to provide a cooling service. Consequently, we expanded the range of species under investigation, extending the range of studied plant traits (all of which could contribute to temperature regulation). The light leaf colour and hairiness of the species that cooled best in our early experiments, along with the succulence as a feature of many drought-adapted species, prompted us to consider these leaf traits in more detail in a subsequent study. All of these traits contribute to the regulation of leaf temperature (Vaz Monteiro, 2015; Vaz Monteiro et al., 2016) and thus potentially to the environmental and building cooling. We were interested in understanding the mechanisms which enable plants with these traits to regulate leaf temperature and therefore indirectly the temperature of the surrounding surfaces and the environment.

Chosen species included *Heuchera* (four cultivars representing a range of leaf colours – from purple to yellow), *Salvia* (three cultivars with different leaf colours and hair length), *Sempervivum* (three cultivars representing different leaf thicknesses, as well as colour and hairiness) (Vaz Monteiro, 2015) (Figure 7.4) alongside *Stachys* and *Sedum* used in a previous study (Blanusa et al., 2013).

Experiments included both the glasshouse and controlled environment work with all chosen species and cultivars, but also outdoor field work with a subset of selected species, representing the widest range of responses detected in controlled environments. Outdoors, plants were grown in 1.5 m × 1.5 m × 0.1 m plots (Figure 7.5), on the experimental grounds at the University of Reading (UK), over two growing seasons. Each plant cultivar was represented by two plots; within each plot, a number of parameters were measured. The measurements included continuous monitoring (and logging) of substrate temperature (at 10 mm and 60 mm depth) and leaf temperature as well as regular discrete measurements of substrate moisture, leaf stomatal conductance (used via the Penman–Monteith equation to estimate plant transpiration) and albedo. Leaf area indices were determined twice in each season.

In some of the experiments we also attempted to compare plant-induced cooling of the ground (through shading, transpiration and reflection) with the use of artificial shade (pergola) or by applying white paint to the substrate surface to increase reflectance.

In the summer-time experiments in both experimental years (2012 and 2013), we found that the presence of thinner-leaved plants improved substrate cooling (at two depths, 10 and 60 mm), particularly on the hottest days of the experiments (maximum daytime temperature >24°C) compared with the artificial shade (Table 7.1, showing 2013 data), but the presence of succulents (particularly *Sempervivum*) did not.

Herbaceous plants insulated the substrate best; *Salvia* cultivar (*Salvia officinalis* 'Berggarten', with longest leaf hair length in our experiments) and *Stachys* provided most cooling and potential insulation (Table 7.1). This was because they offered more substrate shading (through having a greater LAI) and protection, and had the lowest leaf and canopy temperatures, leading to lower heat release towards the substrate underneath (and therefore the lowest substrate heat fluxes) (data not shown). On the contrary, the succulent *Sempervivum* even warmed up the substrate underneath on the

(a)

(b)

Figure 7.4 Plant species/cultivars used in the experiments: (a) *S. officinalis*; (b) *Sempervivum*; (c) *Heuchera* 'Obsidian' – yellow and 'Electra' – purple).

hottest days during some parts of the day (data not shown). *Sedum* performed intermediately between the best and worst 'coolers'.

Our research showed that water loss by evapotranspiration was the main mechanism that contributed to better cooling of leaves, substrate and air. Therefore, choosing plants which transpire more and keeping them

(c)

Figure 7.4   (Continued)

Figure 7.5   Plots with sensors in use in summer 2013 at the experimental grounds of the University of Reading (UK). General view of the experimental site (left), unvegetated/bare substrate shaded by netting (right).

(sustainably) watered is important for the reduction of temperatures. Using canopies with a greater LAI and presence of light-coloured leaf hairs also had a small positive influence on lowering leaf, surface and air temperatures (Vaz Monteiro, 2015).

The importance of diversity and complexity of plant structure (i.e., larger LAIs and bigger canopies) as well as higher ETp rates for the provision of insulation and cooling by green roofs can also be inferred from other green roof species studies in different climatic conditions (Huang *et al.*, 2008; Liu *et al.*, 2012; Blanusa *et al.*, 2013), and similar examples have been found in green walls too (Cameron *et al.*, 2014).

Table 7.1   Substrate temperatures at 10 mm and 60 mm below the surface

Treatment	Substrate temperature (°C) below surface, 13:00–17:00 h	
	At 10 mm	At 60 mm
Bare substrate	32.5 g	27.4 f
Shaded bare substrate	25.0 cd	23.4 cd
S. officinalis	20.7 a	19.8 a
Stachys byzantine	23.3 bc	21.9 bc
Heuchera, yellow*	29.0 ef	25.1 de
Heuchera, purple	21.9 ab	21.3 ab
Sedum mix	26.8 de	23.9 d
Sempervivum, green	29.1 f	26.4 ef
Least significant difference between the means, LSD	2.25	1.86

*Substrate coverage of yellow *Heuchera* was significantly lower than for other plant treatments (40% vs 100%) due to the frost damage to plants between 2012 and 2013 growing seasons.
Note: Temperatures were measured every 10 minutes in the period 13:00–17:00 h on 10 days when the maximal daily temperature was >24°C, in the period 15 July–31 August 2013. Values are means of two plots per treatment, averaged hourly. Statistical analysis was carried out with a residual maximum likelihood estimation and different letters next to the temperatures indicate means which are statistically significantly different ($p = 0.05$)

7.2.3   Plant Species Choice and Winter-Time Insulation

Although the focus of our research was on detecting the species' differences to provide summer-time cooling, and understanding which plant structural and functional traits are the key to supporting those differences, we were able to make observations relating to the species' potential for winter-time insulation as well. We hypothesised again that extending the range of species away from just succulents will be beneficial for improving winter-time insulation, particularly in cold and overcast weather. Our winter-time outdoor experiments showed that in the climate of southern UK, in the relatively colder weather conditions (represented by maximal daytime temperatures <3°C and when snow cover was present), plant species' choice influenced surface insulation (as measured by substrate temperatures at 10 and 60 mm). For example, in a snow-covered scenario, substrate 60 mm underneath *Stachys byzantina* was 1.8°C warmer than bare, unvegetated (but snow-covered) substrate, with *Sedum* cover being second best, warming up a surface by 1.4°C (Table 7.2). *Sempervivum* performed least well of all the studied plant covers, still significantly warming the substrate compared with bare substrate though (by 0.7°C, Table 7.2). This suggests that in those weather scenarios, the presence of vegetation on the roofs would be beneficial as it would act to increase roof insulation and building temperatures.

On warmer days (maximal air temperature >10°C), however, there were no species differences, but the presence of vegetation reduced the substrate temperature (by up to 2.9°C compared with bare, unvegetated surface) (data not shown). The difference in insulation on mild winter days is likely to be linked to the shading effect created by the plants,

Table 7.2 Substrate temperatures 60 mm below the surface in two types of winter scenario (Vaz Monteiro et al., 2016b)

Treatments	Substrate temperatures at 60 mm from 13:00 to 16:00 h	
	Days with maximum air temperature <3°C	Snow covered
Bare substrate	2.4 a	0.5 a
Salvia	2.5 abc	1.5 c
Stachys	2.8 bc	2.3 3
Heuchera yellow	2.8 abc	1.7 d
Heuchera purple	2.6 abc	1.4 c
Sedum	2.9 c	1.9 d
Sempervivum	2.5 ab	1.2 b
LSD	0.39	0.24

Note: Temperatures were measured every 10 minutes in the period 13:00–16:00 h on 9 days when plots were covered by snow and 10 days when maximal daily temperature was <3°C in January 2013. Values are means of two plots per treatment, averaged hourly. Statistical analysis was carried out with a residual maximum likelihood estimation and different letters next to the temperatures indicate means which are statistically significantly different ($p = 0.05$)

which reduced the radiation reaching the substrate on sunny winter days (Sailor, 2008; Jaffal *et al.*, 2012).

In climates such as that of the UK, winter-time insulation by green roofs is likely to be in the balance (i.e., vegetation providing warming of the surface on some days, while acting to cool on others). As the summer-time benefits can be significant, we suggest that the overall annual service of green roof vegetation will be a positive one (i.e., more benefits from summer-time cooling and insulation and winter-time insulation than from the additional winter-time temperature reduction due to the blocking of solar radiation). This is in agreement with recent findings (Cameron *et al.*, 2015) on a model mini building system clad with vegetation, suggesting that 21–37% reduction in winter heating could be achieved.

7.3　Plant Species Choice and Stormwater Management

Surface flooding in urban areas is likely to become more common due to further increases in urbanisation, as the replacement of vegetation with impervious surfaces will lead to drainage systems being under increased pressure (Nagase and Dunnett, 2012). Additionally, a likely increase in the frequency of intense precipitation events in many parts of the world is predicted by climate change models (IPCC, 2013). Sufficiently deep green roofs with viable, diverse vegetative cover may help to alleviate flood risk by delaying runoff and reducing its volume. Green roofs provide this service through direct interception of rainfall by green roof vegetation, infiltration and storage of water in the green roof substrate and subsequent uptake of water by the vegetation (Stovin *et al.*, 2012). Water taken up by plants may be stored in plant tissues or transpired back to the atmosphere

(Razzaghmanesh *et al.*, 2014). The majority of studies focused on measuring the ability of simple, extensive green roofs to reduce runoff (Van Woert *et al.*, 2005; Carter and Rasmussen, 2006; Graceson *et al.*, 2013), impact of substrate type and depth on runoff volume, and the change in runoff quality and chemical properties (Berndtsson, 2010; Speak *et al.*, 2014). Only a small number of studies investigated the impact of plant species selection on runoff volume (Nagase and Dunnett, 2012; Poë *et al.*, 2015). Differences in plant structure, including canopy size and leaf morphologies, will influence the volume of water that can be intercepted (Nagase and Dunnett, 2012). This study investigated functional groups of plants (forbs, grasses and *Sedum*) on shallow, extensive green roofs and found that grasses as a group reduced the runoff most of all studied species; larger canopy and root system size correlated with better water retention within the system (Nagase and Dunnett, 2012).

In our recent experiments we aimed to understand in more detail the mechanisms that enable different plants (situated on green roofs or in other forms of greening) to perform stormwater management to a greater or lesser degree. We also aimed to identify if some of the mechanisms associated with good provision of the cooling service could also be linked with the provision of other ecosystem services by chosen plants (including runoff reduction). For the experiments we chose plants which in our previous studies enabled the best surface cooling and insulation (Vaz Monteiro, 2015) and also have leaf/canopy properties (e.g., presence of hairs, large LAI, range of transpiration rates) which should enable them to be effective at runoff reduction, but also potentially improving other services such as particle pollutant trapping (Freer-Smith *et al.*, 2005; Blanusa *et al.*, 2015).

Previous studies have identified that the green roof substrate, rather than vegetation, is the main store for rainwater. The retention capacity of green roof substrates depends on substrate type and depth, together with the antecedent substrate moisture conditions (Stovin, 2010; Berretta *et al.*, 2014). The ability of vegetation to restore a substrate's retention capacity following a rainfall event, through uptake and removal of water from the substrate, is therefore crucial as it determines the potential of the green roof system to retain water in subsequent rainfall events. Water uptake from the substrate will vary depending on each species' evapotranspiration rate, so we hypothesised that species' ETp differences would be the main factor contributing to the improvement of water retention within the plant/substrate system. Additionally, however, we were interested in understanding what proportion of the applied water (in a simulated rainfall event) would be directly intercepted and retained within a plant canopy (i.e., what is the additional contribution of the interception by canopy to overall water storage of a green roof system?).

Three low-growing perennial species with varying leaf and canopy characteristics (*Salvia officinalis*, *Stachys byzantina* and *Heuchera* 'Obsidian') that have shown potential for use on green roofs (Vaz Monteiro, 2015) were used in the experiments, along with a typical succulent green roof mix (industrial *Sedum* mix). Plants were grown in an industrial green roof substrate (Meadow Roof Medium, Vital Earth GB Ltd, Ashbourne, Derbyshire, UK). The amount of rainfall captured on the canopy was measured by applying simulated rainfall to individual plants (eight replicates per species) in 2 litre containers where the substrate was saturated with water to full capacity, so any weight change of the plant/substrate system would be due to the 'rainfall' retained on the canopy. We also assessed how species differed in their capacity to restore the substrate's water-holding capacity after a fixed period of time (3 days in our glasshouse-based experiments), due to the differences in their ETp rates, canopy and root system sizes or any combination of those factors.

We found that succulent *Sedum* lost least water in a 3-day experimental period (just under 130 ml on average), with three herbaceous species having relatively similar extent of water losses per container (*Heuchera* and *Salvia* around 250 ml on average followed by *Stachys* with about 220 ml) (Table 7.3). This resulted in substrate moisture content dropping from a full container/substrate capacity of $0.25 \, m^3/m^3$ at the start of experimentation to about $0.10 \, m^3/m^3$ after a 3-day drying period in herbaceous species; however, in the substrate with *Sedum*, substrate moisture was significantly higher after 3 days of drying (Table 7.3), linked to low rates of water loss. *Salvia* also captured most water within the canopy (about 5% of that applied) (Table 7.4). Consequently, when the system's ability to retain water was re-tested after 3 days of drying, *Salvia* retained most 'rainfall' (about 50% of the applied water volume) within the plant/substrate system (closely followed by *Heuchera* and *Stachys*) (Table 7.4). *Sedum* retained only about 30% of 'rainfall' in comparison, the same as bare unvegetated substrate (Table 7.4). Experiments have also shown that depending on the leaf and canopy shape and structure, varying amounts of water slide off the leaves. For example, as much as 20% of the applied water slid off the *Heuchera* canopy, compared with under 3% in *Salvia*. We are conducting further tests to confirm this and understand the detail, but we believe that it is the smooth epidermis and large, umbrella-like structure of the *Heuchera* canopy that contributes to the greater proportion of rainfall sliding off the canopy, in contrast with *Salvias*' hairy, upward-angled leaves and dense canopy.

Table 7.3   Mean substrate moisture content (SMC) of a water-saturated substrate and a substrate after 3 days of drying; cumulative water lost from individual plant containers after 3 days of drying

Species/ substrate	Saturated SMC (m^3/m^3)	Water loss, cumulative (ml)	SMC 3 days post-watering (m^3/m^3)
Bare substrate	0.241	134.9	0.175
Heuchera	0.231	249.8	0.093
Salvia	0.254	262.8	0.111
Sedum	0.264	127.3	0.180
Stachys	0.250	217.4	0.097
LSD (d.f.)	0.0215 (35)	27.49 (35)	0.0154 (35)

Data are mean of eight replicates per treatment with the associated LSD and degrees of freedom (d.f.).

Table 7.4   Mean percentage of water captured on a plant canopy (A) when soil is saturated or (C) after 3 days post-saturation; (B) mean percentage of water sliding off a plant canopy

Species/ substrate	Saturated substrate		After 3 days of drying
	(A) % water captured on canopy	(B) % water sliding off canopy	(C) % water captured in substrate and on canopy
Bare substrate	0.4	3.7	28.6
Heuchera	1.7	20.5	46.1
Salvia	5.1	2.8	50.7
Sedum	3.4	7.1	30.8
Stachys	1.8	6.6	42.7
LSD (d.f.)	2.01 (15)	17.25 (15)	4.42 (35)

Data are mean of eight replicates per treatment with the associated LSD and degrees of freedom (d.f.).

In our minds, this highlights the importance of understanding the biological (i.e., structural and functional) differences between plants that can be used on green roofs and more generally green spaces, because of the impact that those differences can have on the delivery of ecosystem services. Owing to the fact that plants simultaneously perform a number of ecosystem services, success or 'failure' to deliver a single service should not be a reason to exclude a plant from a planting list. However, depending on the main drivers for a plant's installation at a particular location (i.e., cooling of the south side of a building in the northern hemisphere, stormwater retention, abatement of noise or pollution of a building near a busy road), some plant traits might be preferable.

7.4   Greater Plant Variety can Enhance Urban Biodiversity

Early research dealing with the issue of biodiversity was focused primarily on extensive, low-maintenance roofs; it described in depth the ability of species (such as grass mixtures) adapted to dry, exposed conditions and shallow substrates to attract particularly birds and small invertebrates in urban areas (Brenneisen, 2006; Kadas, 2006). Even a relatively simple mixture of grass and succulent cover on the roof, with some variation in substrate depth and the presence of sheltering habitats (e.g., log piles), would serve to increase the biodiversity support of roof spaces (Kadas, 2006). More recent research, however, suggests that increasing the complexity of species' mixtures and encouraging planting that encompasses a range of plant structures will improve a roof's ability to provide biodiversity support (Madre *et al.*, 2013). In this study, for example, roofs composed of a combination of mosses, low-growing succulent plants (*Sedum sp.*), grass mixes, but also woody shrubs such as *Lavandula angustifolia*, *Cotoneaster franchetii* or *Pinus mugo*, were characterised by a significantly increased species richness and the abundance of four arthropods' taxa (spiders, beetles, true bugs and hymenopterans) compared with simpler roofs where no shrubs were present (Madre *et al.*, 2013).

7.5   Plant Choices and Particle Pollution Mitigation

Elevated concentrations of both gaseous and particle pollutants in urban areas can in part be mitigated by urban greening interventions, including green roofs. Concentrations of particulate pollutants are greater at ground level than at roof level (Mitchell and Maher, 2009), so the potential for direct impact of green roofs on particles' mitigation service is proportionally less than their contribution to services such as building insulation/cooling and runoff reduction. The contribution of simple extensive green roofs to direct sequestration of particle pollutants (through dry deposition) has been modelled and shown to be in the range of 100g of particles/m^2 of roof annually, equating to the average annual emissions of one car (Rowe, 2011). There is, however, a potential indirect contribution of green roofs to pollution reduction through reduced coal use (and thus fewer particles released from burning) for energy generation for air-conditioning in situations where building temperatures are lowered by the use of green roofs and walls (Rosenfeld *et al.*, 1998; Rowe, 2011). Extrapolation from a range of plant studies characterising largely tree species' ability to sequester particulate pollutants (e.g., Beckett *et al.*, 2000; Freer-Smith *et al.*, 2005; Blanusa *et al.*, 2016) suggests that there are significant species differences in the ability for pollutants capture, due to leaf or canopy property differences (e.g., larger LAIs usually correlate with better particle capture, as does the presence of structures such as trichomes). Canopy size and structure have an impact on surface roughness and resultant wind turbulence, so plants with larger and more complex canopies create greater surface roughness and more turbulence, and more particles are thus deposited (Speak *et al.*, 2012). Traditional *Sedum* would thus be unlikely to sequester as many particles per unit leaf area as well as per unit area of the roof as a species with larger LAI and rougher leaves (Mitchell *et al.*, 2010). In a study on two in situ roofs in Manchester (UK), for example, it was found that the grasses (*Agrostis stolonifera* and *Festuca rubra*) were more effective than broad-leaved *Plantago lanceolata* and succulent *Sedum album* at the capture of particles in the PM10 range (Speak *et al.*, 2012).

7.6   New Plant Choices and Adaptation of Current Green Roof Systems

Plant survival and green roof installation/maintenance costs will long remain prime considerations in planting choices for green roofs. If the low levels of funding, lack of horticultural knowledge/experience and need for reduced maintenance limit the options, then developing a roof with succulents and grasses might be a way to introduce some ecosystem benefits. These plant groups might not excel in many aspects of ecosystem services provision, but for a number of services (including some biodiversity support, pollutant and noise abatement) would be an improvement on unvegetated, often impervious surfaces. Drought-adapted grass species and succulents will thus remain of interest as green roof planting choices in certain situations.

However, in scenarios where a semi-extensive substrate depth can be afforded and an investment in sustainable irrigation (recycled rainwater, greywater) is possible, then considering and using a wider range of low-growing perennial species with light-coloured leaves, higher LAIs and ETp rates would likely provide more benefits. The total direct cost of roof installation may well be higher in that case, but the argument to support a more diverse plant choice should be linked to the direct and indirect savings and benefits which this planting produces over and above the simple extensive green roof (temperature reduction, more pollutant capture per square metre, etc.).

The change of species from more succulent to more herbaceous, low-growing, sub-shrub and vigorous planting choices would affect roof loads and potential retrofitting costs (at the outset), then water management and maintenance costs of green roofs. This will necessitate the use of sustainably sourced water (e.g., collected rainwater, greywater), extending the substrate depth to increase its water-holding capacity and considering the use of substrate amendments such as biochar (Karhu *et al.*, 2011), silicate granules and hydrogels (Farrell *et al.*, 2013; Savi *et al.*, 2014).

7.7   Conclusions and Future Work

Work within our and other groups is beginning to paint a picture of the importance of plant species' choice to maximise the provision of multiple ecosystem services by green roofs and other forms of green infrastructure. Often it is a similar set of leaf/canopy/plant traits that correspond to better delivery of several services (i.e., large LAI, presence of light-coloured hairs, high ETp rates with a degree of drought adaptation). Using a wider range of plants on green roofs will improve the delivery of a number of ecosystem services. Thus, the scientific and practical challenges will lie in elucidating further issues, such as:

1. The impact of greywater on plants' functioning (and thus the potential for the delivery of services such as cooling) by long-term greywater use. It is clear that irrigation is required for many of those species to provide maximum benefits; however, to do it sustainably, greywater reuse might be an option, but its impact on plant functioning needs to be investigated.
2. Understanding the composite contribution to multiple services by chosen plants. Most of the studies to date focus on one particular service by plants, when it is evident that plants simultaneously perform numerous roles that should now come into focus.
3. Devising simplified tools to enable end users (landscape designers, private owners, policy makers) to choose the most effective plant combinations depending on cost and other constraints.

The challenges for retrofitted green roofs lie additionally in the issues relating to buildings' load-bearing capacities and limited options for installation of water supply. Many of the plants we studied, which exhibit a high capacity for ecosystem services provision, also require additional watering and at least 10–20 cm substrate depth. Thus, adapting existing lightweight systems and developing new systems which are capable of supporting such plants will be required.

References

Akbari, H., Kurn, D. M., Bretz, S. E. and Hanford, J. W. (1997) 'Peak power and cooling energy savings of shade trees', *Energy and Buildings*, 25, 139–148.

Akbari, H., Pomerantz, M. and Taha, H. (2001) 'Cool surfaces and shade trees to reduce energy use and improve air quality in urban areas', *Solar Energy*, 70, 295–310.

Ascione, F., Bianco, N., de' Rossi, F., Turni, G. and Vanoli, G. P. (2013) 'Green roofs in European climates. Are effective solutions for the energy savings in air-conditioning?', *Applied Energy*, 104, 845–859.

Beckett, K. P., Freer-Smith, P. H. and Taylor, G. (2000) 'Particulate pollution capture by urban trees: effect of species and windspread', *Global Change Biology*, 6, 995–1003.

Berndtsson, J. C. (2010) 'Green roof performance towards management of runoff water quantity and quality: a review', *Ecological Engineering*, 36, 351–360.

Berretta, C., Poë, S. and Stovin, V. (2014) 'Moisture content behaviour in extensive green roofs during dry periods: the influence of vegetation and substrate characteristics', *Journal of Hydrology*, 511, 374–386.

Blanusa, T., Vaz Monteiro, M. M., Fantozzi, F., Vysini, E., Li, Y. and Cameron, R. W. F. (2013) 'Alternatives to Sedum on green roofs: can broad leaf perennial plants offer better "cooling service"?', *Building and Environment*, 59, 99–106.

Berndtsson, J. C. (2010) 'Green roof performance towards management of runoff water quantity and quality: a review', *Ecological Engineering*, 36, 351–360.

Blanusa, T., Fantozzi, F., Monaci, F., Bargagli, R. (2015) 'Leaf trapping and retention of particles by holm oak and other common tree species in Mediterranean urban environments', *Urban Forestry & Urban Greening* 14(4), 1095–1101.

Brenneisen, S. (2006) 'Space for urban wildlife: designing green roofs as habitats in Switzerland', *Urban Habitats*, 4, 27–36.

Cameron, R. W. F., Harrison-Murray, R. S., Atkinson, C. J. and Judd, H. L. (2006) 'Regulated deficit irrigation – a means to control growth in woody ornamentals', *Journal of Horticultural Science and Biotechnology*, 81, 435–443.

Cameron, R. W. F., Harrison-Murray, R. S., Fordham, M., Wilkinson, S., Davies, W. J., Atkinson, C. J. and Else, M. A. (2008) 'Regulated deficit irrigation of woody ornamentals to improve plant quality and precondition against drought stress', *Annals of Applied Biology*, 153, 49–61.

Cameron, R. W. F., Taylor, J. E. and Emmett, M. R. (2014) 'What's "cool" in the world of green façades? How plant choice influences the cooling properties of green walls', *Building and Environment*, 73, 198–207.

Cameron, R. W. F., Taylor, J. E. and Emmett, M. R. (2015) 'A Hedera green facade – energy performance and saving under different matirime-temperate, winter weather conditions', *Building and Environment*, 92, 111–121.

Carter, T. L. and Rasmussen, T. C. (2006) 'Hydrologic behavior of vegetated roofs', *Journal of the American Water Resources Association*, 42, 1261–1274.

Costanza, R., d'Arge, R., de Groot, R., *et al.* (1997) 'The value of the world's ecosystem services and natural capital', *Nature*, 387, 253–260.

Coutts, A. M., Daly, E., Beringer, J. and Tapper, N. J. (2013) 'Assessing practical measures to reduce urban heat: green and cool roofs', *Building and Environment*, 70, 266–276.

Dunnett, N. and Kingsbury, N. (2008) *Planting Green Roofs and Living Walls.* Timber Press: Portland, OR.

Fantozzi, F. (2013) *'The mitigation of air pollution by urban trees'*, University of Siena, Siena.

Farrell, C., Ang, X. Q. and Rayner, J. P. (2013) 'Water-retention additives increase plant available water in green roof substrates', *Ecological Engineering*, 52, 112–118.

Freer-Smith, P. H., Beckett, K. P. and Taylor, G. (2005) 'Deposition velocities to Sorbus aria, Acer campestre, Populus deltoides × trichocarpa "Beaupré", Pinus nigra and × Cupressocyparis leylandii for coarse, fine and ultra-fine particles in the urban environment', *Environmental Pollution*, 133, 157–167.

Gates, D. M. (1966) 'Transpiration and energy exchange', *The Quarterly Review of Biology*, 41, 353–364.

Graceson, A., Hare, M., Monaghan, J. and Hall, N. (2013) 'The water retention capabilities of growing media for green roofs', *Ecological Engineering*, 61, 328–334.

Graceson, A., Monaghan, J., Hall, N. and Hare, M. (2014) 'Plant growth responses to different growing media for green roofs', *Ecological Engineering*, 69, 196–200.

Grimmond, S. (2007) 'Urbanization and global environmental change: local effects of urban warming', *Geographical Journal*, 173, 83–88.

Huang, L., Li, J., Zhao, D. and Zhu, J. (2008) 'A fieldwork study on the diurnal changes of urban microclimate in four types of ground cover and urban heat island of Nanjing, China', *Building and Environment*, 43, 7–17.

IPCC (2013) Summary for Policymakers. Climate Change 2013: The Physical Science Basis. Contribution of Working Group I to Stocker, T. F., Qin, D., Plattner, G.-K., *et al.* (eds), *Fifth Assessment Report of the Intergovernmental Panel on Climate Change.* Cambridge University Press: Cambridge.

Jaffal, I., Ouldboukhitine, S.-E. and Belarbi, R. (2012) 'A comprehensive study of the impact of green roofs on building energy performance', *Renewable Energy*, 43, 157–164.

Kadas, G. (2006) 'Rare invertebrates colonizing green roofs in London', *Urban Habitats*, 4, 66–86.

Karhu, K., Mattila, T., Bergström, I. and Regina, K. (2011) 'Biochar addition to agricultural soil increased CH_4 uptake and water holding capacity – results from a short-term pilot field study', *Agriculture, Ecosystems & Environment*, 140, 309–313.

Kluge, M. and Ting, I. P. (1978) *Crassulacean Acid Metabolism: Analysis of an ecological adaptation.* Springer-Verlag: New York.

Köhler, M. (2006) 'Long-term vegetation research on two extensive green roofs in Berlin', *Urban Habitats*, 4, 3–26.

Kolb, W. and Schwarz, T. (1999) *Dachbegrünung – intensiv und extensiv.* Eugen Ulmer: Stuttgart.

Lazzarin, R. M., Castellotti, F. and Busato, F. (2005) 'Experimental measurements and numerical modelling of a green roof', *Energy and Buildings*, 37, 1260–1267.

Liesecke, H. J. (2001) 'Zwiebel- und Knollenpflanzen fuer extensive dachbegruenungen', *Stadt+Gruen*, 50, 133–139.

Liu, T. C., Shyu, G. S., Fang, W. T., Liu, S. Y. and Cheng, B. Y. (2012) 'Drought tolerance and thermal effect measurements for plants suitable for extensive green roof planting in humid subtropical climates', *Energy and Buildings*, 47, 180–188.

Lundholm, J., MacIvor, J. S., MacDougall, Z. and Ranalli, M. (2010) 'Plant species and functional group combinations affect green roof ecosystem functions', *PLoS ONE*, 5(3), e9677.

Madre, F., Vergnes, A., Machon, N. and Clergeau, P. (2013) 'A comparison of 3 types of green roof as habitats for arthropods', *Ecological Engineering*, 57, 109–117.

McPherson, E. G., Herrington, L. P. and Heisler, G. M. (1988) 'Impacts of vegetation on residential heating and cooling', *Energy and Buildings*, 12, 41–51.

Mickovski, S. B., Buss, K., McKenzie, B. M. and Sökmener, B. (2013) 'Laboratory study on the potential use of recycled inert construction waste material in the substrate mix for extensive green roofs', *Ecological Engineering*, 61(C), 706–714.

Mitchell, R. and Maher, B. A. (2009) 'Evaluation and application of biomagnetic monitoring of traffic-derived particulate pollution', *Atmospheric Environment*, 43, 2095–2103.

Mitchell, R., Maher, B. A. and Kinnersley, R. (2010) 'Rates of particulate pollution deposition onto leaf surfaces: temporal and inter-species magnetic analyses', *Environmental Pollution*, 158, 1472–1478.

Molineux, C. J., Fentiman, C. H. and Gange, A. C. (2009) 'Characterising alternative recycled waste materials for use as green roof growing media in the U.K.', *Ecological Engineering*, 35, 1507–1513.

Monteith, J. L. (1965) 'Evaporation and environment'. *Symposia for the Society of Experimental Biology*, Vol. 19, pp. 205–223.

Monterusso, M. A., Rowe, D. B. and Rugh, C. L. (2005) 'Establishment and persistence of Sedum spp. and native taxa for green roof applications', *HortScience*, 40, 391–396.

Nagase, A. and Dunnett, N. (2010) 'Drought tolerance in different vegetation types for extensive green roofs: effects of watering and diversity', *Landscape and Urban Planning*, 97, 318–327.

Nagase, A. and Dunnett, N. (2012) 'Amount of water runoff from different vegetation types on extensive green roofs: effects of plant species, diversity and plant structure', *Landscape and Urban Planning*, 104, 356–363.

Oberndorfer, E., Lundholm, J., Bass, B., *et al.* (2007) 'Green roofs as urban ecosystems: ecological structures, functions, and services', *BioScience*, 57, 823–833.

Oke, T. R. (1987) *Boundary Layer Climates*, 2nd edn. Methuen: New York.

Pahlke, K. (1989) 'Establishing an extensive green cover on roofs – a comparison under practical conditions. Results of a model experiment carried out over three years', *Rasen-Turf-Gazon*, 20, 37–41.

Papadakis, G., Tsamis, P. and Kyritsis, S. (2001) 'An experimental investigation of the effect of shading with plants for solar control of buildings', *Energy and Buildings*, 33, 831–836.

Poë, S., Stovin, V. and Berretta, C. (2015) 'Parameters influencing the regeneration of a green roof's retention capacity via evapotranspiration', *Journal of Hydrology*, 523, 356–367.

Razzaghmanesh, M., Beecham, S. and Kazemi, F. (2014) 'Impact of green roofs on stormwater quality in a South Australian urban environment', *Science of the Total Environment*, 470, 651–659.

Rosenfeld, A. H., Akbari, H., Romm, J. J. and Pomerantz, M. (1998) 'Cool communities: strategies for heat island mitigation and smog reduction', *Energy and Buildings*, 28, 51–62.

Rowe, D. B. (2011) 'Green roofs as a means of pollution abatement', *Environmental Pollution*, 159, 2100–2110.

Sailor, D. J. (2008) 'A green roof model for building energy simulation programs', *Energy and Buildings*, 40, 1466–1478.

Saiz, S., Kennedy, C., Bass, B. and Pressnail, K. (2006) 'Comparative life cycle assessment of standard and green roofs', *Environmental Science & Technology*, 40, 4312–4316.

Savi, T., Andri, S. and Nardini, A. (2013) 'Impact of different green roof layering on plant water status and drought survival', *Ecological Engineering*, 57, 188–196.

Savi, T., Marin, M., Boldrin, D., Incerti, G., Andri, S. and Nardini, A. (2014) 'Green roofs for a drier world: effects of hydrogel amendment on substrate and plant water status', *Science of the Total Environment*, 490, 467–476.

Shashua-Bar, L., Pearlmutter, D. and Erell, E. (2009) 'The cooling efficiency of urban landscape strategies in a hot dry climate', *Landscape and Urban Planning*, 92, 179–186.

Speak, A. F., Rothwell, J. J., Lindley, S. J. and Smith, C. L. (2012) 'Urban particulate pollution reduction by four species of green roof vegetation in a UK city', *Atmospheric Environment*, 61, 283–293.

Speak, A., Rothwell, J., Lindley, S. and Smith, C. (2014) 'Metal and nutrient dynamics on an aged intensive green roof', *Environmental Pollution*, 184, 33–43.

Stovin, V. (2010) 'The potential of green roofs to manage urban stormwater', *Water and Environment Journal*, 24, 192–199.

Stovin, V., Vesuviano, G. and Kasmin, H. (2012) 'The hydrological performance of a green roof test bed under UK climatic conditions', *Journal of Hydrology*, 414, 148–161.

Taha, H., Akbari, H., Rosenfeld, A. and Huang, J. (1988) 'Residential cooling loads and the urban heat island – the effects of albedo', *Building and Environment*, 23, 271–283.

Taiz, L. and Zeiger, E. (2010) *Plant Physiology*. Sinauer Associates: Sunderland.

Van Woert, N. D., Rowe, D. B., Andresen, J. A., Rugh, C. L. and Xiao, L. (2005) 'Watering regime and green roof substrate design affect *Sedum* plant growth', *HortScience*, 40, 659–664.

Vaz Monteiro, M. M. (2015) '*Plants and temperature regulation: the impact of leaf and plant structure and function on leaf temperature and surface energy balance*'. PhD thesis, University of Reading, UK.

Vaz Monteiro, M.M., Blanusa, T., Verhoef, A., Hadley, P., Cameron, R.W.F. (2016a) 'Relative importance of transpiration rate and leaf morphological traits for the regulation of leaf temperature', *Australian Journal of Botany*, 64, 32–44.

Vaz Monteiro, M., Hadley, P., Blanusa, T., Cameron, R.W.F. (2016b) 'Implication of plant selection for building insulation', *Acta Horticulturae*, 1108, 339–344.

Volder, A. and Dvorak, B. (2014) 'Event size, substrate water content and vegetation affect storm water retention efficiency of an un-irrigated extensive green roof system in Central Texas', *Sustainable Cities and Society*, 10, 59–64.

Wong, N. H., Chen, Y., Ong, C. L. and Sia, A. (2003) 'Investigation of thermal benefits of rooftop garden in the tropical environment', *Building and Environment*, 38, 261–270.

Green Roof Retrofitting and Conservation of Endangered Flora

Paul Osmond and John Blair

UNSW, Sydney, Australia

8.0   Introduction

Multiple environmental, social and economic benefits of green roofs are widely reported in the literature, which includes: landmark studies such as Banting *et al.* (2005), Kennedy *et al.* (2008) and Snodgrass and McIntyre (2010); robust cost–benefit analyses from the Center for Neighborhood Technology and American Rivers (2010), the US General Services Administration (USGSA, 2011) and Kats and Glassbrook (2015); and in Australia – a latecomer to green roof research and practice – the pioneering studies of Williams *et al.*, (2010) and Hopkins and Goodwin (2011). However, the question of biodiversity protection and conservation of endangered flora has received much less attention than benefits such as stormwater detention or building energy savings. This chapter provides a brief theoretical context for biodiversity conservation more generally, before examining the current state of play regarding the application of roof greening in the protection of endangered flora. The chapter concludes with the presentation of a research design for a rooftop conservation project which is intended to address some of the knowledge gaps identified. The plant species involved belong to the Eastern Suburbs Banksia Scrub (ESBS), an endangered plant community indigenous to Sydney's coastal region.

Green Roof Retrofit: Building Urban Resilience, First Edition.
Edited by Sara Wilkinson and Tim Dixon.
© 2016 John Wiley & Sons, Ltd. Published 2016 by John Wiley & Sons, Ltd.

8.1   Biodiversity Conservation – a Strategic Overview

Biodiversity conservation – whether conceived for the benefit of future generations of humans or for its own sake – stands alongside climate change mitigation and adaptation as one of the overarching environmental challenges of the 21st century. Paradoxically, the process of urbanisation both enhances and diminishes vegetation biodiversity. As the existing indigenous flora submits to the bulldozer and the chainsaw, a veritable cornucopia of exotic plants sourced from around the world is taking root in the city's public and private gardens. Moreover, together with the spread of those ever-present camp followers that accompany human settlement, a.k.a. 'weeds', the invasion of this new artificial biodiversity challenges remnant native biodiversity on all three levels: community, species and genetic. Although it is neither scientifically defensible nor practical to turn back the tide of neo-biodiversity,[1] it is justifiable to resist the trend towards bio-homogeneity. From this perspective, the effort to retain maximal variety[2] across plant communities, species and genetic information must include strategies for conserving a place's original flora.

Margules and Pressey (2000) have argued for a more systematic approach to conservation planning, which both ensures the representation of a region's biodiversity and separates this biodiversity from processes that threaten its persistence. In the city, this is difficult. Habitat becomes increasingly fragmented into smaller, albeit more numerous, remnant patches (McKinney, 2002) within an inhospitable matrix of developed land. Moreover, species richness generally declines as fragment area decreases (Collinge, 1996). Accordingly, the significance of all types of urban green space for biodiversity conservation grows (Goddard et al., 2010), including rooftops, especially in inner city areas where open space at grade is limited. Moreover, green roofs designed to facilitate habitat conservation on new developments could help resolve the invariable conflicts between ecology and commerce (Gedge and Kadas, 2005), and provide new opportunities for denatured urbanites to re-engage with their environment. With the majority of the world's population now being city dwellers, our main experiences of 'nature' increasingly occur within the urban fabric (Kowarik, 2011).

Remnant indigenous species typically survive, indeed often thrive, in those spaces which are overlooked, unavailable or inappropriate for urban development, including cliffs, gullies, swamps, infrastructure easements and cemeteries. Such spaces are defined primarily by fragmentation, and, thanks to the role of linear easements, connectivity. At this local scale, the 'edge effect'[3] becomes noteworthy. Fragmentation of continuous natural habitat results in

---

[1] We return to the topic of neo-biodiversity or 'novel ecosystems' (Hobbs et al., 2013) later in this chapter.

[2] Ecologically, to build resilience to external disturbance (such as climate change); from an anthropocentric perspective, to build potential for provision of food, fibre, medicines, etc.

[3] Changes in species composition, population and community structure at the boundary between two habitats.

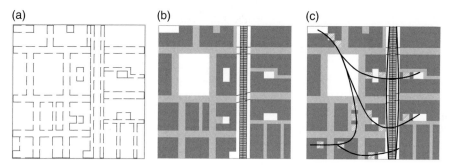

Figure 8.1   (a) Pre-development habitat; (b) fragmented landscape post-development, showing a rail reserve, major park and smaller green spaces; (c) new 'stepping stone' spaces (such as green roofs) link existing parks and reserves. The black lines represent connectivity.

a decrease in the ratio of area to perimeter of the newly created fragments – in other words, longer boundaries. For example, the area-to-perimeter ratio for the intact green space depicted in Figure 8.1(a) is 24:1; the ratio for the dispersed green space in Figure 8.1(b) is just 2.2:1. Although the area of green space in the built-up example is less than one-sixth that of the undeveloped example, the total perimeter is almost twice the length. More edge means more opportunities for fragmented natural habitats to be influenced by surrounding built-up habitats, through exchanges of materials, energy and organisms (Collinge, 1996) – for example, invasive garden escapees and weeds.

As noted above, corridors enable connectivity between habitat fragments, an issue of more relevance to fauna than flora, but nonetheless an opportunity for the spread of organisms (and the exchange of genes) between intact fragments. A detailed meta-analysis by Beier and Noss (1998) found that despite some scepticism about their value, the evidence from well-designed studies suggests that corridors are valuable conservation tools. The sketch in Figure 8.1(c) shows schematically how a series of small retrofitted green spaces such as backyards or green roofs could be planted with indigenous species to act as links between more significant areas of indigenous biodiversity. Although not strictly corridors, such ecological stepping stones can provide stop-off points for birds and invertebrates (Hopkins and Goodwin, 2011) and an opportunity for seeds to disperse, settle and germinate.

Following from the above, the starting point for the preservation and management of remnant indigenous vegetation in urban areas – including examples of rare and endangered species – may be characterised in terms of 'honey pots and spider webs'. The former represent discrete reservoirs of native biodiversity, while the latter represent existing or newly designed connections between them. It is in this context that a city-wide green roof strategy to support biodiversity conservation and enhancement may be fashioned.

Such a strategy, of course, goes beyond the biodiversity conservation objectives articulated in this chapter to address a plethora of co-benefits. This green roof strategy represents a landscape design response to the socio-environmental problems common to built-up places – not just the loss and simplification of ecosystems, but pollution, excessive motor traffic, the overwhelming pervasiveness of artificial structures and also an opportunity to build on the positive aspects of city living.

Before moving from landscape planning at city scale to landscape design at neighbourhood and building scale, several other principles are worth recording:

- In habitat conservation, *individually* insignificant sites become important *collectively* (i.e., as an integrated system).
- An increased number of ecosystem connections and interactions heightens stability and resilience (Naveh and Lieberman, 1990), which underpins design objectives to improve current habitat linkages and establish new ones.
- Full *replication* of the complex plant communities which existed pre-development is not ecologically possible in the city, hence *indication* is the appropriate objective (Osmond, 1994).
- In turn, this can inform a new landscape design aesthetic in which planting is based on context and function in addition to ecology to create ecologically multi-functional landscapes with their own local identity.

Another important consideration is the unavoidable *incrementalism* resulting from private (residential or business) premises becoming the main focus of rooftop greening for nature conservation (as distinct from government and other public buildings), which is crucial to any city-wide rollout. In these circumstances, sites, resources and the time to connect them become available less by design and more as a by-product of the interactions of a myriad of public and private actors. However, while the need to operate in an incremental framework is at odds with outcome-oriented master planning, it does allow for the flexibility and experimentation fundamental to the evolution of a new design/conservation concept. Further, involvement of householders and businesses in green roof installation and maintenance represents a fine example of bottom-up 'reconciliation ecology' – reconciling human and non-human use of urban space to support biological conservation (Francis and Lorimer, 2011). Enlisting community support for local biodiversity conservation is achievable, as evidenced by the numerous bush-care groups operating in the Sydney region. In contrast, the effort involved in public awareness building and citizen training and education to achieve the necessary level of adaptive collaborative management (Henry and Frascaria-Lacoste, 2011) should not be underestimated.

8.2   A Review of Green Roofs in Habitat Conservation

A focus on optimising the *physical* benefits of green roofs, such as stormwater detention, microclimate modification and heating/cooling energy reduction, has meant that a key *biological* variable – plant species – has often been treated as if it were a constant. The conventional response to the objective of ensuring viable plant cover to optimise the above benefits is to install those plants known to perform well on rooftops, such as *Sedum* species (e.g., Monterusso *et al.*, 2005). Although most research relating to green roof biodiversity has focused on fauna (Williams *et al.*, 2014), recent studies from several countries have found that a low-diversity mix of cosmopolitan succulents is not the only solution to plant performance.

Sutton *et al.* (2012), for example, found that many North American prairie and grassland species, subject to harsh growing conditions in their natural habitats, will flourish on extensive green roofs. Across the Atlantic, Madre *et al.* (2014) confirmed the benefits of rooftop greening in creating indigenous habitat, in this case through providing a medium for colonisation by a variety of 'volunteer' flora. 86% of species across 115 roofs were native to the locality (northern France). They found that plant diversity was strongly related to substrate depth, and the taxonomic and functional composition of the colonising plant communities was also shaped by green roof age, surface area, and height and maintenance intensity at building scale (Madre *et al.*, 2014). Ishimatsu and Ito (2013) explored the notion of 'brown/biodiverse' roofs on brownfield (previously developed, now abandoned) sites in the UK. They argue that brownfields provide habitat conditions similar to more natural habitats and can help maintain populations of some rare species. The key, they found, is to preserve the top layer of natural substrate, including existing vegetation, seed bank and soil organisms, for subsequent installation on the roofs of new developments.

The broadly generalisable conclusion from the literature is that indigenous species, which thrive in shallow soils, tolerate drought and are adapted to high winds, extreme temperatures and intense sunlight (particularly dry grassland, coastal and alpine floras; Oberndorfer *et al.*, 2007), are well suited to green roof installation. As Williams *et al.* (2014) point out, however, rare and threatened plant species or communities that do not fall into this category are probably best conserved and managed in situ at ground level at this stage.

The concept of 'novel ecosystems' was mentioned at the beginning of this chapter, referring to the changes in species composition resulting from the interaction between existing native biota, introduced flora and fauna, and the altered physical/environmental conditions of urbanisation. They are defined by human agency, so that these 'intermingled' ecosystems are the result of deliberate or inadvertent human action (Hobbs *et al.*, 2006). While urban habitats can harbour self-sustaining populations of rare and endangered native species, they cannot replace the complete functionality of nature (Kowarik, 2011). However, even intermingled urban ecosystems may support threatened native plants. *Functional diversity* (Van Mechelen *et al.*, 2015) offers one useful framework for designing this kind of ecosystem, including opportunities to incorporate threatened local species. A functional trait is any measurable property of an organism that reflects what it is doing and how it interacts with other organisms and its physical environment. The functional diversity of vegetation is defined by traits such as plant height, longevity, leaf area, succulence and flowering time. Moreover, functional diversity is strongly associated with the provision of ecosystem services.[4] Where there is demonstrable correlation between species biodiversity and functional (trait) diversity, the inclusion of rare indigenous plants with the desired traits in a new green roof assemblage could address the dual objectives of maximising ecosystem services and species conservation. Preservation of threatened species, possibly as part of a biodiverse intermingled ecosystem, thus becomes one way in which the principle of *indication* rather than *replication* of pre-development biodiversity introduced above (Osmond, 1994) may be given practical expression on our urban rooftops through skilful design.

The general principles of urban biodiversity conservation discussed above affirm that the habitat potential of a green roof can only be evaluated in the context of the broader urban landscape. Green roof characteristics like height above ground, available area, human visitation (if any), microclimate and relation to key natural areas in the urban landscape underpin their biodiversity benefits and must be considered in any policies advocating green roofs as habitat (Williams *et al.*, 2014). Blank *et al.* (2013) also point out that establishing a viable network of green roofs would help support biodiversity and serve as stepping stones to shorten links between existing habitats. These two groups of researchers also suggest that there will be difficulties in achieving this with green roofs given the confounding issues of plant health and abundance, substrate depth and roof load-bearing capacity. Finding rooftops in strategic locations to connect the generally fragmented networks of threatened and endangered species, and then managing them, could be demanding. Generating strong levels of collaborative management could meet the challenge, however (Francis and Lorimer, 2011).

The biodiversity research conducted on green roofs can offer a degree of guidance on endangered species, although most of the research has focused on locally abundant species, not necessarily endangered or under threat. One frequently occurring message from the recent literature is that local species exhibit improved performance over the common *Sedum* roof (Lundholm *et al.*, 2010; McIvor and Lundholm, 2011). Nagase and Dunnett (2012) found that *Sedum* roofs had greater levels of stormwater runoff than bare roofs, and McIvor and Lundholm (2011) found surprising performance differences in growth rates and vegetation abundance between the local species used in their study – such as *Carex argyrathra* and *Carex nigra* – and the industry standard green roof succulents, *Sedum acre* and *Sedum spurium*. Perhaps *Sedum* vegetation is popular because it is easier to install, easily modularised and relatively cheap. Kraft (2013: 1) quotes McIvor, a conservation biologist: 'The problem is that *Sedum* plants aren't really performing on green roofs… They're just there.' Apart from not absorbing water as efficiently as other species, at certain times of the year *Sedum* actually absorbs heat instead of deflecting it (Kraft, 2013).

---

[4] Those services which the natural environment provides to humanity – such as food and fibre, carbon sequestration, and cultural and recreational opportunities.

Another frequent theme is the need to match substrate depth and nutrient quality with the desired plant species (McIvor and Lundholm, 2011). Nagase and Dunnett (2011) found that the response to higher levels of organic matter was different for different species, and that species from a nitrogen-rich habitat tended to be encouraged by a high nitrogen content. Similarly, Brenneisen's work (2006) on green roofs in Zurich, Switzerland has shown that the use of natural soils can benefit biodiversity, with useful implications for sustaining endangered species. Australia has a uniquely high proportion of nutrient-poor soils to which (along with fire) much of the continent's native flora is adapted (Orians and Milewski, 2007). Hence, the substrate nutrient status needs to be carefully considered in green roof design using locally indigenous species, irrespective of whether natural or manufactured growing media are selected.

At the same time, little research has been done on the non-plant biota associated with green roofs. McGuire et al. (2013) have pointed out that the microbial biomass and bacterial-to-fungal ratios are higher in ground-level parks than in green roof substrates in New York. The authors suggest that microbial levels may influence plant functionality and propose that microbes and fungi on green roofs may be an underestimated component of these systems. The lesson from these studies is that careful planning around targeted plant species is likely to produce better performance.

8.3   Knowledge Gaps and Further Research

Blank et al. (2013) found that research on green roof biodiversity had increased significantly but still received only a small fraction of the total research effort. Nevertheless, the breadth and depth of current green roof research belies the relative youth of the subject, though there are still substantial knowledge gaps relevant to habitat restoration and conservation. Although tentative evidence suggests green roofs can provide habitat for both generalist and some rare species, Williams et al. (2014) point out that there have not been enough ecological studies globally with adequate replication and controls, or of sufficient duration, to adequately test the proposition that green roofs have sufficient potential to connect to ground-level habitats.

Drawing on a four-year study of plant assemblages on two green roofs in Birmingham, UK, designed to emulate diverse brownfield habitats, Bates et al. (2013) also highlight the need for more medium and long-term studies, and specifically the role of rooftop micro-habitats including the effects of different types of growing media. In their detailed investigation of the rooftop performance of native American grassland species, Sutton et al. (2012) list several significant knowledge gaps, verified by researchers such as Lundholm et al. (2010), MacIvor and Lundholm (2011), Nagase and Dunnett (2011, 2012) and McGuire et al. (2013), and applicable in principle to a wide range of plant communities and climate zones:

- relationships between substrate, root structure and plant growth;
- nutrient turnover and substrate fertility;
- water–plant relations and the role of irrigation;

- roof temperatures and plant performance under extreme conditions;
- soil microbiological diversity.

A case study research design that would address most of these gaps follows. It is framed around the ESBS, Sydney's endangered coastal plant community, but the principles and many of the details are applicable to any jurisdiction interested in applying roof greening to biodiversity and endangered species conservation.

8.3.1   A Research Programme for Conserving Endangered Species on Green Roofs

To quote Williams *et al.* (2014: 1643): 'Ecologists need to work with the industry to evaluate green roof biodiversity and help design green roofs based on ecological principles to maximize biodiversity gains.' While this statement is applicable to most green roof endeavours, intuitively the ESBS community may not need high levels of management. It has displayed considerable resilience in its natural growing conditions, with plant cover in long unburned fragments of ESBS being species poor but the soil seed bank retaining diversity. The intense sunlight, coastal sea breezes (which can be strong) and unusually nutrient-poor Aeolian sands are further evidence of the resilience of the ESBS (Pellow *et al.*, 2015). Artificial conditions on the rooftops of the low-rise buildings typical of this part of Sydney are unlikely to be significantly more challenging.

Objective 3 of the ESBS Recovery Plan is to improve the conservation management of the community (NSW Department of Environment and Conservation, 2004: 10–12): 'To restore, and where practical, connect and enlarge remnants through appropriate management.' Since the area of ESBS is declining (Perkins *et al.*, 2012), one possible way of arresting the loss is to follow the reconciliation ecology concept and establish new sites in the form of green roofs, which represent considerable potential for urban conservation given the limited opportunities for establishing new parks and reserves in urban areas (Francis and Lorimer, 2011).

8.3.2   The Endangered Community of the Eastern Suburbs Banksia Scrub

The ESBS is a shrub-dominated and largely sclerophyllous heath community on nutrient-poor Aeolian dune sand, confined to the coastal suburbs of Sydney, NSW, Australia (NSW Scientific Committee, 2002). The ESBS consists of a minimum of 63 separate plant species, is near extinct (Perkins *et al.*, 2012), and is listed at the state and national levels as an endangered ecological community. It covered approximately 5300 ha at the time of European settlement in 1788, but is now a highly fragmented 145 ha on about 24 sites (Figure 8.2). Less than 3% of its original area remains (NSW Department of Environment and Conservation, 2004) and several small fragments are under imminent threat of development and exhibit quite high levels of degradation (Perkins *et al.*, 2012: 224; Pellow *et al.*, 2015).

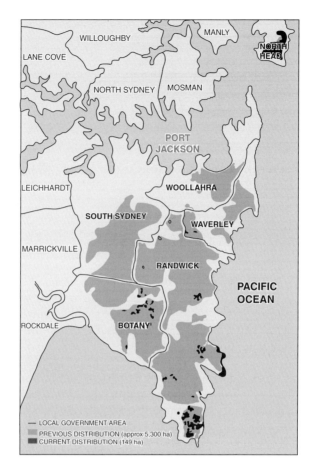

Figure 8.2   Location of ESBS sites.
Source: NSW Department of Environment and Climate Change (2009).

Figure 8.3   The 'scrub' in rich profusion.
Source: NSW Department of Environment and Conservation (2004).

Common species in the ESBS community (Figure 8.3) include over-storey 4–5 m trees like the Heath-leaved Banksia (*Banksia ericifolia*), Old Man Banksia (*B. serrata*), Coast Teatree (*Leptospermum laevigatum*) and Tree Broom-heath (*Monotoca elliptica*); sub-shrubs and ground-cover species like *Epacris* spp., Pink Wax Flower (*Eriostemon australasius*),

Variable Sword Sedge (*Lepidosperma laterale*) and Grass Tree (*Xanthorrhoea resinifera*). The ESBS is a predominantly fire-adapted community, highly dynamic and characterised by periodic ecological disturbance, regenerating by re-sprouting and germinating from the soil seed bank (Bradstock *et al.*, 1995; NSW Department of Environment and Climate Change, 2009).

The ESBS community was the first ecological community to be listed as endangered under the NSW Threatened Species Conservation Act 1995. It has also been listed as endangered under the Australian Government's Environment Protection and Biodiversity Conservation Act 1999. Both statutes required a recovery plan, which was approved in 2004, followed by best-practice guidelines (NSW Department of Environment and Climate Change, 2009) and management plans for a limited number of sites.

The degree and extent of regeneration from the persistent seed bank following restoration at one of the medium-size sites were 'sensational' (Perkins and McDonald, 2012: 132). The total number of native species increased only slightly over the six years (2001–2007), from 31 to 35 species, but there was a dramatic increase in abundance and distribution across the site (Perkins *et al.*, 2012).

In all management units, the removal of weed or heavy shade was sufficient to trigger germination of a range of species in most of the treated quadrats, although germination still occurred in poorer-condition plots without the addition of seeds. Practitioners also found that discarding the thick leaf-litter layer and debris crust was important in that it revealed the more natural Aeolian sandy soil and simultaneously removed weedy and nutrient-rich top soils. This is an important finding given the intention to raise species *indicative* of the ESBS on trial green roofs in coastal Sydney. It is also pertinent in a more general sense that plant resilience in the ESBS's case has been remarkable, a characteristic that bodes well for its transfer to the environment of green roofs, which are normally viewed as extreme. It certainly raises confidence that conservation objectives might readily be achieved with some plant species, whether endangered or more abundant.

8.4   A Model Research Design for Species Conservation

8.4.1   Extensive or Intensive Roofs?

The selection of extensive versus intensive roofs will depend on the vegetation structure desired at maturity. However, the height and canopy cover possible on intensive roofs is unlikely to occur in Sydney, where most green roof retrofits will take place on buildings that do not generally have the load-bearing capacity for thick substrates and luxuriant vegetation. A further issue connected with green roofs, at least in Sydney, is noise and privacy. Local councils often place access restrictions on development approvals – except for maintenance (Wise, 2011; Knierem, 2014). It may mean that extensive roofs will be favoured, since they are not especially conducive for passive relaxation and avoid the possible need for structural upgrades for intensive roofs. Ironically, access restrictions may mean that conservation objectives for establishing threatened or endangered species on roofs can be more easily met. As noted above, the ESBS grows on nutrient-poor sands but supports a density and variety of vegetation more normally associated with the deeper and richer substrates of intensive roofs, which then become more attractive as recreation space for building occupants.

8.4.2   Research Objectives

The research should be long term – four to five years - to allow monitoring of plant condition and especially to observe a full cycle of seed planting and germination, growth into young seedlings, maturation, further seed generation by the maturing plants and natural germination. The research in this case would have the overall goal of supporting Objective 3 of the ESBS Recovery Plan (NSW Department of Environment and Conservation, 2004) and helping to combat the apparent ongoing loss of species and restricted gene pool in some fragments of the ESBS (Perkins *et al.*, 2012). However, the framework suggested here would be applicable broadly to green roof research and biodiversity conservation.[5] Moreover, such research not only implements endangered plant species conservation but also offers more general ecosystem benefits.

Specific objectives for the ESBS are as follows:

(i)   Develop the green roofs as new sites to establish 'indicator' species of the ESBS and track their relative performance on natural and artificial substrates of different depths (Figure 8.4).

(ii)   Establish the ability of green roofs to act as a conservation medium and seed bank for a range of species within the ESBS community.

(iii)   Support the reintroduction of species now absent from remnant sites.

(iv)   In particular, use the green roof sites to re-establish ESBS species that are sensitive to being crowded out by more vigorous and resilient native species (e.g., *Acacia* spp.), which are no longer controlled by fire (Gill, 1981; Tozer and Bradstock, 2002).

(v)   Support species that do not form soil seed banks (e.g., *Banksia* spp.) and those whose seed banks are not persistent.

(vi)   Test the ability of green roofs to mimic natural ground-level habitats with a view to scaling up their role more generally in the conservation of threatened and endangered species.

(vii)   Gauge the effectiveness of green roofs to act as stepping stones for nectarivorous birds and insects (e.g., native bees) that may help with pollination.

(viii)   The project will necessitate cross-disciplinary contact among UNSW researchers as well as collaboration with external partners such as

---

[5] The authors will seek funding to implement this research design and propose to use two derelict green roofs at the UNSW campus, each 73 m at first-floor level, to test the suitability of roof greening as a strategy for ESBS conservation. The roofs are on student accommodation and are about 20 m apart.

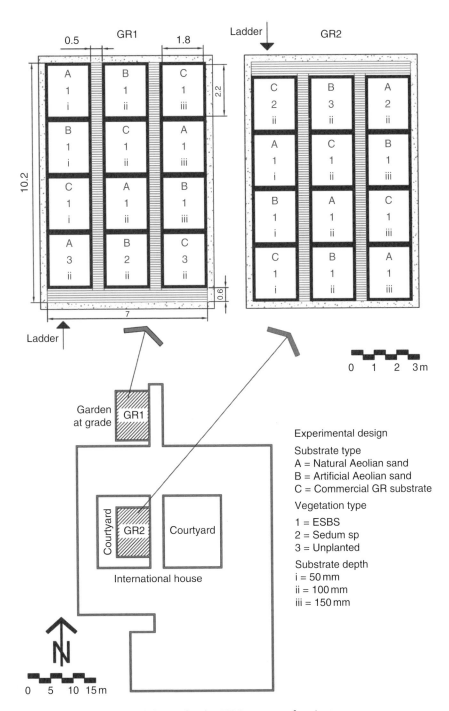

Figure 8.4 Experimental design for the ESBS green roof project.

the City of Randwick and its community nursery; industry sources of materials for infrastructure and substrates; and organisations that have worked on site restoration of the ESBS or who are familiar with restoration principles.

8.4.3   Guiding Principles for ESBS Regeneration

(i)   The relationship often existing between substrate depth and fertility and plant abundance (e.g., Brenneisen, 2006; Madre *et al.*, 2014) may not exist in the case of the ESBS, since lush vegetation can exist on infertile and relatively thin sands. Consequently, the guiding principle should be to match conditions on the green roof closely with those enjoyed by the natural community (e.g., Oberndorfer *et al.*, 2007; Razzaghmanesh *et al.*, 2014; Williams *et al.*, 2014). This may seem self-evident, but it is likely to be critical to success.

(ii)   Matching tactics should also test the ESBS Aeolian sand mantle for soil micro-organisms and fungal populations and ensure representative communities are included in the green roof substrate (McGuire *et al.*, 2013).

(iii)   The green roof installation should employ features found at grade, such as rocks and tree branches, to provide suitable microclimates as well as shade (from companion plants) and sunny areas to encourage plant diversity (Köhler, 2006). Features like tree branches many need to be fabricated from lightweight materials to minimise roof loads.

(iv)   The planting design should maximise ecosystem services by increasing the functional diversity of species planted, within the constraints imposed by substrate depth.

(v)   Irrigation will not be used, since Razzaghmanesh *et al.*'s (2014) findings regarding improved plant survival rates with supplementary watering do not apply to the higher precipitation levels experienced by Sydney and the ESBS is drought adapted.

(vi)   Successful implementation will require a detailed monitoring plan in order to track progress in achieving objectives.

8.4.4   Preparatory Steps

(i)   The sites currently do not have fixed access from ground level. Access compliant with the New South Wales Workplace Health and Safety Act 2011 will be constructed and green roof infrastructure installed on both roofs (membrane, drainage layer, root barrier and substrate).

(ii)   Roofs will be prepared for planting by removing existing weeds, scoria and rubbish.

(iii)   The roofs will each be subdivided into 12 approximately 4 m² test beds according to a modified Latin square design based on substrate type.

(iv)   Three substrate types will be intalled: samples of the natural Aeolian sand mantle of the ESBS from a fragmentary site about to be developed; a manufactured sand mantle, which closely mimics the original ESBS substrate; and a standard commercial green roof growing mix, all inoculated with suitable micro-organisms.

(v)   Three substrate depths will be used: 50 mm, 100 mm and 150 mm.

(vi)   The experimental design will include two test beds of *Sedum* spp. as controls, and two unplanted beds. The latter are included to test the substrates' capacity to facilitate germination of 'volunteer' seeds. This will include seeds from the soil seed bank for the natural Aeolian sand, and airborne seeds for the articfial Aeolian sand.

(vii)   ESBS seedlings and seeds will be sourced from the community nursery operated by Randwick City Council. Randwick is the Sydney local government area (LGA) containing the greatest proportion of remaining ESBS, and also the LGA in which the university is situated.

8.4.5   Monitoring

The following monitoring programme is proposed for the two green roofs:

a)   Assess ESBS species survival, viability and growth through performance parameters such as re-sprouting and self-germination propensity, leaf area index, plant coverage and plant abundance compared with the same plants on restored ESBS fragments described above and managed by the NSW Office of Environment and Heritage.

b)   Assess native faunal biodiversity (avian, reptilian, invertebrate) through data collection and application of suitable diversity indices.

c)   Collect and germinate seed to evaluate the viability of the green roof as a seed orchard for selected ESBS species.

d)   Evaluate the seeding and germination potential of ESBS species which have had reproduction difficulties in cultivation.

e)   Record the volunteer plants on the unplanted natural and manufactured ESBS substrates.

8.4.6   Expected Outcomes

(i)   Performance parameters for selected plants in the ESBS endangered community on green roofs (e.g., viability, growth rates and vigour); ESBS performance parameters tested against several types of substrate.

(ii)   Green roof performance vis-à-vis faunal biodiversity (invertebrate and avian).

(iii)   Capacity of green roofs to provide ESBS seed orchard services.

(iv)   Provision of seeds for distribution to the four local councils that still have remnants in their area; NSW government agencies, especially the Department of Environment, Climate Change and Water and the Office of Environment and Heritage.

8.5   Conclusions

Green roof benefits such as stormwater detention and reduction of building heating and cooling energy needs are well researched, relatively easy to quantify and widely understood by built environment professionals. Much less attention has been paid to the potential of rooftop greening as a strategy for biodiversity protection and conservation of endangered vegetation in our densifying cities. Nonetheless, work done to date on this topic suggests that green roofs may have an important role. For example, the harsh conditions associated with growing plants on a structure mimic the circumstances frequently associated with the persistence of remnant indigenous flora, including threatened species, at grade.

Urban ecosystem conservation and management strategies include the development of networks of reserves and corridors – 'honey pots and spider webs' – to maximise resilience and diversity. Strategies may also include establishment of functional 'novel' or intermingled plant communities in circumstances where spatial fragmentation and loss of biodiversity mean that it is not possible to replicate a city's pre-development natural communities. In this situation, *indication* rather than *replication* of original ecosystems becomes a design objective. This is also the default scenario where extensive green roofs – which automatically exclude the use of trees and larger shrubs – are installed to supplement conventional ground-level conservation efforts.

While the relatively sparse literature on roof greening as a vegetation conservation strategy offers some general principles, specific case studies are important both to test and to validate these principles, and to contribute to the cumulative experience needed to inform future practice. Australia is known for its unique flora and fauna, but less positively for its record of extinctions over the past 200 years. On the contrary, individual native species and fragmented communities such as Sydney's Eastern Suburbs Banksia Scrub manage to survive even in highly built-up areas. The ESBS is introduced here as the focus for a five-year programme with the objectives of evaluating the role of green roofs in the management of this particular community and addressing the more general research gaps around roof greening and indigenous plant conservation identified above. Such a research agenda will hopefully contribute to establishing green roofs as a viable conservation strategy with outcomes applicable at international as well as local scale.

References

Banting, D., Doshi, H., Li, J. and Missios, P. (2005) Report on the Environmental Benefits and Costs of Green Roof Technology for the City of Toronto. Ryerson University, Toronto.

Bates, A. J., Sadler, J. P. and Mackay, R. (2013) 'Vegetation development over four years on two green roofs in the UK', *Urban Forestry & Urban Greening*, 12, 98–108.

Beier, P. and Reed, N. (1998) 'Do habitat corridors provide connectivity?', *Conservation Biology*, 12(6), 1241–1252.

Blank, L., Vasl, A., Levy, S., *et al.* (2013) 'Directions in green roof research: a bibliometric study', *Building and Environment*, 66, 23–28.

Bradstock, R. A., Keith, D. A. and Auld, T. D. (1995) 'Fire and conservation: impera-
tives and constraints on managing for diversity'. In Bradstock, R. A., Auld, T. D.,
Keith, D. A., *et al.* (eds), *Conserving Biodiversity: Threats and solutions*. NSW
National Parks and Wildlife Service: Sydney; pp. 323–333.

Brenneisen, S. (2006) 'Space for urban wildlife: designing green roofs as habitats in
Switzerland', *Urban Habitats*, Vol. 4: Dec.

Center for Neighborhood Technology and American Rivers (2010). *The Value of
Green Infrastructure*. CNT and American Rivers: Washington D.C.

Collinge, S. K. (1996) 'Ecological consequences of habitat fragmentation: implications for landscape architecture and planning', *Landscape and Urban Planning*,
36, 59–77.

Francis, R. and Lorimer, J. (2011) 'Urban reconciliation ecology: the potential
of living roofs and walls', *Journal of Environmental Management*, 92(6),
1429–1437.

Gedge, D. and Kadas, G. (2005) 'Green roofs and biodiversity', *Biologist*, 52(3),
161–169.

Gill, A. M. (1981) 'Adaptive responses of Australian vascular plant species to fires'.
In Gill, A. M., Groves, R. H. and Noble, I. R. (eds), *Fire and the Australian Biota*.
Australian Academy of Science: Canberra.

Goddard, M. A., Dougill, A. J. and Benton, T. G. (2010) 'Scaling up from gardens:
biodiversity conservation in urban environments', *Trends in Ecology & Evolution*,
25(2), 90–98.

Henry, A. and Frascaria-Lacoste, N. (2011) 'The green roof dilemma – discussion of
Francis and Lorimer', *Journal of Environmental Management*, 104, 91–92.

Hobbs, R. J., Arico, S., Aronson, J., *et al.* (2006) 'Novel ecosystems: theoretical and
management aspects of the new ecological world order', *Global Ecology and
Biogeography*, 15, 1–7.

Hobbs, R. J., Higgs, E. and Hall, C. M. (eds) (2013) *Novel Ecosystems: Intervening
in the new ecological world order*. John Wiley & Sons: Chichester.

Hopkins, G. and Goodwin, C. (2011) *Living Architecture: Green Roofs and Living
Walls*. CSIRO: Collingwood, Vict.

Ishimatsu, K. and Ito, K. (2013) 'Brown/biodiverse roofs: a conservation action for
threatened brownfields to support urban biodiversity', *Landscape and Ecological
Engineering*, 9, 299–304.

Kats, G. and Glassbrook, K. (2015) Washington D.C. Smart Roof Cost–Benefit
Report. District of Columbia Department of General Services, Washington,
D.C.

Kennedy, J., Haas, P. and Eyring, B. (2008) 'Measuring the economic impacts of
greening: the Center for Neighborhood Technology green values calculator'. In
Birch, E. and Wachter, S. (eds), *Growing Greener Cities: Urban Sustainability in
the Twenty-First Century*. University of Pennsylvania Press: Philadelphia, PA.

Köhler, M. (2006) 'Long-term vegetation research on two extensive green roofs in
Berlin', *Urban Habitats*, Vol. 4: Dec.

Kowarik, I. (2011) 'Novel urban ecosystems, biodiversity, and conservation',
Environmental Pollution, 159, 1974–1983.

Kraft, A. (2013) 'Why Manhattan's green roofs don't work – and how to fix them',
Scientific American, 17 May.

Lundholm, J., MacIvor, J. S., MacDougall, Z. and Ranalli, M. (2010) 'Plant species
and functional group combinations affect green roof ecosystem functions', *PLoS
ONE*, 5(3), e9677.

Knierem, C. (2014) Personal interview with Mr Chris Knierem, professional builder
and green roof installation specialist, 23 September, Sydney, Australia.

MacIvor, J. S. and Lundholm, J. (2011) 'Performance evaluation of native plants suited to extensive green roof conditions in a maritime climate', *Ecological Engineering*, 37, 407–417.

Madre, F., Vergnes, A., Machon, N. and Clergeau, P. (2014) 'Green roofs as habitats for wild plant species in urban landscapes: first insights from a large-scale sampling', *Landscape and Urban Planning*, 122, 100–107.

Margules, C. R. and Pressey, R. L. (2000) 'Systematic conservation planning', *Nature*, 405, 243–253.

McGuire, K. L., Payne, S. G., Palmer, M. I., *et al.* (2013) 'Digging the New York city skyline: soil fungal communities in green roofs and city parks', *PLoS ONE*, 8(3), e58020.

McKinney, M. L. (2002) 'Urbanization, biodiversity, and conservation', *BioScience*, 52(10), 883–890.

Monterusso, M. A., Rowe, D. B. and Rugh, C. L. (2005) 'Establishment and persistence of Sedum spp. and native taxa for green roof applications', *HortScience*, 40(2), 391–396.

Nagase, A. and Dunnett, N. (2011) 'The relationship between percentage of organic matter in substrate and plant growth in extensive green roofs', *Landscape and Urban Planning*, 103, 230–236.

Nagase, A. and Dunnett, N. (2012) 'Amount of water runoff from different vegetation types on extensive green roofs: effects of plant species, diversity and plant structure', *Landscape and Urban Planning*, 104, 356–363.

Naveh, Z. and Lieberman, A. S. (1990) *Landscape Ecology, Theory and Application*. Springer-Verlag: New York.

NSW Department of Environment and Climate Change (2009) *Best Practice Guidelines: Eastern Suburbs Banksia Scrub*. NSW DECC: Sydney.

NSW Department of Environment and Conservation (2004) *Eastern Suburbs Banksia Scrub Endangered Ecological Community Recovery Plan*. NSW DEC: Sydney.

NSW Scientific Committee (2002) *Eastern Suburbs Banksia Scrub in the Sydney Basin Bio-region: Endangered Ecological Community Listing, Final Determination*. NSW Scientific Committee: Sydney.

Oberndorfer, E., Lundholm, J., Bass, B., *et al.* (2007) 'Green roofs as urban ecosystems: ecological structures, functions, and services', *BioScience*, 57(10), 823–833.

Orians, G. H. and Milewski, A. V. (2007) 'Ecology of Australia: the effects of nutrient-poor soils and intense fires', *Biological Reviews*, 82(3), 393–423.

Osmond, P. (1994) 'Environmental sustainability and inner-urban landscape design'. A Vision for a Greener City: National Greening Australia Conference, Fremantle, 4–6 October.

Pellow, B., Lambert, J. and Lambert, G. (2015) 'Impacts of fire, thinning and herbivory on species diversity in Eastern Suburbs Banksia Scrub', *Ecology Consulting*, 3, 25–26.

Perkins, I. and McDonald, T. (2012) 'Speaking multiple languages: practice, management and ecology. Interview with Ian Perkins', *Ecological Management and Restoration*, 13(2), 126–134.

Perkins, I., Diamond, J., SanRoque, G., *et al.* (2012) 'Eastern Suburbs Banksia Scrub: rescuing an endangered ecological community', *Ecological Management and Restoration*, 13(3), 224–237.

Razzaghmanesh, M., Beecham, S. and Kazemi, F. (2014) 'The growth and survival of plants in urban green roofs in a dry climate', *Science of the Total Environment*, 476/477, 288–297.

Snodgrass, E. and McIntyre, L. (2010) *The Green Roof Manual: A Professional Design Guide to Design, Installation and Maintenance*. Timber Press: Portland, OR.

Sutton, R. K., Harrington, J. A., Skabelund, L., MacDonagh, P., Coffman, R. R. and Koch, G. (2012) 'Prairie-based green roofs: literature, templates, and analogs', *Journal of Green Building*, 7, 143–172.

Tozer, M. G. and Bradstock, R. A. (2002) 'Fire-mediated effects of over storey on plant species diversity and abundance in an eastern Australian heath', *Plant Ecology*, 164, 213–223.

USGSA (2011) *The Benefits and Challenges of Green Roofs on Public and Commercial Buildings*. USA General Services Administration: Washington D.C.

Van Mechelen, C., Van Meerbeek, K., Dutoit, T. and Hermy, M. (2015) 'Functional diversity as a framework for novel ecosystem design: the example of extensive green roofs', *Landscape and Urban Planning*, 136, 165–173.

Williams, N. S. G., Rayner, J. P. and Raynor, K. J. (2010) 'Green roofs for a wide brown land: opportunities and barriers for rooftop greening in Australia', *Urban Forestry & Urban Greening*, 9(3), 245–251.

Williams, N., Lundholm, J. and McIvor, S. (2014) 'Do green roofs help urban biodiversity conservation?', *Journal of Applied Ecology*, 51(6), 1643–1649.

Wise, T. (2011) Personal interview with Mr Timothy Wise, development planner with the council of the City of Sydney, 22 August, Sydney, Australia.

Urban Food Production on Retrofitted Rooftops

Sara Wilkinson and Fraser Torpy
UTS, Australia

9.0   Introduction

In this chapter the issues of food security, human health, population, access to nutritious food sources and the carbon impact of current food production methods are discussed. The potential for urban rooftop food production is examined, as well as the typical features required of rooftops for successful outcomes. Australia ranks as the 18th most urbanised country in the world out of 195 countries, with 89.2% of its population living in towns and cities. With predictions that 2.2 billion more people will be living in cities by 2050, Sydney is a good city to investigate this aspect of green roofs. Significant amounts of urban regeneration are underway as the city seeks to reintroduce mixed uses, including residential land use in the CBD, and to maintain liveability. Not only does urban food production present an opportunity for inhabitants to maintain contact with the natural world in high-density environments, but it also allows younger generations to learn where food comes from and to get an appreciation for the natural world. The chapter describes empirical research into rooftop food production conducted on campus at the University of Technology Sydney; including social, environmental and economic aspects, as well as setting out typical specifications and considerations in respect of bed systems. The main focus is on the technical, environmental and economic aspects of larger-scale food rooftop production. Finally, the chapter concludes by discussing the potential on a city-wide scale for urban food production as well as on an individual building basis.

This chapter discusses the potential for using modular, intensive green roof technology to create rooftop vegetable gardens on existing buildings with a view to minimising food miles, shortening the supply chain and

Green Roof Retrofit: Building Urban Resilience, First Edition.
Edited by Sara Wilkinson and Tim Dixon.
© 2016 John Wiley & Sons, Ltd. Published 2016 by John Wiley & Sons, Ltd.

reducing the carbon footprint of growing and transporting food. The research considers the economic and environmental benefits of *retrofitting* existing buildings with green roofs for owners and investors, and the desirable social and psychological impacts on the inhabitants – including the potential betterment of the community by utilising roof space for urban agriculture.

9.1   Green Roof Retrofit and Urban Food Production

'Roofs can represent up to 32% of the horizontal surface of built-up areas' (Frazer, 2005), and many have the potential to become urban farmland. There are many successful established examples, such as Eagle Street Rooftop Farm, which has over $500\,m^2$ of intensive green roof sustaining an organic vegetable farm located on a warehouse rooftop in Greenpoint, Brooklyn, NY (Rooftop Farms, 2013). The use of existing urban horizontal spaces as farmland increases the food security of a city. As global temperatures rise and crops fail, and droughts become more frequent and severe, it will become increasingly desirable to equip urban dwellers with the ability to cultivate food, or to encourage urban farmers to produce food locally. Difficulties in harvesting and transporting crops long distances from regional production areas to urban centres as the global transport energy transitions from oil may also play a role in the general decentralisation/urbanisation of food production. Concomitant to these outcomes are the social benefits and the financial and environmental imperatives. A green roof offers a building and its surrounding environment many benefits. These include stormwater management, improved water runoff quality (Mentens, 2006; Hilten, 2008), improved air quality in the urban canyon (Yang *et al.*, 2008), prolonged durability of the roof skin (Köhler, 2002), increased efficiency of energy use in buildings (Castleton, 2010) and a reduction of the urban heat island effect (Rizwan *et al.*, 2008). Other benefits also include enhanced architectural interest and biodiversity (Castleton, 2010: 62) as well as reintroducing the natural world into the anthropogenic environment.

As millions face starvation globally and the proliferation of food waste becomes endemic, a report released by the Institute of Mechanical Engineers (Fox, 2013) estimated 'that 30–50% (or 1.2–2 billion tonnes) of all food produced is lost before reaching a human stomach'. Some reasons are poor engineering and inefficient agricultural practices, inadequate transport and storage infrastructure. Urban rooftop farming has the potential to ameliorate some of these problems by shortening the food supply chain. With claims that food security will become an issue in future because of the expanding global population, the opportunity to reduce food wastage through inefficiencies in harvesting and/or storage should be explored. A further issue arises where, through commercial decisions made by food retailers, there is destruction of crops in the field due to overproduction because it is no longer profitable to harvest and sell the produce.

Rooftop agriculture has the potential to create healthier communities in both alimentary and psychological ways. Urban rooftop agriculture could provide access to fresh, healthy, nutritious produce due to the reduced time spent in transit and storage. City dwellers and workers are increasingly detached from nature, and this contributes to rising stress levels and dissatisfaction with contemporary society (Shephard, 1982). Kellert and Wilson (1995) claimed that 'humans have a profound need for regular contact with the natural environment for continued wellbeing'. 'Rooftop gardening means taking up an inspiring, ecological and productive activity, and developing new links with the food chain, the seasons, the environment and the community' (Germain, 2008).

A supplementary social benefit of rooftop agriculture may be community volunteer programmes whereby residents and workers engage in food production. Eagle Street Rooftop Farm in Brooklyn, NY (Rooftop Farms, 2013) operates a small community-supported agriculture (CSA) programme and an onsite farm market which caters to local restaurants. It utilises trained interns and urban farming apprentices and hosts volunteers during growing seasons. In partnership with the Growing Chefs organisation, the farm hosts educational and volunteer programmes to bring city dwellers closer to their food source (Growing Chefs, 2013). Whilst there are many successful examples of urban agriculture in the northern hemisphere, it is surprising that Sydney has so few examples of rooftop urban food production, and to date, no empirical studies as to its viability.

Climate and local weather conditions have a considerable impact on what can be grown and the duration of the growing season. With regard to prevailing weather conditions, Sydney is located in a temperate climatic zone with rainfall spread throughout the year. Annual meteorological data for 2012 showed 1213.6 mm of rainfall, a mean maximum temperature of 22.7°C and a mean minimum of 14.4°C (Australian Bureau of Meteorology, 2013). Sydney's annual sunshine averages almost seven hours a day (City of Sydney, 2013), with Sydney's rainfall an average 11 wet days per month. Overall, these are good conditions for growing food currently. But what is predicted in the future? New South Wales Government Agencies and the University of New South Wales have been developing climate change forecasts for the NSW State Plan regions and Sydney's weather is projected to become hotter over all seasons (2–3°C), with summer rainfall projected to increase by 20–50% and winter rainfall projected to decrease (NSW Environment and Heritage, 2015). The pattern of the El Niño–Southern Oscillation cycle is projected to continue, but with higher temperatures than currently experienced. El Niño years are likely to continue to be drier than average and become hotter. La Niña years are likely to continue to be wetter than average and also to become warmer. In El Niño events, water stress is projected to be more intense due to higher temperatures. During La Niña years, storms with heavy downpours are projected to be more frequent (Plan, 2008). Given these predictions of climate change impact on Sydney's growing seasons, rooftop farmers will need to adapt their taxonomic palette.

A further consideration is the characteristics of the building stock and the numbers of potential consumers for the food produced. In June 2011, the City of Sydney LGA housed 169,505 people (Australian Bureau of Statistics, 2015), with the CBD covering $25\,km^2$ and a population density of $6780.2/km^2$ (City of Sydney, 2013). Based on previous studies of the potential for green roof retrofit (Osmond, 2012), it is possible that 17–20% of Sydney rooftops could accommodate intensive green roofs. There are over 17.5 million square metres of built form within the CBD. Whilst no data exists regarding the potential for vegetated rooftop gardens, given that there are $17.5\,km^2$ of roofs with a 20% intensive green roof potentiality factor, approximately $3.5\,km^2$ of roof space is available to support urban agriculture in containerised garden beds (Osmond, 2012).

9.2   Stakeholders and Urban Food Production

There are a number of stakeholders involved in urban food production. The regulators include urban and regional planners, building code regulators, food regulators and public health and safety regulators. Each regulator covers a different aspect of urban food production from food standards to minimum building safety standards where food may be grown. The urban and regional planners take a longer-term and wider perspective in respect of trying to develop policies and guidelines that will lead to liveable cities and settlements for the community with regard to social, economic and environmental sustainability. This remit gives them a broad interest in urban food production within the urban environment, as well as significant power to influence the variables, which can lead to greater levels of food production.

For the community, people have the ability to engage in, and to adopt, urban food production in various ways. To date, this has typically been in private gardens on a household basis or in community gardens on a wider scale. Community gardens are typically at ground level and can be located on private or council-owned land. Typically, land values increase in city centres, and here there is less land available for garden activities; herein lies the opportunity for rooftop gardening and to use space that typically has no active use. Generally, the community is keen to engage in gardening and the positive social outcomes associated with it, as discussed in greater detail in Chapter 10.

The owner stakeholder group are diverse and can comprise private individuals and commercial organisations. The land-use types which can support rooftop food production are very varied and include retail, residential (multi-unit and individual household), commercial office and industrial buildings. The key criteria are for a relatively shallow-sloping, well-drained, accessible rooftop with good access to sun and a water supply. As noted above, there is a large area of rooftops in city centres which could support food production, however, to date in capitalist economies there are barriers to uptake. The main one is that owners are reluctant to allow agricultural production on their rooftop due to perceptions of increased maintenance liabilities or potential overloading of the roof or drainage problems. Wilkinson *et al.* (2016) posited that the adoption of rooftop licences in

Sydney would assuage the fears of owners by setting out start and termination dates for rooftop food production, along with a schedule of condition at commencement and an agreement to make good any wants of repair at the termination. Furthermore, there is an, as yet, untapped opportunity for owners to gain income from rooftops and potentially to add to their corporate social responsibility (CSR) profile. The argument for CSR is that in allowing rooftop food production, the owner indirectly adds to biodiversity, improves air quality and reduces stormwater runoff and the urban heat island effect. There are plans to pilot the rooftop licence in Sydney, Australia in 2016. Another model with greater social sustainability, and again which can feature in CSR, is where food produced on the rooftop is donated to charities. Owner-occupiers have fewer barriers related to legal entities around access to, and use of, roofs. Where food is produced commercially for distribution or sale to the public, then legislation in respect of food supply and food safety applies.

To date, very few commercial food producers are found in city centre rooftops globally, and this may be due to perceived costs of production and economies of scale. In times of restricted food supply, countries like Cuba have turned to wide-scale urban food production, including rooftop food production to feed the people. Rooftop food production is likely to appeal to niche markets, to supply local cafes or food co-operatives, or small retailers. Therefore, larger commercial producers are less likely to enter this market, with their production focused around peri-urban and rural areas. It is likely that over time, the barriers to urban food production will diminish as food security issues become more known to the wider public. At this point an enlightened community will see benefits in having a local food supply, so that younger members of the society are able to learn directly where fresh food comes from and how it grows.

9.3   Contamination and Air-Quality Issues

As agriculture within the bounds of urban settlement increases, the ecosystem services provided by intensively disturbed urban soils previously used for residential, waste management and industrial purposes will play a more central role in the future of human development (Luo et al., 2012). The growing of urban crops for human consumption, with the simultaneous reduction in air pollutants, as well as stormwater management, are the major services sought. Timely, intensive study of these soils is thus a pressing concern. Whilst the development of intensive agriculture in densely populated urban areas presents many problems, the major concern for human health is the contamination of crops due to the close proximity of past or current polluting activities (Wiseman et al., 2013; Galal and Shehata, 2015a). Given that pollutant concentrations will be unevenly distributed across urban areas dependent on land use (e.g., Luo et al., 2012), an understanding of both pollutant distribution and remediation techniques and their limitations, along with the contaminant uptake mechanisms of the crops themselves, is essential for the safe expansion of urban farming activities.

The major sources of urban soil pollutants are a vast range of industrial processes and emissions from road traffic. Vehicular traffic contributes to urban soil pollution primarily from exhaust emissions, but also through the wear of components such as brakes and tyres (Zereini *et al.*, 2012). In recent years, it has been shown that heavy metal levels in soil and vegetation have increased considerably as daily traffic increases (Onder and Dursun, 2006). Farmaki and Thomaidis (2008) reported increased concentrations of the metals lead, copper, zinc and palladium in the urban environment, including the topsoil, highways and streets. Areas with highly elevated metal concentrations were generally located in industrial and residential areas, roadsides and crowded commercial districts (Cicchella *et al.*, 2008; Alyemenia and Almohisen, 2014). Further, vehicular traffic emissions are of concern as they consist of gaseous pollutants (Laschober *et al.*, 2004), which may remain in the air for some time, but most are deposited in roadside soils and plant materials near the road. These toxins can enter plant tissues directly via rain and dust and be taken up from the soil through the root system (Jozic *et al.*, 2009).

Luo *et al.* (2012) reviewed heavy metal concentrations from different cities around the world, finding very wide variations between the concentrations of all metals, ranging from safe to extremely high levels (e.g., 37 mg/kg of lead in Moscow to 395 mg/kg in Chicago urban soils). This variability was directly related to either the predominant industries or traffic patterns in the cities, but also the age of the cities, population density, environmental regulations and local climates.

9.3.1   Types of Pollutant

Heavy metals are the primary pollutants of concern within the context of the contamination of urban food crops. Heavy metal pollution is becoming a growing global problem as the global population increases, and urbanisation and industrialisation expand. Organic pollutants make up a lower proportion of total soil contamination than do metals (De Nicola *et al.*, 2015), and are bioaccumulated by plants and translocated amongst plant tissues (Zhang *et al.*, 2015). This class of pollutants is generally considered of lower concern in food crops, and will not be considered further.

Metals of major concern include cadmium, exposure to which can lead to various cancers and renal dysfunction syndromes (Żukowska and Biziuk, 2008). Lead exposure can lead to a broad range of conditions, notably in the nervous, skeletal, circulatory, enzymatic, endocrine and immune systems (Li *et al.*, 2015). In addition, exposure to high levels of chromium, arsenic, mercury, copper, zinc and nickel is also of significant health concern (Chen *et al.*, 2005). Furthermore, the replacement of lead in automotive fuel with methylcyclopentadienyl manganese tricarbonyl (MMT) has the potential to lead to high levels of manganese in urban soils from exhaust pollution (Brault *et al.*, 1994).

In urban environments, lead is the heavy metal toxicant of most concern (see Lu *et al.*, 2015). There is growing evidence that lead levels in many urban soils are at or above levels that warrant vigilance, including both industrialised areas and non-industrial urban areas, across both developing and developed countries (Laidlaw and Taylor, 2011; Lu *et al.*, 2015). The greatest single source of soil-borne lead comes from its prior use in motor vehicle fuels. Mielke *et al.* (2011) estimated that approximately 1.4 million tonnes of lead in the US environment came from this source between 1950 and 1982, when its use ceased, resulting in a median concentration of 16.5 mg/kg soil throughout that country, with far higher levels in urban areas. Other sources of lead include smelting and many other industrial processes (e.g., Lu *et al.*, 2015). Lead-containing house paint was once considered a major source, however its contribution has become less significant compared with other sources after its use has been progressively reduced since the 1980s (Laidlaw and Taylor, 2011).

Once any of the heavy metals are present in soil, they persist indefinitely (Peña-Fernández *et al.*, 2015), and long-term exposure to some metals, even in low concentrations, can cause health problems, especially in foetal development (Grandjean and Landrigan, 2006). Lead has been associated with health effects including decreased academic achievement, attention deficit hyperactivity disorder, learning and conduct difficulties in both children and adults, at levels below many international health standards (5 μg/dL blood) (Taylor *et al.*, 2012). Anthropogenic derived lead behaves differently in the biosphere to naturally occurring forms, as it is concentrated in carbonate, iron and manganese hydroxide soil fractions, which are easily absorbed by living organisms. Whilst human blood lead concentrations decreased markedly once it ceased being used as a fuel additive (Thomas *et al.*, 1999), its presence in soil, especially that in which food plants are grown, is still a health concern.

9.3.2   Most Urban Soils are Contaminated

Most urban land worldwide is affected by some environmental pollution. Mitchell *et al.* (2014) analysed the substrate from 54 urban gardens in New York, USA and found that 70% produced at least one sample that exceeded health regulation levels for at least one pollutant. Lead is the most common contaminant found in levels that are high enough to cause health concerns (Angotti, 2015), with children especially being susceptible (Centers for Disease Control and Prevention, 2013). Mireles *et al.* (2012) tested urban soils in the cities of Zacatecas and Guadalupe in Mexico that had experienced both long-term mining and increasing traffic activity, to assess whether residents might be at risk of exposure. The authors found high levels of caesium, zinc, arsenic and antimony relative to US and Mexican regulatory standards. Clarke *et al.* (2015) assessed urban garden soils in Los Angeles, USA for heavy metals, finding increased soil concentrations with proximity to roads for lead, arsenic and cadmium. Neighbourhood age was also associated with lead levels, which the authors concluded was due to the previous use of lead-based paints. Karim *et al.* (2015) found metal contamination of the urban soils of Karachi, Pakistan to be moderate to moderately severe for lead and moderate for chromium and copper. Peña-Fernández *et al.* (2015) found that cadmium, copper, lead and zinc contamination in the urban soils of an urban area in Madrid, Spain could be attributed to traffic emissions, while arsenic, nickel and beryllium originated from industrial pollution. Chen *et al.* (2005) found high levels of copper and lead in urban parks in Beijing, China, and associated these pollutants with anthropogenic sources. Qing *et al.* (2015) found moderate to high soil concentrations of cadmium, zinc, copper and lead in an industrial city in northern China. Highly industrialised areas of Bangladesh have been found to be heavily polluted with a range of metals; Islam *et al.* (2015) showed that soils contaminated with tannery waste, metal-work industry pollution and electrical waste were heavily contaminated with nickel, copper, arsenic, cadmium and lead. Cadmium was of particular concern in this study, and was most likely sourced from smelting operations (Islam *et al.*, 2015). Thus it is apparent that urban soil contamination is widespread, although concentrations vary on both large scales (i.e., between cities) and at a finer level, between different sites depending on exposure to current and past polluting activities. Thus, urban garden designers need to be cognisant of previous activities in the area, especially when food production is proposed, and to make provision for adequate testing of produce, as well as soils, air quality and water supply.

9.3.3   Do Contaminants Accumulate in Urban Crops?

Many studies have investigated heavy metal levels of crops grown in contaminated soils. The conclusions drawn from these studies are quite inconsistent, leading to difficulty in predicting whether crops grown in an area with a specific contaminant profile will be of concern to health, or which crop species accumulate contaminants at higher rates. Furthermore, it is unknown whether the contaminant levels in urban-grown produce are higher than those from commercial agriculture, where the substrates have a long history of fertiliser and pesticide use (Angotti, 2015).

A study in Brescia, Italy examined whether proximity to long-term ferroalloy industry sites could be associated with higher concentrations of toxic metals in home-grown vegetables (Ferri *et al.*, 2015). They found aluminium, cadmium, iron, manganese, lead and zinc were all higher in garden soils close to the plants, in contrast to remote reference sites. Spinach plants were found to have high concentrations of lead, and to a lesser extent cadmium. The other crop tested – turnips – did not have high metal concentrations.

Hibben *et al.* (1984) compared lead and cadmium in food crops between gardens in Brooklyn, New York, which suffers from increased environmental metal concentrations due primarily to air pollution, and the same plant species grown in an unpolluted suburban area. The authors found low levels of cadmium in both sites in all plants, and only higher lead concentrations in radish and lettuce leaves in the Brooklyn sites, concluding that the levels of these metals in urban crops are unlikely to be a health concern.

The bioaccumulation of metals by a range of crop plants in highly cadmium-contaminated soil in China was tested and several crops accumulated cadmium at unsafe levels, including Chinese cabbage and lettuce (Hu *et al.*,

2013). A greater number of crops did not accumulate cadmium. Hu *et al.* (2013) concluded that crop species where the stems and leaves are eaten are more likely to cause health problems – the authors recommend avoiding such crops on contaminated soils. In contrast, McBride (2013) concluded that root vegetables such as carrots may concentrate some metals at a greater rate than leafy crops and recommended avoiding such crops in suspected soils.

Sipter *et al.* (2008) tested metal accumulation in vegetables grown in soil heavily contaminated with mine tailings in Hungary. Despite very high soil metal levels, only moderate concentrations of cadmium and lead, and no arsenic, were detected in all crops, including fruit, leaf and root species. Given that the population in the sampled area is generally non-mobile, and people spend their entire lives consuming these crops, the authors calculated lifetime exposure rates and concluded that the consumption of vegetables did not pose a high health risk. Soil exposure, however, was noted as a potential hazard, especially for children. In contrast to these findings, Finster *et al.* (2004) tested vegetables grown in contaminated residential gardens in Chicago, USA, finding metal concentrations in numerous crops that were far higher than those detected by Sipter *et al.* (2008), which clearly represented a significant health hazard. These high levels included detergent-washed plant tissues, negating the presence of adherent contaminated soil. It should be noted that Chicago is well known to possess highly contaminated soil in parts of the urban area (Witzling *et al.*, 2011; Luo *et al.*, 2012). Säumel *et al.* (2012) detected varying levels of metals in a range of vegetables grown in urban Berlin, with proximity to traffic a major determinant of the contamination level.

Wild and commercially grown mushrooms exposed to high traffic in Berlin, Germany were tested for heavy metals (Schlecht and Säumel, 2015). Wild mushrooms contained metals that exceeded EU standards in most cases, despite being thoroughly cleaned before testing. Cultivated varieties, in contrast, did not exceed the limits. It is thus possible that some fungi accumulate metals from the soil at a different rate to plant material – vegetables sampled from the same areas contained far lower concentrations of contaminants. Schlecht and Säumel (2015) prudently recommended further research into the health consequences of the consumption of wild fungi from heavy traffic areas.

The presence of fairly high levels of metals in soils does not always indicate contaminated vegetables. McBride (2013) found that a range of crops grown in soil with up to 400 mg/kg lead and 100 mg/kg arsenic produced vegetables with concentrations of both contaminants below the limits of international health standards. Similarly, Warming *et al.* (2015) tested the concentrations of seven toxic metals in both leafy and root crops grown in urban areas of Copenhagen, Denmark. The levels of all metals found were within an acceptable range, and were not related to the concentrations in the soil, which ranged from very low to very high across the three sites sampled.

McBride *et al.* (2014) conducted a study to assess the relationship between soil and vegetable lead levels. Whilst a number of samples exceeded EU standards, the authors concluded that in general, urban-grown vegetables should be safe for consumption. A critical observation made in McBride *et al.*'s

(2014) study was that many high metal levels detected in urban crops are a result of soil particle adherence or incorporation into plant tissues, thus reinforcing the necessity of careful cleaning of vegetables grown in potentially contaminated soil before consumption. The authors concluded that accidental soil ingestion posed the greatest exposure risk in urban food production, rather than the consumption of contaminated produce.

9.3.4   Mitigating Urban Crop Contamination

Owing to the inconsistency in the conclusions drawn from the literature, there is no universally recommended means of mitigating the potential of urban crop contamination. There are, however, a range of techniques for the amelioration or avoidance of toxic produce, all of which should be effective to varying degrees, and more so in combination.

Contaminated soil can be treated to reduce or remove the contaminants, either by remediating the soil or replacing it altogether. Historically, soil replacement has been the most common solution (Angotti, 2015). Whilst simple, this method can be expensive, does not address the problems with the existing soil, and relies on the assumption that the imported soil is of greater quality than the existing substrate, generally with no testing being performed (Angotti, 2015). If uncontaminated replacement soil is used, however, this method will clearly lead to reduced levels of heavy metals in crops (Mitchell *et al.*, 2014).

Phytoextraction and phytoremediation involve using sacrificial plants to concentrate and remove pollutants from a contaminated environment (Peng *et al.*, 2008). This process involves growing plants known to accumulate pollutants, with harvesting and disposal of plant materials off-site. This method is far less commonly used, as it is often thought to be time consuming – in the range of years to decades – and the technology is unfamiliar to most urban gardeners (Angotti, 2015).

The selection of phytoextraction species has received significant research attention. Galal and Shehata (2015a,b) tested the capacity of several environmental weed species as bioaccumulators of heavy metals in polluted roadway soils. They found that the capacity of the plants to bioaccumulate heavy metals was generally limited to below that of the concentration in the soil, with some translocation of the metals from roots to shoot parts of the plants demonstrated for most plant species and pollutants. For example, the wetland plant *Phragmites australis* has been shown to be an effective bioaccumulator of aluminium, iron and manganese (Wang and Jia, 2009). Jambhulkar and Juwarkar (2009) tested the capacity of six plant species to accumulate metal pollutants from a fly ash dump in Nagpur, India. The authors detected bioaccumulation of iron, manganese, nickel, zinc, copper, chromium and lead, with the species *Cassia siamea* accumulating all metals at higher concentrations than the other tested plants, suggesting that hyperaccumulator species exist. Such species may be useful for the remediation of highly metal-contaminated soils prior to crop sowing, especially if the simpler methods are ineffective in a specific area.

Soil treatments may also be used to effectively reduce contaminant levels or capacity to enter plant tissues. The progressive amendment of contaminated soil with compost has been used with some success (Angotti, 2015; Clarke et al., 2015), but as this method does not physically remove metals from the substrate, the only means by which they can be removed are still through consumption of crops or windblown dust – neither of which are desirable outcomes. McBride et al. (2013) tested whether soil lead transfers into leafy vegetable crops could be reduced by adding a range of soil amendments including composts, peat, calcium phosphate, gypsum and iron oxide. All additions were generally unsuccessful. Low pH, however, unquestionably increases the solubility, and thus the uptake rate of many metals (McBride, 2013). Increasing the soil pH above 6.5 should thus lead to reduced rates of metal transfer, and can generally be recommended for all potentially contaminated soils, in combination with testing of crops if high levels of contamination are suspected.

McBride et al. (2013) noted that one of the main reasons why these amendments are unsuccessful is that the main mechanism by which lead contaminates crops is through soil adhesion. Ferri et al. (2015) similarly observed that washed spinach had lower metal concentrations than unwashed produce, leading to the recommendation that urban-grown produce should be washed thoroughly before consumption. This practice is strongly recommended for all crops grown in urban areas for the reduction of contamination.

Perhaps the simplest way to minimise the potential for crop contamination is to select sites with a reduced likelihood of contamination. Clarke et al.'s (2015) study indicated that locating plots further from roadways was associated with decreasing metal concentrations. Rooftops potentially offer a good location. Säumel et al. (2012) found that whilst contamination levels in urban vegetables were higher in high-road-traffic areas, the presence of buildings or vegetation barriers between crops and roads substantially reduced crop metal contamination. Witzling et al. (2011) noted that raised beds can result in lower soil metal levels. Findings that the soils from urban parks and recreational areas have far lower levels of contaminants than industrial or high-traffic areas in China (Luo et al., 2012) is evidence that with some targeted a priori field testing, safe areas for urban food production should be available in even the most populous of cities.

Overall, although a number of studies have raised the possibility that under certain conditions, metal contamination of urban-grown produce may be of concern for our health, it is more likely that the outcomes of eating greater quantities of fresh fruit and vegetables will provide far greater health benefits (Guitart et al., 2014) than the generally minor risks associated with contamination. Despite inconsistent literature regarding the mitigation of crop contamination from polluted soils, it can safely be recommended that the selection of areas less likely to harbour high contaminant levels, maintaining high soil pH and organic matter, and careful cleaning of produce before consumption should lead to minimal risks, without the expense of phytoextracting or replacing existing soils.

9.3.5   Urban Gardens and Air Quality

There is a growing body of literature supporting the hypothesis that plants can play a major role in ameliorating poor ambient air quality. This is in line with the larger body of literature from indoor urban environments, where plants have been shown to reduce or remove virtually all types of air pollutants (e.g., Orwell *et al.*, 2004, 2006; Torpy *et al.*, 2014). Although limited studies to date have examined urban air-quality effects from urban food gardens, recent evidence (Irga *et al.*, 2015) indicates that plants other than mowed grass have a major influence on a number of air pollutants in urban areas. Irga *et al.*'s (2015) study found that the local density of all components of urban vegetation – other than grass – had the greatest influence on the proximal air quality of any variables measured, which included rainfall and traffic density. It is reasonable to expect that many urban food crops could provide the same subsidiary health benefits to the urban environment. Tong *et al.*'s (2015) finding that urban food gardens can remove airborne particulate matter supports this hypothesis. The finding that the leaves from tree species in polluted environments may accumulate higher levels of toxic metals than the same species in uncontaminated environments (Hu *et al.*, 2014) suggests another area of research that may yield dividends, although the resulting contamination of crops with airborne contaminants such as heavy metals is of concern, as described previously. It is suggested that following the recommendations given in Section 9.3.5 should reduce the toxic effects of above-surface plant contamination to a safe level in the same way that they reduce soil-sourced contaminants.

Green roofs have been theorised to improve outdoor air quality by collecting particulate matter, filtering noxious gases and reducing building CO_2 emissions by reducing demands on air-conditioning systems through keeping a building at thermal comfort levels (Refahi and Talkhabi, 2015). Substantial research has shown that green roof systems in densely populated areas can effectively remove tonnes of air pollutants annually (Yang *et al.*, 2008; Rowe, 2011). Indirectly, vegetation facilitates evapotranspiration and thus cools surfaces and can shade a building's roof to help lower indoor temperatures and thus decrease the need to use air conditioning (Heisler, 1986). Yang *et al.* (2008) found through a modelling procedure that 19.8 ha of green roofs with canopies of herbaceous plants, short grass and deciduous trees in Chicago, USA effectively removed 85 kg ha^1 yr^1 of air pollutants from 2006–2007. Currie and Bass's (2005) study estimated that 109 ha of green roofs can account for the annual removal of 7.87 tonnes of air pollutants. Tan and Sia (2005) measured the concentrations of sulphur oxides and particulate matter on a 4000 m^2 roof before and after the installation of a roof garden. They recorded a 6% reduction in sulphur oxides and a 37% particulate matter reduction. There is thus significant potential for roof gardens to provide subsidiary benefits in air-quality improvement. The empirical degree to which they do this, and the specifics of how much of which pollutants are removed and whether this removal interacts with food quality, are both areas in need of further study. The following section reports on a research project at UTS to grow food on retrofitted campus rooftops, where many of the issues identified above were investigated and analysed.

9.4   The Research Design and Methodology

This research uses empirical evidence derived from growing plants and vegetables on three rooftops at UTS, New South Wales, Australia during 2013 and 2014. UTS is located in Ultimo on the fringe of the CBD and was founded in 1988, although it can trace its origins to the 1870s. In 2013 the university had just under 38,000 students, taught in buildings having a mix of architectural styles which reflect the different periods in which the buildings and grounds were constructed and renovated. The university offers self-catered student accommodation in five buildings. Gumal Ngurang housed one of the rooftop sites, and is the second-largest complex located on the busy Broadway street. It is a high-density inner-city location and offered great potential to learn about issues related to urban food production.

Three different types of rooftop garden beds are described in three illustrative case studies. The research is qualitative, sharing the three basic assumptions identified by Patton (1980) of being naturalistic, holistic and inductive. Naturalism involves seeing the phenomenon in its naturally occurring state, in this case by visiting the three sites to observe what has taken place. The holistic aspect involves looking at the whole problem to develop a more complete understanding of the influencing factors and variables with regard to three different approaches to rooftop food production in Sydney. Figure 9.1 shows the location of the university and rooftop in the centre of Sydney. The inductive approach is derived from the literature review, whereby a picture of the problems and issues emerges as the researcher becomes more familiar with the topic area. A literature review identifies which areas need to be addressed.

An advantage of case study research is that it is a flexible method, which can be adapted during the research (Robson, 2003). With this research, three different beds are evaluated on three different roofs and so it is not possible to make an exact comparison of outputs. However, that is not to

Gumal housing, Broadway

Main UTS campus including science and DAB buildings

Figure 9.1   Location of UTS campus and project rooftops.

say that the conclusions drawn from the study are not valid. A limitation of the technique is that the researcher does not sample widely enough and that studies may represent the peripheries and not the average (Robson, 2003). However, Yin (1989) observes that the case study is concerned with analytical and not statistical generalisation. Care was taken to ensure the conclusions drawn are noted as being analytically general rather than statistically representative. The criticism of the case study as a 'soft option' was rejected as the method requires preparation, knowledge of procedures (in this case food production on Sydney rooftops) and analytical skills (Robson, 2003). It is soft only in the sense that no hard and fast rules exist for the researcher to follow. The means of data collection was through observation and direct experience, which was deemed most suitable because it allowed the researcher to collect identical data from each site (Moser and Kalton, 1979). Records were kept on biodiversity, watering, weather, bed costs, planting, dates, fertilisers used and crop yields.

9.4.1   Case Studies

The first task was to find suitable roofs on the university campus. After a number of visits to rooftops it was found that there were issues such as accessibility or uses which precluded other activity, such as telecommunications equipment. A third roof was discounted as it was heavily overshadowed and had poor orientation. Property managers were a significant factor, and finally the team met one who was also a gardener. This staff member was helpful and knowledgeable, and took the team to several potential roofs before a joint decision was arrived at. The Science Faculty had test beds on their roof and permission was given to position another bed there. Finally, the researchers' home faculty has a roof space directly outside the staff kitchen and the DAB Faculty Manager gave permission to site the V Garden beds there.

9.4.2   Gumal Student Housing

This roof, located at ninth-floor level on Broadway, Sydney faces southeast. The construction is reinforced concrete with an impervious tiled covering. The roof is designed for access and has a concrete perimeter wall approximately 1200 mm high, 600 mm wide and 800 mm deep, which is planted out along a recessed top surface. There is lift access to level 9. It is exposed and open to the wind and sun. The garden bed chosen for this site was a recycled plastic raised bed supported on a timber-frame trestle. The UV-resistant recycled plastic was extremely light, easily assembled and its dimensions were 3300 mm long × 1200 mm wide × 300 mm deep. See Figures 9.2 and 9.3.

A 3600 × 1200 mm² trestle was constructed from 90 × 45 mm² treated pine frames, braced with galvanised strapping tied together using a 90 × 45 mm² treated pine rail top and bottom. The frames were prefabricated off-site to minimise the noise impact during construction, and for easier transportation.

Figure 9.2   Gumal bed under construction.

Two sheets of ply $1800 \times 1200\,mm^2$ formed the top of the trestle and supported the plastic framework for the bed.

A layer of food-grade rubber waterproofing membrane, ethylene propylene diene monomer (M-class EPDM rubber), was placed over the timber trestle as weather protection. The plastic pod was positioned on the membrane and a bead of food-grade silicone sealed the base of the garden bed and held it in place. At one end a floor drain was installed and sealed with silicone, and using a spirit level and some small plastic wedges, the end of the trestle furthest from the floor drain was raised slightly to facilitate drainage. A layer of 20 mm drainage cell sheeting was placed across the floor of the bed with a layer of geotextile fabric laid over the drainage cells to keep the soil and plant roots from blocking the drain. A layer of fine gravel 20 mm deep was laid onto the geotextile fabric, followed by another layer of

Figure 9.3 Gumal bed planted out.
Source: Wilkinson.

geotextile fabric. The bed was divided into two sections for different grow-ing media; one was filled with an organic composted cow manure and gar-den soil mixture and the other a lightweight engineered substrate with a mixture of coir bark, perlite P400, Canadian peat, 0–8 mm composted pine bark, trace elements, calcium nitrate, coarse granular dolomite, gypsum, superphosphate, zeolite 1–3 mm and magrilime. Both beds were top dressed with a compressed pelletised organic seaweed fertiliser (Seamungus) and mulched with lucerne hay. Both were fertilised topically fortnightly with an organic fish emulsion and Seasol (a seaweed tonic) was applied topically once a month.

The beds were planted out with eggplant, zucchini, basil, carrots, beet-root, lettuce, chilli, capsicum, silverbeet, celery, rocket, mizuna and mari-golds. These beds were planted out in November 2013 and the cost for the two beds was $1350.62 plus labour.

9.4.3 Science Roof

This roof is located at seventh-floor level on the corner of Harris Street and Thomas Street in Sydney and faces northwest. The construction comprises reinforced concrete with an impervious covering. The roof is protected with walled structures approximately 3 m high to three sides and a glazed screen to the Thomas Street elevation. The garden bed chosen for this site was a plastic wicking bed.

The bed was a pond purchased at a cost of $280 with a 320 litre capacity and dimensions of $1500\,mm \times 750\,mm \times 300\,mm$ high. The reservoir in the bed was created by laying 100 mm agricultural drainage pipe across the base of the pond. A short section of tube was positioned vertically from the bottom of the pond up to the top (in a place where the overflow was visible). This was the filler tube, for which a section of agricultural pipe was used. A hole, to accommodate a 30 mm threaded tank outlet, was drilled into the pond shell at the height presented by the top of the agricultural pipe, 100 mm from the base. The outlet had a washer to eliminate leaks. The overflow outlet was located as close as possible to the rooftop drain to minimise the trip hazard created by a hose. Geotextile fabric was placed on the agricultural pipe to prevent the soil and roots from entering the reservoir and to allow the capillary or wicking action to irrigate the garden bed. Figures 9.4 and 9.5 show the bed immediately following planting in December 2013 and then four weeks later in January 2014.

Figure 9.4   Wicking bed on Science roof (December 2013).
Source: Wilkinson.

Figure 9.5   Wicking bed on Science roof (January 2014).
Source: Wilkinson.

The bed was filled with soil and compost to a depth of approximately 200 mm. It was top dressed with a compressed pelletised organic seaweed fertiliser (Seamungus). The bed was filled with water through the vertical filler tube until it overflowed from the outlet. It was topped up over the two days while the soil conditioned and after this initial phase it was topped up with 30–40 litres of water every five to six days. The bed was planted with a mix of eggplant, zucchini, basil, carrots, beetroot, lettuce, chilli, capsicum, silverbeet, celery, rocket, mizuna and marigolds. After planting, the bed was mulched with lucerne hay and fertilised topically fortnightly with an organic fish emulsion and Seasol (a seaweed tonic) was applied topically once a month. The bed was planted out in December 2013, which is summer in Sydney, Australia. The total cost of the bed was $412 plus labour.

9.4.4   Vertical Gardens

This roof is located at fifth-floor level on Harris Street in Sydney. The roof faces northwest. The roof construction comprises reinforced concrete with an impervious tiled covering. The roof is designed for access and has a concrete parapet approximately 1200 mm high and 200 mm deep to one side. Two sides are flanked by buildings that rise to a height of 7 floors and 20 floors. The remaining edge has a metal-framed glazed fence and overlooks an internal courtyard at fourth-floor level. The roof is enclosed on all sides by tall buildings. In summer months, when the sun is high, there are around six hours of direct sunlight on the roof, however in winter months there is

Figure 9.6   V Gardens on level 5 roof.
Source: Wilkinson.

minimal direct sun. Furthermore, the buildings do lead to very high wind levels at times. There is lift access to level 5, however there are steps out onto the roof terrace area, which made transportation less easy. The beds were supplied by V Gardens, Sydney. The beds have a timber frame and a large base bed with a series of metal-framed horizontal trays to a height of 1600 mm. The horizontal trays are approximately 150 mm deep. One bed has a self-watering system on a 12 volt timer, which utilises a submersible 12 volt pump and drippers. It is powered by a battery, which is recharged by photovoltaic cells and the sun. The reservoir at the base of the garden houses the submersible pump and acts as a wicking bed for the lowest garden. The second bed is identical in design apart from the irrigation system and wicking bed. See Figures 9.6 and 9.7.

These beds were planted with a variety of herbs including basil, mint and oregano and vegetables such as lettuce, eggplant, silverbeet and capsicums. Larger root vegetables such as carrots and beetroots were grown in the base bed. The beds were planted out in November 2013.

9.4.5   Results and Interpretation

Social

There was considerable interaction and interest from staff within the faculties where the beds were sited around the university. This interest was focused on what had been planted, and whether anyone could join in to water the plants and harvest the food. Without prompting, staff in the

Figure 9.7   V Garden with wicking bed.
Source: Wilkinson.

Design, Architecture and Building faculty put up a wall calendar with a pen in the staff kitchen to record whether the plants had been watered. When watered, the staff member or person simply ticked the date and others knew when the plants had been watered. It is a simple system, and few plants died despite a record-breaking hot, dry Sydney summer. People asked and talked about the plants regularly and would often describe the meals they cooked with the plants and the flavour of the herbs and vegetables they used. Other staff – such as security guards – also expressed interest in the rooftop gardens, imparting tips and guidance where they thought it was needed. One staff member, upon learning that the beds were an experiment to see what could be grown on Sydney rooftops, noted that: 'this is why the Cubans survived and the North Koreans starved to death'. They have given advice also about the timing of the watering and care of the plants. Students approached the researchers when attending the gardens at Gumal and chatted freely about the plants. A journalism student from Germany decided to write about the gardens for her assignment. Industrial design students used the gardens and rooftop agriculture in their major design projects. Overall, the social interactions were high and positive.

Economic

The costs of the beds varied, as did the amount of growing space between the three roofs. The costs were reasonably affordable, although it would take many years to grow sufficient food to pay back the initial costs.

Environmental Considerations

The three locations experienced different weather conditions to some extent. For example, the Gumal rooftop is exposed to sun and high winds, which desiccated the plants on a number of hot summer days. The beds needed more watering due to accelerated evapotranspiration. The Science roof was sheltered from wind on three sides, and the plants received more shade during the hottest months, resulting in less leaf burn and water stress. High winds were experienced in the DAB roof area and although the V Garden's construction, with the weight centred at the base, meant that neither structure was affected by the winds, some of the larger vegetables were badly battered on these occasions. The DAB roof is surrounded by high buildings on all four sides and consequently during autumn and winter periods less direct sun was experienced on the roof, which affected growing rates. However, in the summer, plants on this building had more respite from intense heat and direct sunlight.

In terms of thermal performance, the installation of rooftop gardens inevitably results in some reductions in air-conditioning-system cooling loads. Owing to the inherent thermal properties of shading, the temperature under the raised bed was significantly lower and this provided a reduction in the temperature of the roof covering. With the wicking bed and its direct surface contact, higher levels of thermal performance would be expected. No data was recorded on temperatures in the rooms directly below the beds, as the air-conditioning (A/C) systems in the building would ameliorate any temperature changes caused by the roof garden, but this is worth exploring in the future, especially with regard to any effects on the energy use of the A/C systems. Given the absorptive properties of the growing media, there was a noticeable diminution in the amount of water entering the rainwater drainage systems of each of the roofs as a result of the installation of the garden beds. The Gumal beds had plastic tanks sited below the drainage outlet, and this allowed the researchers to ascertain the approximate amounts of rainwater runoff from the beds compared with the rainfall recorded in a rain gauge. The Science roof beds drained onto the roof and into an open drainage channel. No silting of the drains occurred on any of the roofs as the geotextile fabric ensured only water passed through the textile.

With regard to attracting biodiversity, as soon as all three roofs were planted, insects appeared. Native and European bees were spotted on all sites. On the Gumal roof, a group of sulphur-crested cockatoos (*Cacatua galerita*) visited the site on the first day and uprooted the majority of the plants. Protective screens of wire mesh were fixed temporarily to deter the birds. Both yellow and orange lady beetles encamped within just a few weeks, and within all the beds worms were seen on a regular basis. No actual tests have been conducted on air quality around the beds, but it should be the case that the air will have higher levels of oxygen and lower carbon dioxide as the plants photosynthesise.

Physical and Location

Access to the three roofs varied. Gumal was always intended for public access and had good conditions from the basement car park to the rooftop. There are good water and power sources on this roof. The recycled plastic garden beds were delivered in a long lightweight tube, which fitted into the lift. The prefabricated trestle frames and the pine sheet were heavy and cumbersome but could fit in the lift, as did substrates and membranes. The 3600 mm rails had to be carried up the fire stairs. Once assembled, these beds were very heavy and not easily relocated.

With the Science roof, access was via a goods lift from the car park to level 7. However, due to the sensitivity and security concerns of the science labs, special access had to be negotiated for the researchers and no public access was possible. With the DAB rooftop there is lift access to the floor but the space planning and configuration of offices meant there was a circuitous route to get the V Garden to the rooftop. Fortunately, the units were not too heavy for two people to carry. The DAB roof does not have a water or power supply, and therefore water had to be transported from the adjoining staff kitchen to the gardens. Although a solar-powered pump on the larger bed with wicking provided irrigation to that bed, it required topping up with water on a regular basis. Table 9.1 summarises the three bed types and their respective performance.

Table 9.1   Three bed types and performance

	Bed 1 – Science roof wicking bed	Bed 2 – Gumal raised bed	Bed 3 – V Garden
Transportability and assembly	Very easy	Difficult. Some carpentry skills required	Units easily transported with two people and a trolley but location presented a challenge
Ease of working	Low to ground	Easy	Very easy
Costs/sq. m of growing area	Medium	Very high	High
Ease of watering	Easy	Manual, every other day in summer	Easy
Plant growth	Very good	Varied	Good
Water usage	Low	Medium to high	Medium
Exposure to wind	Low	High	High
Exposure to excessive summer sun/heat	Medium	High	Medium
Biodiversity attracted to bed	Very good	Very good	Good

9.4.6   Findings

This section of the chapter reports on three rooftops set up in 2013 in Sydney for the production of food. The social, economic, environmental and physical aspects of the installation are described. Despite varying conditions on all three rooftops, production over the summer period in 2014 was good. There were different challenges with all three roofs, due to the physical environment and environmental conditions. The social impacts were overwhelmingly positive in all respects. Economically there was variation in the costs of the beds and the amount of skill and labour required for installation and setup, however there are options to suit most budgets. In this project, plants were tested for the presence of heavy metals; initially, moderate levels of lead were found in the soil (see Section 9.3.2), which were bio-remediated in subsequent crops.

9.5   The Carbon Footprint of Food Grown on Demonstration Beds

Currently, fresh food consumed in cities is trucked great distances. It has been estimated that the cost of transport of a $1 supermarket lettuce head is around 40 cents (Midmore, 2011). Using the Australian Greenhouse Office (2006) *Factors and Methods Workbook*, it is possible to calculate that a diesel-powered truck (manufactured post-2004) with an average carrying capacity of 24 tonnes has an average fuel consumption of 2.10 km/litre and average CO_2 emissions of 42.8 kg/tonne of freight. The University of Queensland conducted a 'lifecycle assessment study' of lettuce using a technique approved in 1998 by Standards Australia (Kershaw and Gafel, 2008). It concluded that to transport a 1 kg lettuce would create 0.0005 kg CO_2 emissions/kg lettuce/km.

Initially it was intended that the carbon footprint of growing vegetables in our demonstration rooftop gardens might easily be calculable by keeping a log of trips made to and from the gardens, however, once the gardens had been constructed, except for several replantings, almost all journeys over the 389 days to date were made by pushbike or walking. There were obviously elevator rides, and a log was kept, but as a conceptual model of urban rooftop farming, where it is assumed that the food will be consumed in situ, this seems somewhat irrelevant because if the gardens were being maintained by residents of the building, then those elevator rides would be incorporated into a daily routine anyway regardless of whether there was a rooftop garden or not.

However, this almost zero-carbon output can be compared with the carbon footprint calculations of commercially grown foodstuff which is trucked from a market garden/farm to a depot, from a depot to a retailer and then once purchased, transported to a residence, quite often by car, train or bus. The Australian Greenhouse Office (2006) calculates petrol as producing 2.7 kg of GHG emissions per litre combusted, and it calculates diesel as producing 2.9 kg of GHG emissions per litre combusted. If an average inner-city car consumes 8 litres/100 km (or 12.5 km/litre) and a typical short round trip from home to purchase vegetables of 6 km is assumed, then approximately 1.296–1.392 kg of GHG emissions is produced per trip. Based on a weekly shopping trip, total transport GHG emissions are 67.392–72.384 kg p.a. It is also worth noting the estimate that the vegetable industry contributes close to 60% of the GHG emissions within horticulture (Deuter, 2008), and this figure includes cultivation as well as transport.

9.6   Potential Reductions in Carbon Footprint

The carbon footprint of food, or 'food miles', measures the transport distance travelled by food products between production and consumption. Food can travel by ship, plane, rail or road transport, each having a different degree of environmental impact. Trucks vary from light commercial to heavy articulated vehicles, and fuel type can be diesel or unleaded petrol. Most food in Australia is transported by road (Gaballa and Abraham, 2007). Another variable to take into account is whether the trucks are full or partly full, as this affects fuel consumption and GHG emissions. When the sustainability of food is considered, food miles are an important part of the complete lifecycle assessment. A further consideration is that food transported over long distances and stored for long periods can have severely reduced nutritional value when it arrives at the point of consumption (Gaballa and Abraham, 2007). In some countries, supermarkets (e.g., Tesco in the UK) label food miles on some products for consumers (Pretty *et al.*, 2005). Lengthy storage times are causing concern, and more local production may be favoured in future, however some areas do not suit local production due to soil and climate conditions. Any analysis of the embodied energy of food must acknowledge that food miles are one part of the food production system and are related to fossil-fuel input, and GHG emissions occur at many, if not all, stages (Gaballa and Abraham, 2007). Another variable is packaging. There is little empirical research on food miles in Australia, and this research makes some preliminary estimates with regard to the carbon footprint of the current supply of City of Sydney LGA food compared with the rooftop production model.

The formula for calculating emissions estimates was sourced following the guidelines in the Australian Greenhouse Office (2006) *Factors and Methods Workbook* as follows:

$$\text{Emissions}(TCO_2 - e) = \text{Distance}(km) \times \text{Fuel Consumption Rates}(FCR)(1/km)$$
$$\times \text{Emissions Factor}(EF) \text{ per fuel type}(TCO_2 - e / kl) / 1000$$

Emission estimates using this formula are calculated for an average food-transporting truck transporting 1 tonne of truck mass and 1 tonne of food mass. Weighted averages are used to calculate an average truck, average truck mass, average fuel consumption rate of an average fuel and average emissions factor. Emissions estimates are based on data from the Australian Bureau of Science and the Australian Greenhouse

Table 9.2 Food miles and carbon emissions in Sydney, Australia

Food item	Transport (km)	Emissions: 1 tonne of food item transported by road (transport km × 0.0002205 T CO_2-e)	Emissions: 1 kg of food item transported by road (g CO_2-e)
Tomatoes	1618	356.8	357
Lettuce	54	11.9	12
Carrots	311	68.6	69
Onions	782	172.4	172

Source: Adapted from Gaballa and Abraham (2007).

Office and some data was not available for all years, consequently some inaccuracy may exist. Table 9.2 illustrates the food miles and carbon emissions for four vegetables, two of which were grown in the UTS rooftop garden beds.

It is apparent that for the four vegetables above, lettuce has the smallest carbon footprint, partly due to it representing the smallest distance travelled. Typically these vegetables require little processing and packaging, and are sold in their original form and therefore have lower carbon footprint compared with other foods such as bread or meat products. With the four vegetables in Table 9.2, however, it would appear that growing tomatoes and onions in the CBD would have the greatest impact on reducing carbon food miles as they have the highest footprint. This estimate is to be treated with caution, as the calculation was based on information provided by third parties and there was some incomplete information. Source data also varies from year to year. However, the estimates do give consumers some idea of the comparative levels of carbon food miles between vegetables. For example, the adoption of intensive production techniques may produce higher yields. Further research is required to fully assess the impacts and vulnerabilities of the Australian, NSW and Sydney food system. Food labelling is recommended so that consumer awareness is raised with regard to carbon food miles. Such awareness may lead to a greater desire to adopt increased urban food production, especially on retrofitted rooftops. Furthermore, the potential health impacts of eating fresher, locally grown food cannot be understated. Such knowledge would lead to deeper understanding of the environmental and social impacts of our food systems.

Wilkinson *et al.* (2013) estimated that, if the 15% of City of Sydney LGA rooftops identified by Osmond (2012) as suited for green roofs were used to grow lettuces, then 405,000 kg could be grown in total, leading to a reduction of 4860 kg of CO_2-e. Were tomatoes grown, the emissions reduction would be greater. Based on a typical yield for the Sydney area of 300 tonnes of organic tomatoes per hectare (Scoop it, 2012), and with a total estimated area of 1.6875 km² (or 168.75 ha) available for food production, the total production of tomatoes would be 50,625 tonnes. Therefore, a reduction of 18,073 kg of CO_2-e could be achieved if all suited rooftop space was given over to tomato production.

9.7   Conclusions

This chapter has described issues of food security, human health, population, access to nutritious food sources and the carbon impact of current food production methods, mostly in reference to Sydney, Australia, although the issues are pertinent to other cities and countries. Furthermore, the research reported here relates to university property, which has different drivers and ownership patterns to high-density residential and commercial property. It is possible, however, to adapt the model to residential and commercial property, and this is being proposed in ongoing research into urban food production. The potential for urban rooftop food production was examined, and the typical features required in rooftops for successful outcomes were discussed. Clearly there are social health and wellbeing benefits for those engaged in food production, and local production will increase awareness of food security issues and carbon food miles. The chapter described research conducted at UTS in rooftop food production including social, environmental and economic aspects, as well as setting out the specifications and considerations in respect of bed systems. The issue of contamination of urban sites and soils was described in detail; this is a significant issue that must be addressed to ensure safe, healthy food is grown on rooftops. Each site and city will have slightly different locational issues to contend with, however it is possible to grow contaminant-free food with care and planning.

The technical environmental and economic aspects of larger-scale food rooftop production were described, along with some initial modelling on production potential. McClintock and Cooper (2009) concluded that 5–10% of Oakland's fruit and vegetable requirements for a population of 423,000 could be met from 486 ha of food production on 495 aggregated public land sites. Toronto estimated that 10% of cities' food needs could be grown within the city boundary (MacRae et al., 2010), on rooftops and in public spaces. The potential for Sydney is modelled here, albeit at a very rudimentary level, however it does show the scope for urban rooftop food production and, as the city grows by approximately 2000 people per week, it is an option we will need to consider increasingly. The stakeholders were described, along with their drivers and concerns in respect of rooftop food production. These concerns are not insurmountable; it is largely a case of being risk adverse in the face of adopting a practice that is new and unknown. Given guidelines and experience, these concerns will be addressed and the overall positive aspects of urban food production socially and environmentally will prevail. In Sydney, further research is needed into other methods of urban food production such as vertical urban farming and more intensive modes of production.

References

Alyemenia, M. N. and Almohisen, I. A. A. (2014) 'Traffic and industrial activities around Riyadh cause the accumulation of heavy metals in legumes: a case study', *Saudi Journal of Biological Sciences*, 21, 167–172.

Angotti, T. (2015) 'Urban agriculture: long-term strategy or impossible dream? Lessons from Prospect Farm in Brooklyn, New York', *Public Health*, 129, 336–341.

Australian Bureau of Meteorology (2013) www.bom.gov.au.

Australian Bureau of Statistics (2015) www.censusdata.abs.gov.au/census_services/getproduct/census/2011/quickstat/LGA17200?opendocument&navpos=220.

Australian Greenhouse Office (2006) *Factors and Methods Workbook*. Available at: s3.amazonaws.com/zanran_storage/www.minkvote.no/ContentPages/2483521100.pdf.

Brault, N., Loranger, S., Courchesne, F., Kennedy, G. and Zayed, J. (1994) 'Bioaccumulation of manganese by plants: influence of MMT as a gasoline additive', *Science of the Total Environment*, 153, 77–84.

Castleton, H. (2010) 'Green roofs; building energy savings and the potential for retrofit', *Energy and Buildings*, 42, 1582–1591.

Centers for Disease Control and Prevention (2013) 'Childhood lead poisoning data, statistics, and surveillance,' available at: www.cdc.gov/nceh/lead/data/index.htm.

Chen, T.-B., Zheng, Y.-M., Lei, M., *et al.* (2005) 'Assessment of heavy metal pollution in surface soils of urban parks in Beijing, China', *Chemosphere*, 60, 542–551.

Cicchella, D., De Vivo, B., Lima, A., Albanese, S., McGill, R. A. R. and Parrish, R. R. (2008) 'Heavy metal pollution and Pb isotopes in urban soils of Napoli, Italy', *Geochemistry: Exploration, Environment, Analysis*, 8(1), 103–112.

City of Sydney (2013) 'aboutsydney', available at: www.cityofsydney.nsw.gov.au/aboutsydney/CityResearch/AtAGlance.asp.

Clarke, L. W., Jenerette, G. D. and Bain, D. J. (2015) 'Urban legacies and soil management affect the concentration and speciation of trace metals in Los Angeles community garden soils', *Environmental Pollution*, 197, 1–12.

Currie, B. and Bass, B. (2008) 'Estimates of air pollution mitigation with green plants and green roofs using the UFORE model', *Urban Ecosystems*, 11, 409–422.

De Nicola, F., Baldantoni, D., Sessa, L., Monaci, F., Bargagli, B. and Alfani, A. (2015) 'Distribution of heavy metals and polycyclic aromatic hydrocarbons in holm oak plant–soil system evaluated along urbanization gradients', *Chemosphere*, 134, 91–97.

Deuter, P. (2008) 'Defining the impacts of climate change on horticulture in Australia', *Garnaut Climate Change Review*. Cambridge University Press: Cambridge.

Farmaki, E. G. and Thomaidis, N. S. (2008) 'Current status of the metal pollution of the environment of Greece—a review', *Global NEST Journal*, 10, 366–375.

Ferri, R., Hashim, D., Smith, D. R., *et al.* (2015) 'Metal contamination of home garden soils and cultivated vegetables in the province of Brescia, Italy: implications for human exposure', *Science of the Total Environment*, 518/519, 507–517.

Finster, M. E., Gray, A. K. and Binns, H. (2004) 'Lead levels of edibles grown in contaminated residential soils: a field survey', *Science of the Total Environment*, 320, 245–257.

Fox, T. E. (2013) *Global Food, Waste Not Want Not*. Institute of Mechanical Engineers: London.

Frazer, L. (2005) 'Paving paradise', *Environmental Health Perspectives*, 113, 457–462.

Gaballa, S. and Abraham, A. B. (2007) *Food Miles in Australia: A Preliminary Study of Melbourne, Victoria*. CERES Community Park, Brunswick, Victoria. Available at: www.theage.com.au/ed_docs/food_miles.pdf.

Galal, T. M. and Shehata, H. S. (2015a) 'Bioaccumulation and translocation of heavy metals by *Plantago major* L. grown in contaminated soils under the effect of traffic pollution', *Ecological Indicators*, 48, 244–251.

Galal, T. M. and Shehata, H. S. (2015b) 'Impact of nutrients and heavy metals capture by weeds on the growth and production of rice (*Oryza sativa* L.) irrigated with different water sources', *Ecological Indicators*, 54, 108–115.

Germain, A. E. (2008) *Guide to Setting Up Your Own Edible Rooftop Garden.* Alternatives and the Rooftop Garden Project. Available at: archives.rooftopgar dens.ca/files/howto_EN_FINAL_lowres.pdf.

Grandjean, P. and Landrigan, P. J. (2006) 'Developmental neurotoxicity of industrial chemicals', *The Lancet*, 368, 2167–2178.

Growing Chefs (2013) www.growingchefs.ca/.

Guitart, D. A., Pickering, C. M. and Byrne, J. A. (2014) 'Color me healthy: food diversity in school community gardens in two rapidly urbanising Australian cities', *Health & Place*, 26, 110–117.

Heisler, M. (1986) 'Effects of individual trees on the solar radiation climate of small buildings', *Urban Ecology*, 9, 337–359.

Hibben, C. R., Hagar, S. S. and Mazza, C. P. (1984) 'Comparison of cadmium and lead content of vegetable crops grown in urban and suburban gardens', *Environmental Pollution (Series B)*, 7, 71–80.

Hilten, R. (2008) 'Modeling stormwater runoff from green roofs with HYDRUS-1D', *Journal of Hydrology*, 358(3/4), 288–293.

Hu, J., Wu, F., Wu, S., Sun, X., Lin, X. and Wong, M. H. (2013) 'Phytoavailability and phytovariety codetermine the bioaccumulation risk of heavy metal from soils, focusing on Cd-contaminated vegetable farms around the Pearl River Delta, China', *Ecotoxicology and Environmental Safety*, 91, 18–24.

Hu, Y., Wang, D., Wei, L., Zhang, X. and Song, B. (2014) 'Bioaccumulation of heavy metals in plant leaves from Yan'an city of the Loess Plateau, China', *Ecotoxicology and Environmental Safety*, 110, 82–88.

Irga, P. J., Burchett, M. D. and Torpy, F. R. (2015) 'Does urban forestry have a quantitative effect on ambient air quality in an urban environment?', *Atmospheric Environment*, 120, 173–181.

Islam, M. S., Ahmed, M. K., Habibullah-Al-Mamun, M. and Masunaga, S. (2015) 'Potential ecological risk of hazardous elements in different land-use urban soils of Bangladesh', *Science of the Total Environment*, 512/513, 94–102.

Jambhulkar, H. P. and Juwarkar, A. A. (2009) 'Assessment of bioaccumulation of heavy metals by different plant species grown on fly ash dump', *Ecotoxicology and Environmental Safety*, 72, 1122–1128.

Jozic, M., Peer, T. and Turk, R. (2009) 'The impact of the tunnel exhausts in terms of heavy metals to the surrounding ecosystem', *Environmental Monitoring and Assessment*, 150, 261–271.

Karim, Z., Qureshi, B. A. and Mumtaz, M. (2015) 'Geochemical baseline determination and pollution assessment of heavy metals in urban soils of Karachi, Pakistan', *Ecological Indicators*, 48, 358–364.

Kellert, S. R. and Wilson, E. O. (1995) *The Biophilia Hypothesis.* Island Press: Washington D.C.

Kelly, M. J. (2008) *Britain's Building Stock. A Carbon Challenge.* Available at: www. lcmp.eng.cam.ac.uk/wp-content/uploads/081012_kelly.pdf.

Kershaw, W. and Gaffel, J. (2008) *The Australian Dairy Manufacturing Industry Sustainability Report 2007/2008.* Available at: dmsc.com.au/wpcontent/ uploads/2011/03/admsr0708.pdf.

Köhler, M. (2008) 'Green facades – a view back and some visions', *Urban Ecosystems*, 11(4), 423–436.

Laidlaw, M. A. S. and Taylor, M. P. (2011) 'Potential for childhood lead poisoning in the inner cities of Australia due to exposure to lead in soil dust', *Environmental Pollution*, 159, 1–9.

Laschober, C., Limbeck, A., Rendl, J. and Puxbaum, H. (2004) 'Particulate emissions from on-road vehicles in the Kaisermühlen-tunnel (Vienna, Austria)', *Atmospheric Environment*, 38, 2187–2195.

Li, Z. Y., Ma, Z. W., Kuijp, T. J., Yuan, Z. W. and Huang, L. (2014) 'A review of soil heavy metal pollution from mines in China: pollution and health risk assessment', *Science of the Total Environment*, 468/469, 843–853.

Li, J., Jia, C., Lua, Y., Tang, S. and Shimb, H. (2015) 'Multivariate analysis of heavy metal leaching from urban soils following simulated acid rain', *Microchemical Journal*, 122, 89–95.

Lu, Y., Song, S., Wang, R., *et al.* (2015) 'Impacts of soil and water pollution on food safety and health risks in China', *Environment International*, 77, 5–15.

Luo, X.-S., Yu, S., Zhu, Y.-G. and Li, X.-D. (2012) 'Trace metal contamination in urban soils of China', *Science of the Total Environment*, 421/422, 17–30.

MacRae, R., Gallant, E., Patel, S., Michalak, M., Bunch, M. and Schaffner, S. (2010) 'Could Toronto provide 10% of its fresh vegetable requirements from within its own boundaries? Matching consumption requirements with growing spaces', *Journal of Agriculture, Food Systems, and Community Development*, 1(2), 105–127.

McBride, M. B. (2013) 'Arsenic and lead uptake by vegetable crops grown on historically contaminated orchard soils', *Applied Environmental Soil Science*, 2013, 1–8.

McBride, M. B., Simon, T., Tam, G. and Wharton, S. (2013) 'Lead and arsenic uptake by leafy vegetables grown on contaminated soils: effects of mineral and organic amendments', *Water, Air & Soil Pollution*, 224, 1378.

McBride, M. B., Shayler, H. A., Spliethoff, H. M., *et al.* (2014) 'Concentrations of lead, cadmium and barium in urban garden-grown vegetables: the impact of soil variables', *Environmental Pollution*, 194, 254–261.

McClintock, N. and Cooper, J. (2009) Cultivating the Commons: An assessment of the potential for urban agriculture on Oakland's public lands. Department of Geography, University of California, Berkeley. Available at: www.oaklandfood. org/media/AA/AD/oaklandfood-org/downloads/27621/Cultivating_the_ Commons_COMPLETE.pdf.

Mentens, J. (2006) 'Green roofs as a tool for solving the rainwater runoff problem in the urbanized 21st century?', *Landscape and Planning*, 217–266.

Midmore, D. E. (2011) 'Roof-top gardens an option for green roof-tops and self-sufficient fresh food production', *Rural Industries Research and Development Corporation*, 067(11).

Mielke, H. W., Laidlaw, M. A. S. and Gonzales, C. R. (2012) 'Estimation of leaded (Pb) gasoline's continuing material and health impacts on 90 US urbanized areas', *Environment International*, 37, 248–257.

Mireles, F., Davila, J. I., Pinedo, J. L., Reyes, E., Speakman, R. J. and Glascock, M. D. (2012) 'Assessing urban soil pollution in the cities of Zacatecas and Guadalupe, Mexico by instrumental neutron activation analysis', *Microchemical Journal*, 103, 158–164.

Mitchell, R. G., Spliethoff, H. M., Ribaudo, L. N., *et al.* (2014) 'Lead (Pb) and other metals in New York city community garden soils: factors influencing contaminant distributions', *Environmental Pollution*, 187, 162–169.

Moser, C. and Kalton, G. (1979) *Survey Methods in Social Investigation*. Dartmouth Publishing: Aldershot.

New South Wales Environment and Heritage (2015) 'About climate change in NSW', available at: www.climatechange.environment.nsw.gov.au/About-climate-change-in-NSW/Understand-climate-change.

Onder, S. and Dursun, S. (2006) 'Air borne heavy metal pollution of *Cedrus libani* (A. Rich) in the city centre of Konya (Turkey)', *Atmospheric Environment*, 40, 1122–1133.

Orwell, R. L., Wood, R. A., Tarran, J., Torpy, F. R. and Burchett, M. (2004) 'Removal of benzene by the indoor plant/substrate microcosm and implications for air quality', *Water, Air & Soil Pollution*, 157, 193–207.

Orwell, R. L., Wood, R. A., Burchett, M., Tarran, J. and Torpy, F. R. (2006) 'The potted-plant microcosm substantially reduces indoor air VOC pollution. (ii) Laboratory study', *Water, Air & Soil Pollution*, 177, 59–80.

Osmond, P. (2012) *Green Roofs and Walls Perception Study – Final Report and Recommendations*. University of New South Wales, Sydney.

Patton, M. Q. (1980) *Qualitative Research and Evaluation Methods*. Sage Publications: Thousand Oaks, CA.

Peña-Fernández, A., Lobo-Bedmar, M. C. and González-Muñoz, M. J. (2015) 'Annual and seasonal variability of metals and metalloids in urban and industrial soils in Alcaláde Henares (Spain)', *Environmental Research*, 136, 40–46.

Peng, K., Luo, C., Lou, L., Li, X. and Shen, Z. (2008) 'Bioaccumulation of heavy metals by the aquatic plants *Potamogeton pectinatus* L. and *Potamogeton malaianus* Miq. and their potential use for contamination indicators and in wastewater treatment', *Science of the Total Environment*, 392, 22–29.

Plan, N. G. (2008) *Summary of Climate Change Impact Statement*. NSW Government, Department of Environment and Climate Change, Sydney.

Pretty, J. N., Ball, A. S., Lang, T. and Morison, J. I. (2005) 'Farm costs and food miles: an assessment of the full cost of the UK weekly food basket', *Food Policy*, 30(1), 1–19.

Qing, X., Zong, Y. and Lu, S. (2015) 'Assessment of heavy metal pollution and human health risk in urban soils of steel industrial city (Anshan), Liaoning, Northeast China', *Ecotoxicology and Environmental Safety*, 120, 377–385.

Refahi, H. and Talkhabi, H. (2015) 'Investigating the effective factors on the reduction of energy consumption in residential buildings with green roofs', *Renewable Energy*, 80, 595–603.

Rizwan, A. M., Dennis, L. Y. and Chunho, L. I. U. (2008) 'A review on the generation, determination and mitigation of urban heat island', *Journal of Environmental Sciences*, 20(1), 120–128.

Robson, C. (2003) *Real World Research*. Blackwell: London.

Rooftop Farms (2013) www.rooftopfarms.org.

Rowe, D. B. (2011) 'Green roofs as a means of pollution abatement', *Environmental Pollution*, 159, 2100–2110.

Säumel, I., Kotsyuk, I., Holscher, M., Lenkereit, C., Weber, F. and Kowarik, I. (2012) 'How healthy is urban horticulture in high traffic areas? Trace metal concentrations in vegetable crops from plantings within inner city neighbourhoods in Berlin, Germany', *Environmental Pollution*, 165, 124–132.

Schlecht, M. T. and Säumel, I. (2015) 'Wild growing mushrooms for the Edible City? Cadmium and lead content in edible mushrooms harvested within the urban agglomeration of Berlin, Germany', *Environmental Pollution*, 204, 298–305.

Scoop it (2012) '300 tonnes tomatoes per hectare', available at: www.scoop.it/t/organic-farming/p/995411992/2012/01/17/300-tons-tomatoes-per-hectare.

Shephard, P. (1982) *Nature and Madness*. University of Georgia Press: Athens, GA.

Sipter, E., Rozsa, E., Gruiz, K., Tatrai, E. and Morvai, V. (2008) 'Site-specific risk assessment in contaminated vegetable gardens', *Chemosphere*, 71, 1301–1307.

Tan, P. and Sia, A. (2005) 'A pilot green roof research project in Singapore', Proceedings of Third Annual Greening Rooftops for Sustainable Communities Conference, Washington D.C., 2–6 May.

Taylor, M. P., Winder, C. and Lanphear, B. P. (2012) 'Eliminating childhood lead toxicity in Australia: a call to lower the intervention level', *Medical Journal of Australia*, 197, 493.

Thomas, V. M., Socolow, R. H., Fanelli, J. J. and Spiro, T. G. (1999) 'Effects of reducing lead in gasoline: an analysis of the international experience', *Environmental Science & Technology*, 33, 3942–3948.

Tong, Z., Whitlow, T. H., Landers, A. and Flanner, B. (2015) 'A case study of air quality above an urban roof top vegetable farm', *Environmental Pollution*, in press.

Torpy, F. R., Irga, P. J. and Burchett, M. D. (2014) 'Profiling indoor plants for the amelioration of high CO_2 concentrations', *Urban Forestry and Urban Greening*, 13, 227–233.

Wang, H. and Jia, Y. (2009) 'Bioaccumulation of heavy metals by *Phragmites australis* cultivated in synthesized substrates', *Journal of Environmental Sciences*, 21, 1409–1414.

Warming, M., Hansen, M. G., Holm, P. E., Magid, J., Hansen, T. H. and Trapp, S. (2015) 'Does intake of trace elements through urban gardening in Copenhagen pose a risk to human health?', *Environmental Pollution*, 202, 17–23.

Wilkinson, S. J., Ghosh, S. and Page, L. (2013) 'Options for green roof retrofit and urban food production in the Sydney CBD', Proceedings of the RICS COBRA Conference, New Delhi, India.

Wilkinson, S., van der Kallen, P., Teale, A. and Antoniades, H. (2016) 'Retrofitting cities for tomorrow's world'. In Eames, M., Dixon, T., Hunt, M. and Lannon, S. (eds), *Transforming the Commercial Property Market in Australian Cities: Contemporary practices and the future potential of green roof retrofits*. John Wiley & Sons: Chichester.

Wiseman, C. L. S., Zereini, F. and Püttmann, W. (2013) 'Traffic-related trace element fate and uptake by plants cultivated in roadside soils in Toronto, Canada', *Science of the Total Environment*, 442, 86–95.

Witzling, L., Wander, M. and Phillips, E. (2011) 'Testing and educating on urban soil lead: a case of Chicago community gardens', *Journal of Agriculture, Food Systems, and Community Development*, in press.

Yang, J., Yu, Q. and Gong, P. (2008) 'Quantifying air pollution removal by green roofs in Chicago', *Atmospheric Environment*, 42, 7266–7273.

Zereini, F., Alsenz, H., Wiseman, C. L. S., *et al.* (2012) 'Platinum group elements (Pt, Pd, Rh) in airborne particulate matter in rural vs. urban areas of Germany: concentrations and spatial patterns of distribution', *Science of the Total Environment*, 416, 261–268.

Zhang, Y., Luo, X.-J., Mo, L., Wu, J.-P., Mai, B.-X. and Peng, Y.-H. (2015) 'Bioaccumulation and translocation of polyhalogenated compounds in rice (*Oryza sativa* L.) planted in paddy soil collected from an electronic waste recycling site, South China', *Chemosphere*, 137, 25–32.

Żukowska, J. and Biziuk, M. (2008) 'Methodological evaluation of method for dietary heavy metal intake', *Journal of Food Science*, 73, 21–29.

Social Aspects of Institutional Rooftop Gardens

Sumita Ghosh, Ilaria Vanni and Angela Giovanangeli
UTS, Australia

10.0   Introduction and Objectives

Across the world, rooftop gardens are a common feature of the contemporary city. In fact, rooftop gardens have a long history that dates back to antiquity, with the earliest documented roof gardens identified as the hanging gardens of Semiramis (present-day Syria), considered to be one of the seven wonders of the ancient world (Oberndorfer *et al.*, 2007: 824). In more recent times, however, literature on rooftop gardens links the origins of these spaces to environmental concerns that took place in Germany when, at the turn of the 20th century, gardens were installed on roofs to counteract the damage of solar destruction on roof structures (Oberndorfer *et al.*, 2007: 825), followed in the 1970s by environmental policies and technologies on stormwater management, energy conservation and urban habitat provision (Oberndorfer *et al.*, 2007: 827). Similarly, work on urban planning refers to the way modern cities over the last 50 years have been designed around the use of the car and the decline of the community (Zande, 2006: 206), arguing that some city planners have shifted values in the way that they consider urban structures to reflect sustainable design, including rooftop gardens (Zande, 2006: 210). Today, rooftop gardens cover one in every ten buildings in Europe and are mandated in Germany, Switzerland and France, as well as in Japan (Litichevskaya, 2011).

While the origins of modern rooftop gardens demonstrate a concern for the natural and built environment, the reasons for, and benefits of, rooftop gardens are known to include other factors. Rooftop gardens have been incorporated onto building structures to serve either public or private interests, as well as ornamental and/or functional purposes.

Media articles have documented the way rooftop gardens visually enhance spaces, such as the rooftops of hotels or dams (Beauty and Environmental

Green Roof Retrofit: Building Urban Resilience, First Edition.
Edited by Sara Wilkinson and Tim Dixon.
© 2016 John Wiley & Sons, Ltd. Published 2016 by John Wiley & Sons, Ltd.

Benefits, 2009; Fujita Kanko Incorporated, 2012), particularly where green space is limited and the roof garden is seen as a way of being connected with the outdoors and with landscaping (Hoffman, 1983; Wilkerson, 2010). Furthermore, rooftop gardens are seen as a way of maximising the opportunities associated with the value of properties and projects (Wilkerson, 2010). Media and scholarly articles on rooftop gardens identify the therapeutic effects of rooftop gardens in places such as hospitals, where the garden is considered an advantage to the wellbeing of patients (Wilkerson, 2010; Davis, 2011; Solnik, 2011).

The aim of this chapter is to explore the social life of rooftop gardens. It does this through a case study analysis of two rooftop gardens in higher-density areas of inner-city Sydney, Australia, as well as a comparative analysis of eight institutional rooftop case studies from around the world. Out of the two rooftop gardens in Sydney, the first case study, is on the rooftop garden set up on the roof of Gumal, a UTS student housing building in Ultimo that has a Roof Gardening Club for UTS staff and students. UTS is an important educational institution, located in Sydney CBD, where social aspects of a rooftop garden were analysed considering the aspirations of staff and students as a workplace community. The second case study is the 107 Projects rooftop garden on the roof of a retrofitted warehouse (area: 1700 m²) in Redfern (107 Projects, 2015). 107 Projects is a multidisciplinary creative space opened in 2012, including, in addition to the rooftop terrace and adjacent space, a gallery, performance space, bar and cafe, studio and workshop areas. Milkwood Permaculture, one of the resident organisations at 107 Projects, is a social enterprise focusing on permaculture education (Milkwood, 2015). Permaculture is understood as 'a creative design process based on ethics and design principles' (Permacultureprinciples, 2015), rooted in the reproduction and use of patterns and relationships occurring in nature.

Finally, varying objectives and social needs of rooftop gardens are explored in eight institutional rooftop case studies in different educational institutions in different countries of the world. The main objectives of this chapter are:

- To comprehend the social aspects of community development and aspirations, motivations, expectations and satisfactions of participants through rooftop food production in educational institutions.
- To explore how the evolving ecology of human and non-human elements created through permaculture principles on the 107 Projects rooftop garden designed by Milkwood Permaculture generate forms of sociality.

10.1   Social Aspects, Productivity and Sustainability Potential of Rooftop Gardens

Increasing literature on rooftop gardens refers to the importance of these spaces in the context of urban consumption. The term 'urban consumption' could be viewed very differently from various disciplinary and research perspectives (Miles and Paddison, 1998; Newton, 2011). It could extend beyond traditional understanding of purchasing goods to include consumers' participation and reproduction of physical spaces in urban contexts as well as the creation of culture-specific and meaningful ways of life (Miles and Paddison, 1998). Newton (2011: 13) identified that determinants of urban resource consumption on the supply side are indirect and are influenced by urban form, technology, design innovation and materials used and reused, while the demand-side determinants are direct and include social milieu, household (practice and structure) and individual (structural and behavioural) attributes. Urban gardens on rooftops are part of a range of different typologies of regenerative green infrastructure provisions and food production systems in urban areas, such as plots on public land assigned to individuals or families, community gardens in abandoned and/or vacant areas, and individual or common gardens in either yards, balconies or the rooftops of buildings (Gorgolewski *et al.*, 2011; Orsini *et al.*, 2014). The contributions of urban horticulture to city food supplies have been estimated in a number of cities across the world. For instance, in Toronto (Canada), Peck (2003) found that from a total of 650,000 m^2 of 'greened' rooftops growing vegetable crops, an annual total yield of 4.7 million kg of produce could be harvested. Subsequently, Kaethler (2006) states that in Vancouver (Canada) it is easy to find rooftop gardens producing food above supermarkets, restaurants and social housing.

A range of studies have addressed the role played by urban vegetable gardens in improving human wellbeing through the provision of both ecosystem services and food supplies to city dwellers (Matsuo, 1995; Brown and Jameton, 2000; McClintock, 2010; Orsini *et al.*, 2014). For instance, rooftop gardens may reduce a city's ecological footprint (EF) through the reduction of pollution and noise, the absorption of carbon dioxide (CO_2) emissions and control of the UHI effect by shading (Malcevschi *et al.*, 1996; Wackernagel and Rees, 1996; Shin and Lee, 2005). Rooftop gardens can contribute to the biodiversity in the urban environment and achieve more sustainable conditions for new habitat creation (Bennett, 2003; Khandaker, 2004; Miller, 2005; Maas *et al.*, 2006; Sanyé-Mengual *et al.*, 2013). Furthermore, in countries such as South Africa or the USA, limited urban space and poverty have been the reasons behind rooftop projects where the growing of vegetables provides inexpensive food to locals (Johannesburg Rooftop Garden, 2012; Lt. Governor Simon Awards, 2012). Meanwhile, a number of research papers argue that the rate of urbanisation is increasing over time and that food production sites should increasingly be located near main consumption centres (Matsuo, 1995; Brown and Jameton, 2000; McClintock, 2010; Orsini *et al.*, 2014).

Rooftop gardens for urban consumption are sites for collaboration between artists and community in the growing of food (Franklin, 2011). In some instances, the creative structural elements of the garden are designed and built by local artists using recycled and reclaimed materials, while the sharing of knowledge on how to grow food is seen to have an educational and community impact as a result of spaces that bring people together and teach them about production systems (Franklin, 2011; Gorgolewski *et al.*, 2011).

Rooftop gardens producing food, on institutional and office buildings in higher-density developments, have notably been the particular focus of research on urban agriculture within built environments. Integrating rooftop gardens in urban developments could provide significant social, environmental and economic values for the users and urban residents. Unused roof spaces in such structures are utilised effectively to recreate meaningful and easily accessible places for users, while regenerating ecologies of lost green open spaces successfully within denser urban environments. Rooftop gardens in institutional and office buildings are seen to create places where people engage in different ways in various activities, enhancing place-making (Gehl, 1987). People from different socio-economic backgrounds work together in a social networking space growing food to improve community engagement (Foss et al., 2011). Even viewing a roof with green grass for 40 seconds could enrich mental concentration, as found in a University of Melbourne, Australia study (Lee et al., 2015). Urban design theories highlight that the 'imageability' of a city is primarily cognitive and based on people's perception, reasoning and rational thinking (Lynch, 1960). Responsive design of physical environments could affect people's choices for seven different qualities of built environments: permeability (access or no access to places); variety (different types of use available); legibility (clarity around understanding of opportunities that a built environment offers); robustness (the degree to which places can be used by people for different purposes); richness (people's choice of sensory experience); visual appropriateness (people's perceptions on the detailed appearance of place and the choices available); and personalisation (to what extent people can put their own identity on a place) (Bentley et al., 1985). Unused spaces are utilised for various purposes in rooftop gardens. They enable urban regeneration and renewal processes, promote people's engagement with different types of social activities and community building, interactions with nature, development of sustainability awareness, creation of local identities and new ways of re-imagining human environments. Montgomery's (1998) review of a number of urban design approaches to successful place-making identified three basic qualities: '… successful urban places must combine quality in three essential elements: physical space, the sensory experience and activity' (Montgomery, 1998: 96). Rooftop gardens provide access to physical spaces, enable tangible, perceptive and psychological experience of working with soil, plants, sun and fresh air in natural environmental settings, and motivate carrying out physical activities through gardening practices. Thus, rooftop gardens become an important constituent of successful place-making and urban regeneration in cities and towns.

In the USA, some practical examples of rooftop urban agriculture that are driving social networking and creating new spaces for community building and interactions are: Eagle Street Rooftop Farm (2015) and Brooklyn Grange Rooftop Farm (2015) in New York; Uncommon Ground (2015), Chicago; and Boston's Higher Ground Farm (Boyer, 2013). For instance, Eagle Street Rooftop Farm is located on the third-floor warehouse roof of Broadway Stages in Brooklyn and covers 6000 ft^2 or 557 m^2 (Eagle Street Rooftop Farm, 2015). It produces organic vegetables and supplies vegetables to an on-site market and local restaurants, conducts farm educational programmes, supports a small CSA programme and has Italian honey beehives as part of the farm (Gordon, 2010; Eagle Street Rooftop Farm, 2015). Brooklyn Grange Rooftop Farm includes two rooftop organic vegetable farms with a land area of 2.5 acres or 1 hectare and produces over 22,680 kg of food annually (Brooklyn Grange Rooftop Farm, 2015). New York City's largest apiary, with more than 30 naturally managed honey beehives, is located on this farm (Brooklyn Grange Rooftop Farm, 2015). Uncommon Ground, Chicago is comparatively small, with an area of 60 m². It produces 317 kg of vegetables, such as peppers (capsicums), lettuce, tomatoes, beans, mustard greens and herbs, in the raised rooftop beds and supplies a considerable share of vegetables to the Uncommon Ground Restaurant in addition to educational programmes (Perasso, 2012).

In the UK, the Business Improvement District for Bloomsbury, Holborn and St Giles in London has rooftop gardens on office buildings producing vegetables with the aim of reducing food miles, enhancing carbon and thermal performance benefits, encouraging user engagement and increasing business productivity (Mavrogordato, 2013). Lend Lease, a transnational construction company, has a rooftop garden for staff at its Regents Park office in London, with a biodiversity roof attached which has a 'bug hotel' to encourage local biodiversity (Wilkinson, 2015a). Furthermore, wild flowers are also grown on two green roofs of the law firm Mischon de Reya and the Trade Union Congress to help increase the local bee population (Mavrogordato, 2013). These rooftop gardens are crucially important for the surrounding communities, staff members, clients and visitors to these buildings and environments.

In the Australian context, a rooftop garden at 131 Queen Street, Melbourne, Victoria acts as a social gathering space for building occupants; rented for functions, it is an important initiative under the Inner Melbourne Action Plan (IMAP) (City of Melbourne, 2015; University of Melbourne, 2015). Meanwhile, St Canice Kitchen Garden, Kings Cross, Sydney, a rooftop food garden on the roof of the Refugee Centre, founded by Woods Bagot and designed by PEPO Botanic Design, is creating 'flexible space for communal gatherings and social events' (Woods Bagot, 2015). More information on this garden is included later in the chapter. Australian media articles have been placing significant emphasis on the emerging social importance of rooftop gardens (Sydney Morning Herald, 2008; Carlyon, 2014; Zhou and Stolz, 2014).

10.2   Methodology

Recent academic writing on social issues connected with aspects of rooftop and urban gardening tends to see rooftops as possible sites of urban agriculture and for the purpose of greening the city or in relation to urban food systems. A 'rooftop garden' is different from a 'green roof' in terms of different technical requirements and performance potential. Similarly, a 'rooftop garden in an institutional setting' is different from a 'community garden on a rooftop' in terms of ownership patterns, mode of operation and user types. A 'rooftop garden' is a very specific typology of an urban food production space that has been focused on in this chapter.

Three methodological approaches adopted for case study-based research are: comparative analysis of eight university rooftop garden case studies; semi-structured interviews with UTS Roof Gardening Club and 107 Projects; a sensory ethnography approach. A comparative analysis of eight university rooftop gardens that are growing food was conducted to understand their objectives, aspirations, motivations, achievements and social contributions.

This chapter applies interviews and sensory ethnography research methods to understand the social aspects of rooftop gardens in inner-city Sydney through two selected case studies: UTS rooftop garden, managed by staff and student members of the UTS Roof Gardening Club and 107 Projects rooftop garden, designed and managed by Milkwood Permaculture. Both rooftop case studies share similar characteristics: they are located in the inner city of Sydney in high-density suburbs, Ultimo and Redfern, which are in the process of urban regeneration and renewal. Both rooftops have limited access: while one is on the roof of Gumal, a UTS student residence, supported and funded by the City of Sydney's Environmental Grant Programme, the other is part of a multidisciplinary creative space, 107 Projects, developed as part of the City of Sydney's Accommodation Grant Programme, a community programme that leases city buildings to community groups at no or reduced rent. Both spaces have been designed within the building guidelines imposed by, respectively, a university and a city council, and with the workplace and resident community in mind: on the one hand, resident and non-resident students and staff members; on the other hand, a mixture of artists, permaculture students, permaculture urban gardeners and visitors during special events. This chapter adds to the body of literature by providing an analysis of two rooftop gardens that captures the experience, imagination and expectations of gardeners and visitors. These two different methodological approaches for the analysis of two Sydney case studies allow for a textured analysis of the way people both imagine and experience rooftop gardens, which, we contend, can help researchers to unpack different understandings of the concept of 'social' when talking about rooftop gardens. Articulating the way gardens are imagined and experienced, in turn, boosts our understanding of the way rooftop gardens can have an impact on social and cultural practices.

While comparative analysis focuses on unfold contrasts, similarities or patterns across the case studies, the semi-structured interviews explore the untold stories of the aspirations, motivations and hopes of the gardeners. A sensory ethnographic approach, participant observation and visual methods allow an understanding of people's socio-cultural practices in rooftop gardens. These research methods are distinctly different from each other in terms of their mode of enquiry, analytical methods and interpretations of results, but these methods together generate a very good understanding. Details of the three methods are outlined further in the following three sections. In addition to these, a discussion of St Canice Kitchen Garden, located on the roof of the Refugee Centre at Kings Cross, Sydney, is included in Section 10.3.4.

10.2.1   Comparative Analysis of Eight University Rooftop Garden Case Studies

Very limited research has been conducted specifically to understand the social issues and contributions of institutional rooftop gardens using qualitative methods such as surveys and interviews. Owing to the non-availability of relevant data in this field, a comparative analysis of similar and important rooftop garden case studies in educational institutions has been chosen. This provides a snapshot of the significance and potential of emerging rooftop gardens in universities and their connections to social aspects of university communities. This desktop analysis of eight rooftop gardens located in different educational institutions has been conducted using Internet resources and publications to comprehend conditions, objectives, roles and contributions of rooftop gardens. These case studies are evaluated for four criteria (produce; goals and motivations; achievements and outcomes) to provide evidence on their achievements in multiple domains and to allow the synthesis of information to provide strategic future directions.

10.2.2   Semi-Structured Interviews with UTS Roof Gardening Club

The City of Sydney's Environmental Grant Programme 2013–2014 provided funding support to set up a UTS Roof Gardening Club in 2014 on the ninth-floor roof of the UTS student housing building named Gumal in the inner-city Sydney precinct of Broadway. This roof was selected, after several other potential rooftop sites were visited, on the basis of accessibility and health and safety considerations. This roof had been designed for user access, with a lift to roof level. Accessibility to this rooftop garden was limited to UTS staff and student members of the garden using security access cards. Interviews were conducted with the UTS Roof Gardening Club participants. The key qualitative research objectives were:

1. To understand the motivations, perceptions and influences that guide social participation.
2. To know the expectations of participants to create a successful urban place.
3. To understand the hopes and types of activity that would satisfy the participants the most.
4. To delineate useful ways for long-term management and funding of the garden.

The research to date, however, has been very limited in exploring and identifying the motivations and aspirations of participants in the setting-up stage of a rooftop garden in an institutional setting. While the UTS Roof Gardening Club was comprised of a small number of members at an early stage, the insight into how the members' aspirations, motivations and satisfactions are intertwined with the social aspects through rooftop food production in its initial stage is highly important. These members are likely to have significant interests, pioneering motivations, awareness and sound abilities to initiate a social change and to reflect upon the social aspects of urban food production – especially in a workplace context. Sample sizes are governed by the nature of the qualitative research project (Silverman, 2013). A total of eight semi-structured interviews representing a 67% response rate were conducted based on a carefully designed questionnaire with a total of 17 questions. Although eight interviews is a small number, it is adequate and valuable as each participant was a highly suitable and competent respondent for the interviews and the sample met reliability and validity criteria for qualitative research (Silverman, 2013). The duration of the interviews with the UTS Roof Gardening Club members ranged from 30 to 40 minutes. An ethics approval from the UTS Human Resource Ethics Committee (HREC) was sought for conducting the interviews. These interviews were conducted after obtaining consent from the respondents. A number of factors – previous experience, motivations, expectations and satisfactions, influences, time commitment, management and financial contributions – associated with growing food were analysed.

10.2.3   107 Projects Rooftop Garden: A Sensory Ethnography

Sensory ethnography is best defined as a set of practices based on qualitative methodologies such as participatory observation, ethnographic interviews and visual methodologies like video and photography (Pink, 2007, 2009). The starting point of sensory ethnography is that the way we understand the world and our meaning-making practices are always emplaced and result from a form of embodiment that exceeds the body–mind duopoly to bring in the senses. Howes (2005: 7), one of the first anthropologists to attend to the senses, explains this as the emerging paradigm of emplacement, a 'sensuous interrelationship of body–mind–environment', where environment is understood as 'a bundle of sensory and social values'. To understand this entanglement of social and sensory values, this section follows specifically Pink's (2009: 64) work on sensory ethnography as a 'process of learning through the ethnographer's own multisensory, emplaced experience'. The emphasis on emplacement is key to the study of others' experiences in specific environments, such as rooftop gardens. In turn, the study of emplaced experiences opens up the possibility to understand the impact of the lived and sensory experience on social and cultural practices. The researcher takes part in the same experience as others, and supports the understanding of this experience through continuous narrative unstructured interviews. This kind of methodology enables the researcher to comprehend if and how the material and sensory characteristics of an environment, activity or event have an effect on others' perceptions, behaviours and opinions.

On a practical level, attending to sensorial experiences involves the researcher paying attention to her/his own embodied experiences and to other people's practices, including in her/his methods the consideration of, for instance, smells, taste, touch and movement in addition to the more traditional focus on the visual in participant observation (Pink, 2009, 2012). For this research on rooftop gardening this meant participating in the gardening activities, for instance planting, sitting in the garden, watering plants, harvesting, talking about the smells, feel, taste of produce, learning particular skills, socialising with fellow gardeners, strolling around, sharing food and stories, and documenting the site and interactions with photography.

It also involved short, informal interviews carried out as part of the general 'being in the garden', as standard ethnographic practice, where, as pointed out by Pink, there is no clear distinction between observation and interviews (Pink, 2009: 83). These two methods are intertwined and these conversations are akin to unstructured interviews. In the context of sensory ethnography, interviews are understood as emplaced and embodied instances in which meaning is made and knowledge shared beyond the sharing of verbal information (Pink, 2009: 83).

It is common for gardeners to talk of their gardens in terms of sensorial experiences of colours, touch, smell, sounds and of their body in relation to the garden (Tilley, 2006). 'For most of the time appreciating the garden is thus a synesthetic experience involving all the five human senses – sight, smell, touch, sound and taste, which usually intermingle and feed into each other' (Tilley, 2006: 312).

In addition to this, as any gardener will confirm when asked about any aspect of tending to their garden, gardening is a practice that cannot be understood only by talking. A variety of sensory ways of sharing knowledge and apprehending garden practices – such as how one needs to touch, taste, smell and look at the changes to determine the health and needs of a garden – were observed during the fieldwork. In short, good gardening is a full-body experience, and gardening knowledge can only be transferred through the sharing of those experiences, rather than simply through verbal communication.

It follows that to understand others' social experiences in a garden, a sensory dimension and understanding need to be taken into consideration. To do so, one of the following subsections will provide an analysis of the rooftop designed by Milkwood Permaculture, one of the resident organisations at 107 Projects. The chapter will continue with a narrative illustrating the rooftop garden as an environment constituted through a bundle of social and sensory values (Howes, 2005).

10.3   Main Findings

10.3.1   Comparative Analysis of Eight Rooftop Gardens in Universities

Some notable examples of rooftop gardens in educational institutions exist, such as those at Concordia University (Concordia Food Coalition (CFC), 2015) and Trent University (Blyth and Menagh, 2006), both in Canada, or the University of Maryland's rooftop garden on South Campus Dining Hall, Ellicott Community Diner in the USA (University of Maryland, 2010). The rooftop gardens are responsible for biodiversity protection; improvement in health, mental wellbeing and livelihoods; sharing of knowledge and a 'culture of sustainability' in students and staff, as demonstrated in a number of universities. Table 10.1 compares the eight rooftop gardens growing food in different universities.

In Table 10.1, the areas of the rooftop gardens vary from small to larger and a variety of vegetables are produced on the roof and vertical walls, developed with appropriate technologies and in raised planter boxes. The harvesting capacities of these roof gardens vary too. Kaestart University, Thailand has applied a 900 cm² green roof mat, a vertical green block with attached containers for planting and a bio-façade for climbing plants (Alimurung, 2012; Sunakorn, 2012). New Jersey Institute of Technology, USA has raised planters for growing food and aims to supply fruits and vegetables to up to 9000 university students (Heyboer, 2010). The most important goals identified are: improving access and daily supply of fresh fruits and vegetables; building resilience and food security in case of an emergency; improving and recreating urban ecologies and connections to nature; promoting learning for organic gardening; developing an integrative sustainability approach using a closed-loop food system; creating well-knit institutional communities (Blyth and Menagh, 2006; Heyboer, 2010; Alimurung, 2012; Ducharm, 2015; Rye's HomeGrown, 2015; The Sustainable Campus, 2015). Many of these goals have been achieved already. North Carolina State University, USA and Trent University, Canada have created successful closed-loop food systems by supplying the food produced on the rooftops to campus cafes (Blyth and Menagh, 2006; Kinen-Ferguson, 2015). These rooftop gardening initiatives are supported significantly by the universities and from other funding sources. Outcomes relate significantly to social aspects of staff, students and immediate communities developing a deeper understanding of built environments and food, social responsibility and participation, enhancement of food localism, connectivity, responsiveness and self-sufficiency of supply of food (Table 10.1).

10.3.2   Qualitative Analysis of UTS Roof Gardening Club Semi-Structured Interviews

Demographic data collected showed that 75% of respondents came from an Australian background and were female; 62.5% of respondents came from the 41–60 years age group, while 37.5% were aged 26–40 years.

Half of the respondents had *previous experience in growing food* in home environments, representing intra-generational connections through parents to grandparents and inter-generational links through friends, colleagues and families. Experience of growing culinary herbs, indigenous plants, flowers and different types of vegetables and fruits were common, and gardener types ranged from fairly extensive gardener to non-gardener.

Two key *motivations – professional* and *personal* – for joining the UTS Roof Gardening Club were linked to the 'institutional' quality of a rooftop garden. The *professional* motivation visualised the roof garden as '*a catalyst*' and '*a neutral space*' for community building and people engagement,

Table 10.1 Comparative analysis of eight rooftop gardens in universities

Rooftop garden	Produce	Goals	Motivations and achievements	Outcomes
Oval, Centennial Campus, North Carolina State University, Rayleigh, NC, USA (Kinen-Ferguson, 2015)	Zucchini, squash, peppers, cucumbers, tomatoes and herbs	• To supply fresh vegetables, fruits and herbs to the university's dining hall. • To promote organic gardening and sustainability. • To educate and raise awareness in students and staff through growing food.	• To shorten garden-to-plate distance significantly. • Three months or more waiting time for the food to mature for cooking creates a special culinary experience for diners. • The dining process begins with seed planting. • To increase student participation in the garden. • To understand the garden's therapeutic benefits. • Creates a closed-loop food system within the university. • A self-sufficient kitchen. • Organic composting and water savings up to 70%.	Showcasing special culinary experience of dining for promoting responsiveness, social connectivity and food self-sufficiency with a well-articulated micro local food system
Student Center, New Jersey Institute of Technology, Newark, NJ, USA (Heyboer, 2010)	Kale, leafy greens, greens, beets, lettuces, carrots and turnips 20 m² of raised planters	• To supply fruits and vegetables to up to 9000 university students. • Data collection on the garden to conduct research.	• Joy and happiness to observe the seedlings grow and mature. • Creating living class rooms. • Promoting organic gardening and pesticide-free food. • Importance of 'localness' in making a regenerative productive place in a dense environment. • Localism in urban food production.	Enhancing social aspects, food localism, urban regeneration and immense satisfactions in growing food

(Continued)

Table 10.1 *(Cont'd)*

Rooftop garden	Produce	Goals	Motivations and achievements	Outcomes
Science Building, Brandeis University, Boston, MA, USA (Ducharm, 2015)	Estimated 1588 kg of produce 139 m² rooftop	• To improve food access and health for students and Waltham community. • To educate students and community about importance of growing local food.	• Created by students' initiatives. • Received funding from Schools' Sustainability Fund. • Supplying food to students and wider community. • 100 student and faculty members involved in planting. • Established a campus-based Farmers' Club. • Improved perceptions of growing food through visual demonstrations in the rooftop garden.	Students play an important role in community development and improving participation in workplace and wider communities
Environmental Sciences Building, Trent University, Peterborough, Ontario, Canada (Blyth and Menagh, 2006)	Grows vegetables, fruits and herbs organically	• To act as a learning space. • To improve understanding of local food through bottom-up approach.	• Fresh produce from rooftop supplied to a student-run campus restaurant and an independent co-operative. • Increased awareness of local food culture and interconnectivity. • Appreciating varied availability of seasonal produce. • Food ethics. • Fresh and locally produced food flavours. • Reduced food cost on campus.	Student-led sustainable business creation and education; improved food access; social responsibility and ethical approach to growing

Location	Produce	Objectives	Activities	Outcomes
George Vari Engineering & Computer Centre, Ryerson University, Toronto, Canada (Sloan, 2015; Rye's HomeGrown, 2015)	Eggplants, peppers, squashes, basil, tomatoes and lettuces 1011 m²	• To grow fresh food on campus. • To create a connected community. • To share produce at the university farmers' market.	• Creating 'responsible ecology' and an edible roof. • Reducing environmental impacts. • Growing nutritious food that ripens on the plant. • Collective food-growing interests of students, staff and faculty. • Developing a well-connected university community. • Establishing a closed-loop food system.	Improving urban ecologies in denser environments; co-operative approach to community building and social networking
The Sky Garden, Galbraith Building, University of Toronto, Toronto, Ontario, Canada (Ontario Healthy Communities Coalition, 2015)	Grown in containers: squash, pumpkin, zucchini, heirloom tomatoes, raspberries, herbs and other produce Total 350 kg produce in two years	• To enhance understanding of sustainable food system in wider student population.	• Started in 2010 with students' efforts. • Received university's approval and funding from multiple organisations. • Staff and students involved in management, administration and production. • 90% of the produce supplied to University of Toronto Student Union (UTSU) food bank. • Supply of fresh produce. • Showcasing through tours and training workshops. • Partnership projects run with other student groups.	Importance of students' deeper understanding of food; overall management and monitoring of the garden; unique purpose to supply to food bank for social betterment

(Continued)

Table 10.1 (Cont'd)

Rooftop garden	Produce	Goals	Motivations and achievements	Outcomes
An Integrated Teaching Building (AITB), The Chinese University of Hong Kong (CHUK), Hong Kong, China (The Sustainable Campus, 2015)	Growing fruits and vegetables	• An integrative approach to achieving social, environmental and ecological benefits through rooftop urban farming.	• Participation of up to 50 CHUK staff, students and their families. 'Rooftop Cultivation Project' started in 2014 to: – build community through rooftop urban farming; – promote edible plant growing locally; – improve gardening skills through professional training. • Importance of farming and education. • Food safety. • Reducing food miles and developing 'micro ecology'. • Nurturing human and nature interactions.	Education on urban agriculture; creating and maintaining links between people and nature
7th-Floor roof, Faculty of Architecture Building, Kaestart University, Bangkok, Thailand (Alimurung, 2012; Sunakorn, 2012)	Chinese spinach, watercress, basil, eggplant, beans and herbs 196 m² urban farm	• To promote food security. • To sustain daily food supply. • To supply food in case of an emergency.	• Supported by funds from Thai Health Promotion Foundation, the Faculty of Architecture and Kasetsart University. • To grow local food, innovative applications of a green roof mat (30 × 30 cm² module), a vertical green block with attached containers for planting and a bio façade for climbing plants such as beans, zucchini, etc.	Building community resilience in food; improving food access using innovative and effective solutions

creating new professional linkages in an informal way and cultivating sustainability responsiveness within the university community. Motivations to share gardening knowledge and practices, gain essential access to nature in a workplace, grow own food and observe how the rooftop garden unravels pathways to a successful social change were significantly important too.

> *'There is a relation between growing together and connecting ...'*
> (Interview M)
> *'... you can share knowledge, in a lovely equal environment ...'*
> (Interview H)
> *'... So it is a very good way to establish a community'* (Interview M)

With easy access and providing some time away from the desk, a workplace rooftop garden could provide immense health benefits and a brilliant way of establishing a well-knit university community, which was unlikely otherwise.

> *'... it is wonderful to get up from a desk and spend an hour pottering in the garden and then go back to your keyboard. I find that a very rewarding way of working'* (Interview H)
> *'... new contacts through the garden club both students and staff ... make those professional linkages ... spending on structured quality time with people ... I find that the garden is a place where you can ... it's a neutral space'* (Interview H)

The *personal* motivation included making friends, sharing and learning gardening techniques, involvement in active exercise through gardening, experiencing nature, sunlight and fresh air, and feeling immense happiness and pride associated with growing fresh and nutritious food.

> *'... wanted to have living things around me'* (Interview L)
> *'... like the experience of being able to eat the things I have grown, having that pride in that this is something I have made* (Interview L)
> *'... how to plant, how to see what seeds work with other seeds so it is just gaining knowledge from people who have a little bit of experience in that'* (Interview K)

Incorporating permaculture principles in gardening, worm farming, mitigating environmental impacts through growing own food, and on-site composting and supporting a sustainable lifestyle were important motivations for participation. Dreams and aspirations to regenerate memories, cultural identities and practices of distant homelands locally resonated prominently through the voices of respondents.

> *'... I come from a culture that produces fruits and vegetables'*
> (Interview M)

These responses parallel some of the research on Vietnamese, Greek and Italian migrants' domestic gardens in Australia, identifying that the

Figure 10.1   Vegetable production at the UTS rooftop garden, Sydney.
Source: Photo by Sumita Ghosh.

production of traditional fruits, vegetables, herbs and flowers is linked to their specific cultural identities, memories and traditional practices, and is dynamic and continuously evolving (Graham and Connell, 2006). Furthermore, the rooftop garden provided access to a highly valued productive space at work to implement aspirations in reality for the participants, as shown in Figure 10.1.

Getting to know someone in the UTS Roof Gardening Club or from other gardening initiatives *influenced* the decisions to join the garden. The predominant *expectations and satisfactions* of the participants were to grow a variety of vegetables, fruits, indigenous edible plants (e.g., warrigal greens), exotic vegetables and medicinal herbs in the garden. Preferred choices were: green leafy vegetables (like lettuce), tomatoes, eggplants, sweet potatoes, zucchini, cucumber, green beans, corn, squash, pumpkin and all-year-round vegetables (e.g., cabbage and brassicas), strawberries, lemons and some tropical fruits such as papaya. Herbs such as thyme, rosemary, basil, oregano, sage, parsley, coriander, marjoram or deal and fennel, and some medicinal plants such as chamomile and turmeric, were favoured. In addition, participants' expectations were also to engage in university community development, sharing knowledge and seeing the garden as *'a space for learning'*.

> *'… it is a space for learning not only for the garden club but for all users of the garden'* (Interview J)

Time commitments vary at different times of the year, during vacation time, at the end of and early in the year, as it is an educational institution. Most of the respondents were ready to commit a couple of hours per week, although this varied from a couple of hours per week to a couple of hours per fortnight. There was restricted access, by security card only, due to the location of the rooftop garden on the student housing building, which limited easy access and engagement in gardening activities. Location and access play important roles in fostering participation and a connected university community.

Some respondents (5 out of 8) supported the need for small financial contributions, while the rest thought that obtaining university funding would be more useful, an aspect which has been noted in some rooftop case studies such as the University of Toronto and Kaestart University (Table 10.1). With regard to managerial expectations of the garden, respondents stated that regular planning meetings, record keeping, allocation of specific responsibilities to members considering individual expertise, and the importance of a leadership role would be essential for the long-term continuity of the garden. Clarity around decisions and the consensus of all members would be vital.

'... all the decisions should be made by consultations and consensus as much as possible' (Interview M)

10.3.3   107 Projects Rooftop Garden, Sydney

The 107 Projects rooftop garden in Redfern is a productive and educational space designed and managed by Milkwood Permaculture. Permaculture is defined as an agricultural process based on ethics and design principles. It guides us to mimic the patterns and relationships we find in nature, and can be applied to all aspects of human habitation, from agriculture to ecological building, from appropriate technology to education and even economics (Holmgren, 2015; Permacultureprinciples, 2015). As it is based on a set of three ethics and twelve design principles, permaculture is a malleable system and its elements can be re-contextualised and adapted to different environments (Crosby *et al.*, 2014). In 2014 Milkwood started a crowdfunding campaign to turn the empty rooftop terrace into an urban permaculture garden for learning workshops, events and talks, and a place in which to create a green space and food system in the city open to community seeds and cuttings swaps. Volunteers backed the project, donating their skills, labour and products. The rooftop garden opened in early 2015 and has since been used as the location for permaculture courses, talks and public events.

The Social Life of the Rooftop

The analysis of these events emphasises the assemblage of different users, residents and organisations and highlights how the garden was produced and is managed according to permaculture ethics and design principles.

Figure 10.2   Milkwood, 107 Projects rooftop garden, Sydney.
Source: Photo by Ilaria Vanni.

As an example, one of these events is briefly sketched here. At the beginning of autumn in 2015, the rooftop garden was part of 107 Projects Open Day (see Figure 10.2). While the majority of visitors were young, white cultural producers linked to the site through art world connections, some older local residents attended the event. The round tanks of the movable food forest had been moved along the edges of the rooftop, so that visitors entered the garden and walked following the wavy borders of planters, and could choose to sit at the tables or along the seats included in the design of the garden beds. Some decided to take up the free botanical illustration class offered, some came for a look, or a chat and a drink in the open air.

During the research fieldwork, visitors to the garden stopped to talk, to exchange opinions on herbs and on the garden, to ask questions about specific design elements or plants, and to suggest ways to fix various plant disease problems. Some visitors walked slowly, savouring the multi-sensory dimension of the garden and patting plants, smelling them, nibbling on leaves and engaging in conversation with fellow visitors. Others sat on the edges of planters, contemplating the garden and talking about different experiences with permaculture, different roles in relation to the garden, and planned future involvement with the rooftop and other community gardens, while still others illustrated what they saw. There were short informal meetings. A local resident stopped to talk about the basil plants and to sniff the scent. While all these interactions were temporary, the frequency and repetition of a variety of events organised on the rooftop garden has enabled

Milkwood to create a group of returning visitors and, as a follow-up to these encounters, a strong digital community that supports the exchange of information and data and functions like a repository of collective permaculture intelligence. The 'social and sensory bundle' (Howes, 2005) engendered by the rooftop garden is part of the discussion below.

Analysis: Permaculture on the Rooftop

107 Projects rooftop garden is seen as an evolving ecology of objects, design, plants, animals, bacteria, people, elements, ideas, policies and principles. It is proposed that this ecology generates particular forms of sociality reflecting permaculture principles in two ways: one is through the design of space that guides certain types of interactions, and the other is through learning permaculture practices. While Milkwood offers courses and workshops in different locations, the rooftop has quickly become a site where people with similar interests and values converge and a community based on a definite set of practices is created.

During the fieldwork for this research it became apparent that the curvy shape of the planters, the vertical gardens along the walls, the movable food forest and the inclusion of seats made with recycled wood (producing no waste being a principle) on the edge of garden beds determined the pace and flow of visitors to the garden, inviting them to walk slowly and to linger in places to touch, smell, taste and talk. It is possible to discern several design principles behind these choices:

- 'observe and interact' in order to learn from the environment;
- 'obtain a yield' and produce abundance;
- 'integrate rather than segregate' in the way plants are located.

Also, in the inclusion of structural elements such as rain tanks to catch and store water in the flow of space, as well as ways of integrating gardeners and visitors in the space. Further, in 'use edges and value the marginal', as in nature, the edge of two spaces or systems is rich in diversity (another principle is 'use and value diversity') and opportunities. The vertical gardens along the perimeter and the seats on the edge of garden beds, for instance, are examples of using an edge, but also of maximising space to produce an abundant yield. At the same time they invite gardeners and visitors to stop, observe and interact with the environment.

Similarly, the ethical values of 'earth care', 'people care' and 'fair share' or exchanging skills geared towards environmental protection, sharing produce, labour and knowledge to give back to and create a community are employed successfully in weekend workshops, including planting, gardening, making seed-raising mixes and seed bombs, and making tomato pasta at the end of summer. It is important to stress that these values are not simply communicated verbally, but they are embodied and put into action. During free workshops the public is welcomed to garden on the rooftop, and acquire new skills and competences in exchange for their labour. It is a type of informal learning, and permaculture knowledge is transmitted by inter-actions, gestures, being together and sharing a sensory dimension and embodied experiences. Unlike in community gardens, the interactions in the 107 Projects rooftop garden are mediated through learning specific skills, and are consequently structured in activities.

These two aspects of the rooftop sociality, learning by permaculture ethics and design principles and through structured activities, means also the absence of the conflictual aspects emerging in many community gardens and described in manuals dedicated to community garden management and conflict resolution (Cultivating Community, 2002; Nettle, 2009, 2014; Newcastle Community Garden Project, 2010; Glenelg North Community Garden, 2013).

10.3.4 St Canice Kitchen Garden, Kings Cross, Sydney

St Canice Kitchen Garden, Kings Cross, Sydney is an excellent initiative to provide health, wellbeing, social connectedness and support communities and patients (as shown in Figure 10.3). The 'GROW' horticulture therapy programme in this garden is supported by funding from the City of Sydney and is organised in meaningful partnerships with Inside Out Organic Soup Kitchen, St Vincent Hospital and Hurricane Duke (Kaziro, 2015). Under this programme, outpatients from St Vincent Hospital, Mental Health Service

Figure 10.3 'GROW' programme at St Canice Kitchen Garden, Kings Cross, Sydney. *Source*: Photo by Sumita Ghosh.

are refereed and can access this garden for therapeutic benefits through gardening and attending workshops. The produce grown in this garden is supplied for food preparation and for sale to the Inside Out Organic Soup Kitchen located at the ground floor of the Refugee Centre, thus forming a closed-loop localised food system. Hurricane Duke provides training and workshops to build organic gardening skills and confidence in patients as well as in refugees and participants from the surrounding communities (Kaziro, 2015). The garden has fruit trees such as lemons, medicinal herbs, different types of indigenous and non-indigenous vegetables, and edible and non-edible flowers to attract bees and insects and provide a visually soothing atmosphere and socially interactive space. Some of the plants are: climbing beans (*Phaseolus vulgaris*), broad beans (*Vicia faba*), warrigal greens (*Tetragonia tetragonioides*), leeks (*Allium porrum*), celery, eggplant, peas, silver beet, spring onions, curry plant (*Helichrysum italicum angustifolium*), borage (*Borago officinalis*), nasturtium (*Tropaeolum*), lavender, calendula, lemon verbena (*Aloysia citrodora*) and others (Kaziro, 2015).

From a social perspective, this garden acts as a shared community meeting place for getting together and making friends. It is unique in its objectives to provide horticulture therapy and build socially inclusive and resilient communities through effective collaborative efforts and partnerships. The participation of a number of volunteers in the garden programme and urban food production showcases their commitment to social responsibility and forms new connections to grow the community. Participants can also take produce home from the garden. The partnership of three organisations in the 'GROW' programme plays a key role in delivering a restorative and remedial outcome to those who are in need, and also extends the opportunities to the wider community. The 'GROW' programme uses a *strength-based approach* and a *community recovery model*, where people recover naturally within a human–nature interactive setting and feel connected, revitalised, relaxed and inspired (Kaziro, 2015). The essences of flowers, plants and activities in the garden provoke participants' associations with happy memories, initiate new learning and create a safe, calming and tranquil environment in the garden with useful healing processes that make positive changes over the lifetimes of the participants (Kaziro, 2015).

10.4   Recommendations, Discussions and Conclusions

The rooftop gardens producing food in universities (Table 10.1) show that they contribute hugely to sustainability, social networking and inclusion, community engagement, education, training and relevant skill development for students, staff and community. This research highlights that the people engagement that takes place through food production on the campus is creating successful social connections, leading to better prospects. Outcomes suggest that there is enhancement in workplace community building, rise of food localism, activation of urban regeneration through innovative place-making for positive engagement, immense joy associated with growing food, promotion of self-sufficiency of food and concern for ethical growing

(Table 10.1). In these case studies, the key components of alternative food systems are: short food supply chains (SFSCs); social embeddedness; quality of the produce and defensive localism (where people value traditional, healthy and fresh local foods such as organically produced vegetables in nearby locations) (Daniels *et al.*, 2008). This comparative analysis demonstrates, therefore, that a significant change is already happening in workplaces too.

In the UTS Roof Gardening Club, participants' previous experiences provided multi-generational connections to growing food. Motivations detailed by participants were shaped by their aspirations, goals and commitment to sustainability. Expectations and satisfaction from growing food, as well as influences that guide these collective engagements in rooftop gardens, are deeply rooted in culture, lived experiences and professional and personal commitments. The key expectation of the UTS Roof Gardening Club members was that the rooftop garden would become a suitable model of social change in the Sydney CBD.

> '... *become a model, I guess of social change and experiments*'
> (Interview K)

Individual time constraints, management of the garden and financial support were key concerns with regard to the long-term continuity of the collective and collaborative effort of the gardening club. Notably, some of the outcomes of the qualitative study from the UTS Roof Gardening Club, although in an early stage, are similar and could effectively be linked to the eight rooftops (Table 10.1). A limitation of this research is that the outcomes of these early-stage interviews provide a snapshot of members' viewpoints at a particular point of time. Over the garden's lifecycle, the perspectives of existing and future members may change or remain unaltered based on the productive potential and quality of engagement offered by the garden. To address this, similar interviews at different stages of this garden could be undertaken to understand these variations, and could form a longitudinal study.

The key findings from the study of the 107 Projects rooftop garden are that the social aspects observed are based around shared interests, such as learning (at any level) about permaculture and related practices, and a shared ethos based on permaculture principles. These principles can easily be applied in everyday practices in other contexts, contributing to a change in the direction towards resilience. In addition, the rooftop garden is extended virtually through a strong online presence, which documents the progress of the garden, offers short 'how to' sections, participates in current debates and creates a digital community.

The 'GROW' horticulture therapy programme at St Canice Kitchen Garden presents an excellent example of working together in partnership with appropriate local organisations and communities to make a difference. This process uniquely integrates and implements ways to contribute to improved social wellbeing and health benefits, creating a sustainable food system, promoting local economic growth, building better communities and connecting to multidisciplinary fields of knowledge on this rooftop garden.

There are also a number of barriers to establishing rooftop gardens in an institutional setting. Generally, there are property or facility managers in institutions responsible for the management of buildings and their rooftops (Wilkinson, 2015b). First, it is difficult and time consuming to provide assurance and gain trust from various gatekeepers, requiring different routes of approach in the process of getting approval to set up a rooftop garden. Second, managers with previous experience in urban food production on rooftops may understand the benefits more easily than managers with very limited or no experience. Third, the installation of a rooftop garden needs to satisfy a set of criteria such as: a certain time line within which a garden would operate; that the garden is safe and accessible to participants, satisfies insurance and legal requirements and has the full support of managers. Fourth, understanding which user groups would be accessing the garden, for example, students, staff, occupants and residents; what type of access they would require (weekly, daily, monthly or other); and their choice of times for gardening activities. The level of access could be restricted depending on various factors. In Gumal rooftop garden, located on the student housing in UTS, access to the garden created some frustration for participants coming from outside the housing (Wilkinson, 2015b).

Different exploratory methodological approaches have been applied in this chapter to understand and observe the social phenomena connecting multiple aspects happening across different institutional rooftop garden settings. Recommendations based on the analysis suggest that setting up more rooftop gardens at suitable locations (mainly higher-density areas of cities) and organising events, open days and cooking classes to encourage social networking, participation and knowledge sharing could facilitate multiple community benefits across different domains. Developing and applying innovative sustainable practices and permaculture principles in the design and planning of rooftop gardens, as well as developing guidelines for rooftop plant selection suggestions, could assist keen but less experienced gardeners immensely. It is important to highlight the social and cultural importance of rooftop gardens. For the long-term continuity of the gardens, appropriate management processes need to be formulated. A framework for creating a localised closed-loop food system – including production, distribution and disposal – and working in partnerships would be critical for uptake. Non-governmental organisations (NGOs), government as well as private organisations, local governments and developers could provide help for this initiative. Future research should focus on conducting transdisciplinary research on rooftop gardens and developing useful integrated approaches with regard to the meaningful uptake of urban agriculture in denser urban settlements. This research has informed a discussion on how building community resilience, social connectedness, and health and environmental benefits could be effectively initiated, developed and integrated using collaborative approaches through institutional rooftop gardens.

Acknowledgement

The researchers would like to acknowledge the City of Sydney for funding provided to the Urban Food Production on Sydney CBD Rooftops through the Environmental Grants Program for the UTS Rooftop.

References

107 Projects (2015) 107projects.org/upstairs-107/.

Alimurung, A. (2012) 'Kasetsart university in Thailand builds an innovative rooftop garden on campus'mpuvailable at: inhabitat.com/kasetsart-university-in-thailand-builds-an-innovative-rooftop-garden-on-campus/.

Beauty and Environmental Benefits Meet on a Rooftop (2009) *Waste Disposal and Water Management in Australia*, Vol. 36, No. 4, p. 21. Available at: search.informit.com.au.ezproxy.lib.uts.edu.au/documentSummary;dn=795969933546281;res=IELENG> ISSN: 0311-3558.

Bennett, A. F. (2003) *Linkages in the Landscape: The Role of Corridors and Connectivity in Wildlife Conservation*. IUCN: Gland, Switzerland.

Bentley, I., Alcock, A., Murrain, P., McGlynn, S. and Smith, G. (1985) *Responsive Environments: A Manual for Designers*. Architectural Press: London.

Blyth, A. and Menagh, L. (2006) 'From the rooftop to the restaurant, a university café fed by rooftop garden', *The Canadian Organic Grower*, Fall, 50–53.

Boyer, M. (2013) 'Boston's higher ground farm will be the second-biggest rooftop farm in the world', available at: inhabitat.com/bostons-higher-ground-farm-will-be-the-second-biggest-rooftop-farm-in-the-world/.

Brooklyn Grange Rooftop Farm (2015) brooklyngrangefarm.com/.

Brown, K. H. and Jameton, A. L. (2000) 'Public health implications of urban agriculture', *Journal of Public Health Policy*, 21, 20–39.

Carlyon, P. (2014) 'Green thumbs emphasise the benefits of roof-top gardens', available at: www.abc.net.au/news/2014-03-20/green-thumbs-emphasise-the-benefits-of-roof-top-gardens/5334744.

City of Melbourne (2015) 'Green roofs', available at: www.melbourne.vic.gov.au/Sustainability/CouncilActions/Pages/Greenroofs.aspx.

Concordia Food Coalition (CFC) (2015) 'Le Campus Potager', available at: www.concordiafoodcoalition.com/cfc-projects/concordia-rooftop-projects/.

Crosby, A. L., Lorber-Kasunic, J. and Vanni Accarigi, I. (2014) 'Value the edge: permaculture as counterculture in Australia', *M/C Journal*, 17(6), available at: journal.media-culture.org.au/index.php/mcjournal/article/viewArticle/915.

Cultivating Community (2002) Milne, G. (ed.), *The Good Practice Guide for Community Gardens*. Available at: communitygarden.org.au/wp-content/uploads/2010/06/Good_Practice_Guide_CG.pdf.

Daniels, P., Bradshaw, M., Shaw, D. and Sidaway, J. (2008) *An Introduction to Human Geography*, 3rd edn. Pearson Education: Oxford.

Davis, B. E. (2011) 'Rooftop hospital gardens for physical therapy: A post-occupancy evaluation', *HERD*, 4(3), 14–43.

Ducharm, J. (2015) 'A group of Brandeis students started a rooftop farm on campus', available at: www.bostonmagazine.com/health/blog/2015/06/04/brandeis-university-rooftop-farm/.

Eagle Street Rooftop Farm (2015) rooftopfarms.org/.

Foss, J., Quesnel, A. and Danielsson, N. (2011) *Sustainable Rooftop Agriculture. A Strategic Guide to City Implementation*. Available at: bieb.ruaf.org/ruaf_bieb/upload/3694.pdf.

Franklin, E. (2011) 'A rooftop gardening project in Toronto with the About Face collective' (an interview with an urban farmer, Natalie Boustead), *Women & Environments International Magazine*, Fall 88/89, 40–41.

Fujita Kanko Incorporated (2012) 'Hotel Chinzanso Tokyo's one-of-a-kind rooftop garden unveils at hotel's rebranding opening in January 2013', *Business Wire*, 12 November.

Gehl, J. (1987) *Life Between Buildings: Using Public Space*. Island Press: London.

Glenelg North Community Garden (2013) 'Conflict process for the community garden', available at: gncg.wordpress.com/2013/10/26/conflict-process-for-the-community-garden/.

Gordon, H. C. (2010) 'Rooftop farming: a visit to Brooklyn's Eagle Street Rooftop Farm', available at: inhabitat.com/urban-farming-a-visit-to-brooklyns-eagle-street-rooftop-farm/.

Gorgolewski, M., Komisar, J. and Nasr, J. (2011) *Carrot City. Creating Places for Urban Agriculture*. Monacelli Press: New York.

Graham, S. and Connell, J. (2006) 'Nurturing relationships: the gardens of Greek and Vietnamese migrants in Marrickville, Sydney', *Australian Geographer*, 37(3), 375–393.

Heyboer, K. (2010) 'Rooftop garden at NJIT student center encourages students to eat organic', available at: www.nj.com/news/index.ssf/2010/09/rooftop_garden_at_njit_student.html.

Holmgren, D. (2015) 'About permaculture', available at: holmgren.com.au/about-permaculture/.

Hoffman, M. (1983) 'Rooftop gardens offer urban communities places of beauty, quiet', *The Christian Science Monitor*, 17 March.

Howes, D. (2005) *Empire of the Senses. The Sensual Culture Reader*. Berg Publishers: London.

Johannesburg Rooftop Garden (2012) 'Johannesburg rooftop garden aims to fight poverty', *States News Service*, 8 November, available at: go.galegroup.com/ps/i.do?id=GALE%7CA307868886&v=2.1&u=uts&it=r&p=&sw=w&asid=8e58420603d5812040893cfa85e7f827.

Kaethler, T. M. (2006) 'Growing space: the potential for urban agriculture in the city of Vancouver', School of Community and Regional Planning, University of British Columbia, available at: bitsandbytes.ca/sites/default/files/Growing_Space_Rpt.pdf.

Kaziro, P. (2015) 'GROW' horticulture therapy programme at St Canice Kitchen Garden, Kings Cross, Sydney (personal Communication).

Khandaker, M. S. I. (2004) 'Rooftop gardening as a strategy of urban agriculture for food security: the case of Dhaka City, Bangladesh', *Acta Horticulturae*, 643, 241–247.

Kinen-Ferguson, C. (2015) 'University dining goes green with rooftop garden', *Technician*, 8 July, available at: www.technicianonline.com/news/article_bd6dab08-07de-11e4-9575-001a4bcf6878.html.

Lee, K. E., Williams, K. J. H., Sargent, L. D., Williams, N. S. G. and Johnson, K. A. (2015) '40-second green roof views sustain attention: the role of micro-breaks in attention restoration', *Journal of Environmental Psychology*, 42, 182–189.

Litichevskaya, J. (2011) 'Reviving the world wonder: why rooftop gardens should cover urban landscapes', *Rutgers Computer & Technology Law Journal*, 37(1/2), 58–92.

LT. Governor Simon Awards (2012) 'LT. Governor Simon awards grant to uptown farmers market dedicated wireless link card machine, tours rooftop gardens', *States News Service*, 23 August, available at: go.galegroup.com/ps/i.do?id=GALE%7CA300653875&v=2.1&u=uts&it=r&p=&sw=w&asid=c0a5c39c5ac0e3ae650391bbe5bb5bdf.

Lynch, K. (1960) *The Image of the City*. MIT Press: Cambridge, MA.

Maas, J., Verheij, R. A., Groenewegen, P. P., De Vries, S. and Spreeuwenberg, P. (2006) 'Green space, urbanity, and health: how strong is the relation?', *Journal of Epidemiology & Community Health*, 60, 587–592.

Malcevschi, S., Bisogni, L. and Gariboldi, A. (1996) *Reti ecologiche ed interventi di miglioramento ambientale*. Il Verde Editoriale: Milan.

Matsuo, E. (1995) 'Horticulture helps us to live as human beings: providing balance and harmony in our behavior and thought and life worth living', *Acta Horticulturae*, 391, 19–30.

Mavrogordato, T. (2013) 'Offices are turning their roofs into edible gardens and bee sanctuaries', available at: www.theguardian.com/sustainable-business/offices-roofs-edible-garden-sustainable-cities.

McClintock, N. (2010) 'Why farm the city? Theorizing urban agriculture through a lens of metabolic rift', *Cambridge Journal of Regions, Economy and Society*, 3, 191–207.

Miles, S. and Paddison, R. (1998) 'Urban consumption: a historiographical note', *Urban Studies*, 35(5/6), 815–823.

Milkwood (2015) 'Milkwood permaculture, 18 July, available at: www.milkwood.net/about/.

Miller, J. R. (2005) 'Biodiversity conservation and the extinction of experience', *Trends in Ecology and Evolution*, 20, 430–434.

Montgomery, J. (1998) 'Making a city: urbanity, vitality and urban design', *Journal of Urban Design*, 3(1), 93–116.

Nettle, C. (2009) *Growing Community Starting and Nurturing Community Gardens*, Health SA, Government of South Australia and Neighbourhood Houses and Centres Association Inc., Adelaide.

Nettle, C. (2014) *Community Gardening as Social Action*. Ashgate Publishing: Farnham, Surrey.

Newcastle Community Garden Project (2010) Cameron, J. and Pomfrett, J. (eds), *A Community Garden Manifesto*, Centre for Urban and Regional Studies, University of Newcastle, Newcastle, UK.

Newton, P. (2011) 'Consumption and environmental sustainability.' In Newton, P. (ed.), *Urban Consumption*. CSIRO Publishing: Australia.

Oberndorfer, E., Lundholm, J., Bass, B., *et al.* (2007) 'Green roofs as urban ecosystems: ecological structures, functions, and services', *BioScience*, 57(10), 823–833.

Ontario Healthy Communities Coalition (2015) www.ohcc-ccso.ca/.

Orsini, F., Gasperi, D., Marchetti, L., *et al.* (2014) 'Exploring the production capacity of rooftop gardens (RTGs) in urban agriculture: the potential impact on food and nutrition security, biodiversity and other ecosystem services in the City of Bologna', *Food Security*, 6(6), 781–792.

Peck, S. (2003) 'Towards an integrated green roof infrastructure evaluation for Toronto', *The Green Roof Infrastructure Monitor*, 5, 4–7.

Perasso, E. (2012) 'A green kitchen starting from the top', Available at: www.finedininglovers.com/stories/green-restaurants-uncommon-ground/.

Permacultureprinciples (2015) permacultureprinciples.com.

Pink, S. (2007) 'Walking with video', *Visual Studies*, 22(3), 240–252.

Pink, S. (2009) *Doing Sensory Ethnography*. Sage: London.

Pink, S. (2012) *Situating Everyday Life: Practices and Places*. Sage: London.

Rye's Home Grown (2015) 'Rooftop garden', available at: ryeshomegrown.word press.com/rooftop-garden/.

Sanyé-Mengual, E., Cerón-Palma, I., Oliver-Solà, J., Montero, J. I. and Rieradevall, J. (2013) 'Environmental analysis of the logistics of agricultural products from roof top greenhouses in Mediterranean urban areas', *Journal of Science, Food and Agriculture*, 93, 100–109.

Shin, D. H. and Lee, K. S. (2005) 'Use of remote sensing and geographical information system to estimate green space temperature change as a result of urban expansion', *Landscape and Ecological Engineering*, 1, 169–176.

Silverman, D. (2013) *Doing Practical Research: A Practical Handbook*, 4th edn. Sage: London.

Sloan, W. (2015) 'Farmers' market to welcome some home grown food', 13 May, available at: www.ryerson.ca/ryersontoday/data/news/2015/05/20150513-farmers-market-to-welcome-some-homegrown-food.html.

Solnik, C. (2011) 'Mather Hospital in Port Jefferson opens rooftop garden', *Long Island Business News*, 19 September.

Sunakorn, P. (2012) 'AKU roof top garden', available at: www.cbit.arch.ku.ac.th/home/index.php?option=com_content&view=%20article%20&id=27.

Sydney Morning Herald (2008) 'Future farms over our heads', available at: www.smh.com.au/news/environment/future-farms-over-our heads/2008/10/11/1223145699162.html.

The Sustainable Campus (2015) 'CUHK's splendid rooftop farm', e-newsletter No. 7, The Chinese University of Hong Kong, available at: www.iso.cuhk.edu.hk/english/publications/sustainable-campus/article.aspx?articleid=61081.

Tilley, C. (2006) 'The sensory dimension of gardening', *Senses and Society*, 1(3), 311–330.

Uncommon Ground (2015) www.uncommonground.com/home.

University of Maryland (2010) 'Rooftop garden – the diner', available at: www.sustainability.umd.edu/content/campus/dining.php#South.

University of Melbourne (2015) 'Growing up rooftop garden', available at: www.growinggreenguide.org/victorian-case-studies/growing-up-rooftop-garden/.

Wackernagel, M. and Rees, W. (1996) *Our Ecological Footprint: Reducing human impact on the Earth*. New Society Publisher: Philadelphia.

Wilkerson, A. (2010) 'Rooftop garden in OKC provides fertile ground for community growth', *Journal Record*, 5 August.

Wilkinson, S. (2015a) 'Lend lease rooftop garden, London', personal communication.

Wilkinson, S. (2015b) 'Barriers to establishing an institutional rooftop garden', personal communication.

Woods Bagot (2015) 'Refugee garden brings community together in Sydney', available at: www.woodsbagot.com/news/refugee-garden-brings-community-together-in-sydney.

Zande, R. V. (2006) 'The advantages of a rooftop garden and other things', *International Journal of Art & Design Education*, 25(2), 205–221.

Zhou, C. and Stolz, A. (2014) 'Rooftop gardens on the rise as inner-city Melbourne grows green', available at: canberratimes.domain.com.au/real-estate-news/rooftop-gardens-on-the-rise-as-innercity-melbourne-grows-green-20140827-108xa5.html.

Cool Roof Retrofits as an Alternative to Green Roofs

Dominique Hes, Chris Jensen and Lu Aye
The University of Melbourne, Australia

11.0 Introduction

In this chapter another means of retrofitting a roof is discussed. This is the 'cool roof' option. The chapter outlines a research methodology and approach adopted to evaluate the cool roof option in Australia over four fieldwork experiments:

1. cool roof retrofit;
2. cool roof modelling for industrial, commercial and residential buildings;
3. preliminary look at green roof versus cool roof retrofit;
4. cool roof and photovoltaics.

The advantages and disadvantages of cool roof specifications are discussed, summarising when the cool roof is most effective at keeping heat out of buildings. The chapter concludes by setting out the circumstances whereby the cool roof option is favoured over a retrofit green roof alternative.

11.1 What is a Cool Roof?

As we have seen in other chapters in this book, there is a significant benefit to retrofitting buildings and focusing effort on how to do this effectively and efficiently. This chapter looks at the opportunities of the outer skin of the roof, specifically using a cool roof treatment. Focusing on cool roof paints (CRP), the chapter outlines the benefits and limitations, as well as briefly referring to alternatives such as green roofs.

Green Roof Retrofit: Building Urban Resilience, First Edition.
Edited by Sara Wilkinson and Tim Dixon.
© 2016 John Wiley & Sons, Ltd. Published 2016 by John Wiley & Sons, Ltd.

A cool roof is typically a treatment that is applied to the roof as paint, but can be an integral part of the outer layers of the roof. It is cool because it reflects the sun's heat and emits absorbed radiation back into the atmosphere at a higher rate than standard materials (Urban and Roth, 2010). These types of roof literally stay cooler, thus reducing the amount of heat held and transferred to the building below, keeping the building at a cooler and more constant temperature. In a retrofit the paint can be applied to existing roofing if its condition is reasonable, while the cool roof material is a larger, more costly replacement option when roofing needs replacement. The research that underpins this chapter is based on four experiments: (1) painting two 15-year-old metal roofs white with different CRP products; (2) an initial look at the comparison for the two white roof retrofits with a green roof retrofit; (3) building two scale brick homes to current insulation standards with black concrete tiles, one painted white; and (4) putting solar panels on the two scale brick homes and measuring the impact of roof colour on PV output.

11.2   Background – How does a Cool Roof Work?

'White' or 'cool' roof paints have a significantly higher reflectivity and thermal emittance compared with normal roof materials and coatings. Cool roof performance may be achieved with additives to the base material, or by applying a CRP to an existing roof.

It is important to note that with modern technology, CRPs need not be white. There are many CRP products which use darker-coloured pigments that have increased the reflectivity in the near-infrared (non-visible) portion of the solar spectrum. With these technologies there are roofs that come in a wide variety of colours and still maintain a high solar reflectance, due to increased reflectivity in the infrared range of the spectrum, without affecting the visible range which dictates colour. However, a darker roof will never be as reflective as a light-coloured roof.

A second benefit of a cool roof is that it reduces the absorption and retention of heat and therefore the contribution to the urban heat island effect, as seen by the reduction in roof temperature for all of the experiments.

11.3   Cool Roof Studies and Measurements

Summarised below are several studies, mostly in the northern hemisphere, using both field measurements and computer simulations that document the energy savings from increasing the solar reflectance properties of buildings, combined with an increased thermal emittance. It is now widely accepted that the higher reflectivity a roof colour has, the lower the solar energy that is absorbed into the building and the lower the surface temperature of the roof will be (Kiehl and Trenberth, 2010).

In a 2001 study by Konopacki and Akbari, the Lawrence Berkeley National Laboratory (LBNL) measured and calculated the reduction in peak energy demand associated with a cool roof's surface reflectivity.

They found that, compared with the original black rubber roofing membrane on the Texas retail building studied, a retrofitted vinyl membrane delivered an average decrease of 24°C in surface temperature, an 11% decrease in aggregate air-conditioning energy consumption and a corresponding 14% drop in peak hour demand. The average daily summer-time temperature of the black roof surface was 75°C, but once retrofitted with a white reflective surface, it measured 52°C. Without considering any tax benefits or other utility charges, the annual energy expenditure on providing comfort was reduced by $7200, or $0.07/sq. ft (0.65 cents/m²).

Akbari and Konopacki (2005) have calculated the cooling energy savings due to the application of heat island mitigation strategies (application of cool materials and increase in vegetation cover) for 240 regions in the United States. It was found that for residential buildings, the cooling energy savings vary between 12% and 25%, for office buildings between 5% and 18%, and for commercial (retail store) buildings between 7% and 17%. In Australia, Miller *et al.* (2015) looked at the benefits of CRP in subtropical and tropical areas; they found measured reductions in temperature (roof surface, roof cavity and non-air-conditioned internal spaces), power (kW) and energy usage (kWh) within their studied buildings.

Other relevant field studies in California and Florida have demonstrated direct cooling energy savings in excess of 20% upon raising the solar reflectance of a roof to 0.6 from a prior value of 0.1–0.2 (i.e., 60% reflectance from 10–20% reflectance). Energy savings are particularly pronounced in older houses that have little or no roof insulation, especially if the roof space contains air distribution ducts for ducted heating and cooling. Akbari *et al.* (2009) observed cooling energy savings of 46% and peak power savings of 20%, achieved by increasing the roof reflectance of two identical portable classrooms in Sacramento, California. Konopacki *et al.* (1998) documented measured energy savings of 12–18% in two commercial buildings in California. In a large retail store in Austin, Texas, Konopacki and Akbari (2001) documented measured energy savings of 12%. The roof of the building was insulated metal, with a black membrane coating pre-retrofit, with a white thermoplastic PVC membrane post-retrofit.

This research showed that there are benefits across most climatic regions, but specifically in those that have a larger cooling rather than heating load. The research suggests that the larger the cooling load, the greater the benefit from the CRP. That is, it is not the building type but its cooling load resulting from energy transfer through the roof; if the CRP reduced the energy ingress, then the energy used to maintain comfort was reduced. The studies reported on in this chapter extend this work by looking at a climatic region that has a high heating load.

11.4   The Experiments

The studies reported on in this chapter include field research on residential-type buildings. Within the modelling component, the data from the fieldwork was used to calibrate a model which was then used to look at the benefit for other building typologies; this ensures greater accuracy between modelled results and reality, as outlined by Akbari *et al.* (1997).

Residential level was focused on due to the practicality of setting up test buildings. Roof performance in a residential building is a balance between summer-time heat reduction performance and winter heat absorption, and this is dependent on the climate within which the building is located. The temperate Melbourne climate (similar to the San Francisco Bay area, Cape Town, Southern France and Northern Spain) is considered to be a heating climate for the majority of the year. As the experiments were set up in a heating climate, it was expected that a cool roof product would increase the heating requirements; thus, given our insulation requirements and the use of the CRP, we wanted to see if the positive impact of summer benefits was greater than the negative impact in winter. The key to the potential impact of the insulation (due to saturation and heat balance between the roof cavity and inside the house) is that in winter the insulation is designed to keep the temperature up to 25°C within the house, while in summer the roof cavity will get to over 50°C, resulting in heat moving into the house. This is reinforced by research such as that of Gentle *et al.* (2011), who noted that the roof surface typically does not present a dominant influence on average winter heating needs in most temperate zones, enhancing the benefits of cool roofs.

11.4.1   Results

The University of Melbourne research team has been looking at CRPs since 2010, with four different experiments underpinning this chapter. The location of the research was eastern metropolitan Melbourne, with coordinates 37°48′49″S, 144°57′47″E.

The site is made up of nine buildings (Figure 11.1), six full scale (A–F) and three one-third scale (G–J). Mixed experiments occurred on the site:

- buildings A and C were used for wall-shading studies;
- building B was the control for buildings A–F;
- buildings D and F had different brands of CRP;
- building E was a green roof;
- building G was a one-third-scale building with another type of CRP used to test the impact of weathering, dirt accumulation and cleaning;
- buildings H and J were one-third-scale brick veneer buildings built to current building standards with dark charcoal concrete roof tiles.

Buildings A–G

The test buildings are of a lightweight construction, typical of Australian housing, and insulation levels are indicative of the 1991 minimum building standards (approximately R1.0 walls and R0.82 ceilings), which would have been in place at the time of construction. The uninsulated timber floors

Figure 11.1   Buildings and location.
Source: NearMap.

and the absence of weather strips to doors resulted in an assumed infiltration rate of approximately two air changes per hour (ACH). The doors and windows were always closed, with the exception of those times access was required for installation and maintenance of equipment. Blinds were installed to north-facing windows in order to mitigate misleading sensor output affected by glare and direct solar gain.

Data collected is depicted graphically in Figure 11.2, and included heat transfer into the roof. Room heat flux sensors at roof and ceiling level measured the transfer of heat into the building through the roof. Vertical and horizontal pyranometers mounted on a steel support above the roof measured the reflected radiation from the roof. Within the building, temperature and humidity were measured to determine the ambient comfort conditions. All sensors were connected to the Internet via the data logger.

The data from the onsite measurements discussed in Experiment 1 was collected between December 2010 and July 2011, specifically in summer (1–14 January) and winter (23 April–8 May, 2–16 June). Results are discussed in relation to internal temperature, reflectance and roof temperature. The summer indoor temperature profiles suggest that the CRP product test buildings maintain a lower internal temperature by 2 or 3°C compared with the control building at the warmest part of the day. This visible difference is most obvious during the warmest parts of the day, however a similar effect can be seen overnight also. The main source of difference seen in the indoor temperatures of these test buildings is solar radiation (Figure 11.3).

When looking at the data from the roof surface temperatures, the impact of the CPR is the most marked. It is clear that the painted roofs have a much lower external temperature. The summer roof temperature profile shows

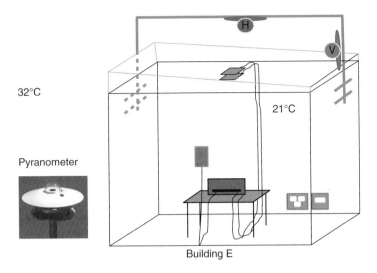

Figure 11.2   Experimental setup.

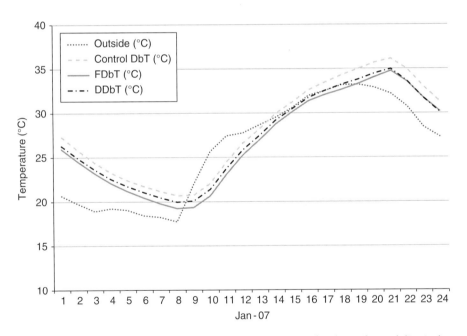

Figure 11.3   Summer indoor temperature across 24 hours (note first letter for each line is the building – i.e. FDbT= building F Dry bulb temperature).

a clear difference of up to approximately 30°C (Figures 11.4 and 11.5). As can be seen, on 6 January 2011 the control roof (zincalume) reaches 68°C whilst the coolest roof is at 35°C.

This difference in the roof temperature is related to the amount of energy that the CRP-painted roofs reflected back off. Figure 11.6 details the energy re-radiated from building D compared with the control building, on 7 January 2011.

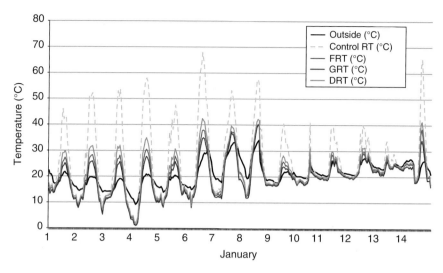

Figure 11.4   Summer roof temperature across 14 days (note first letter for each line is the building – i.e. FRT= building F Roof Temperature).

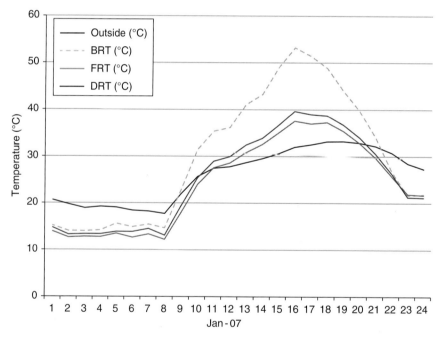

Figure 11.5   Summer roof temperature across 24 hours.

We used the field results to calibrate the simulated model, which was developed in the Transient Systems Simulation Programme (TRNSYS). This simulation showed that for all white roof paints there is a benefit annually of between 0.88 and 1.53 MJ/m². Scaling this up for an average 200 m² home, this would be equal to between 176 and 306 MJ/year. This represents

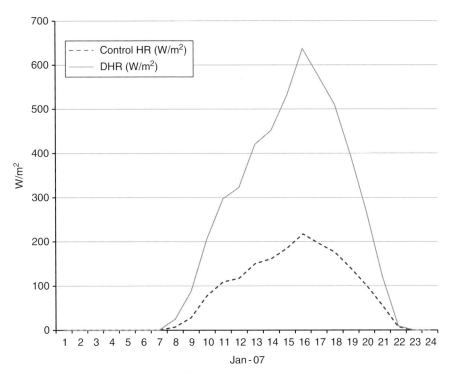

Figure 11.6   Summer roof reflection across 24 hours.

only a small improvement for this type of building (total energy use in this example being 7300 MJ, this represents a 4.2% benefit). With this model the researchers were then able to test some aspects that help to determine when the use of CPR would be most beneficial. The aspects tested were: roof pitch, roof shading, insulation levels and roof-to-wall ratio. For cooling energy the model showed that the steeper the roof slope, the greater the benefit of the CRP (Figure 11.7). Therefore, from this simulation it makes sense to paint sloped roofs if artificial cooling is used. This is also a useful outcome for the central theme of this book: if retrofitting a roof with a steep slope, a green roof is less appropriate.

The simulation of the shading of a roof and the benefit of CRP showed that if a roof is shaded, there is little benefit of the CRP. Owing to the importance of the roof insulation on the impact of the CRP, the model tested whether the location of the insulation (under the roof or over the ceiling) made an impact. Across the year, the difference between using a CRP and not using a CRP can result in an increased roof space temperature of up to 18.5°C (assuming R2.5 insulation fitted to the ceiling). Figure 11.8 shows the temperature of the attic or ceiling space across a year; the highest temperature in the roof space without CRP was 53°C, while at the same time the painted roof was at 36°C.

If the insulation is moved from on top of the ceiling to under the roof (i.e., from between the roof space and the habitable room to between the roof and the roof space), it dramatically reduces the roof space temperature

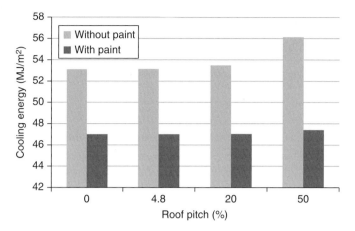

Figure 11.7   Simulated impact of roof pitch and CRP on cooling energy.

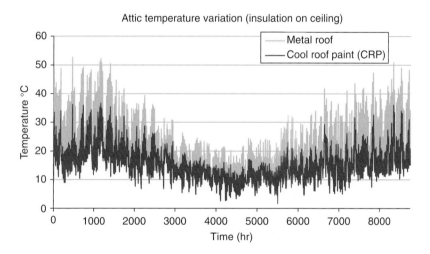

Figure 11.8   Simulated ceiling space temperatures.

to the point where the effect of the CRP is much less significant. In other words, houses with an unvented roof space and insulation only on the ceiling will get a significant benefit from the CRP, as roof space temperatures will otherwise reach over 50°C, which will act to slowly heat the habitable space below. Houses with vented roof spaces, or insulation under the roof material (insulated sarking, aircell or similar) will receive less benefit from the use of CRP, as the heat is not getting into the roof space. The simulation was next asked to provide data on the contribution CRP can have to reducing energy consumption as buildings become taller. Not surprisingly, the fewer the floors and the greater the surface area of the roof space to the external vertical walls, the greater the benefit of the CRP. As such, the CRP is most effective when used on low-rise buildings, which led the researchers to look at industrial-type buildings. It is with these buildings that the greatest benefit was shown.

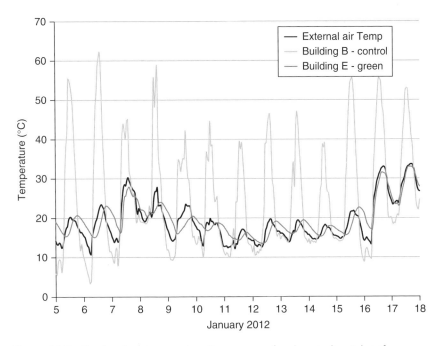

Figure 11.9   Roof surface temperature for green roof and control metal roof.

Because industrial buildings generally do not use energy for heating or cooling, the analysis was instead made on internal comfort conditions. Although this approach results in a direct comparison of performance with and without CRP, it is more difficult to assign a cost saving to the use of the products. The results show that both the CRP and base case roofs result in buildings which are uncomfortable at times, but that the CRP building maintained a significantly lower internal temperature during these times. To illustrate this, as can be seen from Figure 11.9, on a day when the base-case building's internal temperature approached 40°C, the CRP building maintained a temperature of approximately 33°C. This represents a difference of 7°C, or approximately 17% cooler conditions.

To understand the potential energy use consequences for industrial buildings, the model examined two scenarios:

- a high load profile (100 W/m²) representing a process-style building such as manufacturing;
- a low load profile (10 W/m²) representing a storage-style building such as a warehouse.

It was found that if the buildings were heated and cooled, the simulation showed that the cooling energy for both scenarios was significantly reduced (59% reduction for high load, 70% for low load), and that the heating energy was also increased (18.6% for high load, 22% for low load). What is potentially more interesting is that the model showed that without heating or cooling, the CRP would result in a 9% reduction in hours outside the comfort zone (between 18 and 27°C). That is, the facility would be able to continue to operate for a longer period.

Comparison of CRP results with the green roof

The full-scale buildings B, D and F were compared with building E (green roof) to compare the performance of the green roof and that of the cool roofs. The extensive (shallow) green roof was retrofitted on the building and constructed of the following layers above the roof structure: protection layer, drainage layer, filter fabric, substrate and plants. The roof was planted with drought-tolerant succulents and not watered. It was expected that the green roof would reduce the heat transmission through the roof because of shading, evapotranspiration, absorption and the insulating properties or soil and water (Gagliano et al., 2015). The control building (B) was found to have daytime temperatures higher than those of the green roof. The field tests clearly demonstrated low roof temperatures for the green roof compared with a metal roof (Figure 11.9). It should be noted that the maximum temperature reduction coincided with the peak cooling load period. The bulk of the daytime heat gain is the effect of solar radiation absorption, which is usually the most important factor (Suehrcke et al., 2008). Comparing the white and green roofs, the surface temperature clearly shows that the green roof stays much cooler and there is a slight lag, which is expected with the additional thermal mass. The detail in Figure 11.10 is based on one day chosen from 3 months of data collected over 2 years and chosen to reflect a very typical Melbourne day of 35°C.

It was found that when comparing the green, white and control roofs, the internal temperature conditions between the CRP and green roofs varied by around 3°C on a 35°C day (Figure 11.11). Both types of roof retrofit reduced the internal temperature, the white by up to 4°C and the green by up to 7°C. (Remember that the insulation on these retrofits had an R-value below 1; it shows the benefits of the retrofit, which would decrease once the insulation is brought up to standard at an R-value of 2.5.) The graph in Figure 11.11 also shows that the green roofs keep the internal temperature warmer at night, which has negative consequences for night-time comfort and cooling in summer and benefits in winter – as one would expect with the added thermal mass.

Finally, when the researchers looked at the re-radiation of energy from the roofs, it was clear that the green roof did not reflect as much energy as the CRP roofs, or even the old metal roof; instead, it was absorbed by the plants (Figure 11.12).

This would suggest that green roofs are better at reducing the impact of the roof surface on the urban heat island, although cool roofs also have an impact by not holding onto the heat and reflecting it away from the building. Green roofs, as discussed in other chapters, also have many additional benefits – such as providing potential places for ecosystem services, habitat, biophilia, stormwater retention, absorption of emissions, etc.

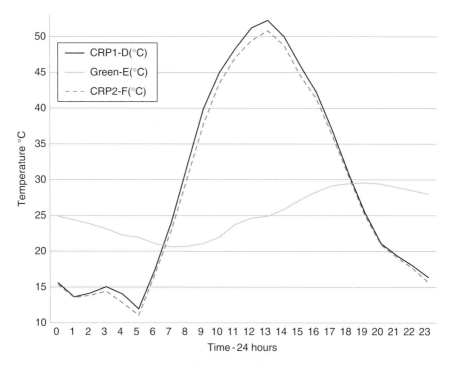

Figure 11.10   Roof surface temperature for green roofs and white roofs (7 February 2012)

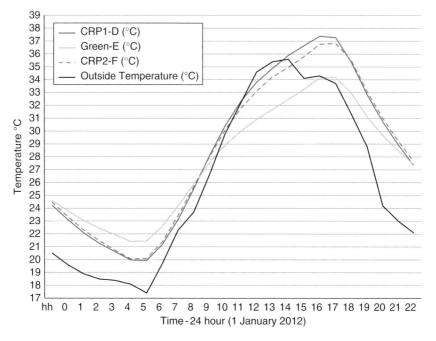

Figure 11.11   Internal temperature (1 January 2012).

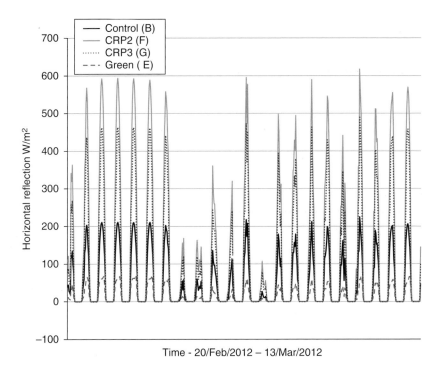

Figure 11.12   Roof horizontal reflection.

11.4.2   Other Residential Building Typologies

Having looked at the lightweight timber buildings, the researchers set up two one-third-scale brick veneer buildings designed to current building-code standards. The buildings were built to one-third the scale of a standard building. Building H had a proprietary cool roof product applied to the concrete tile roof and building J had an untreated charcoal-coloured concrete tile roof. Both had the same orientation (magnetic north), the same design, the same materials, and were constructed to a BCA 6 star equivalent standard (115 MJ/m²). Given the scale and proportions of the buildings, it was not appropriate to 'rate' the buildings at a 6 star performance level, and, as such, the buildings were classified as 'equivalent' to the 6 star standard, in accordance with an accredited rater's experience of typical building standards.

Buildings H and J had a 2000×2000 mm² external base building measurement, with a maximum height of 2250 mm above ground, a single pitch roof of 24.7° (±0.3°). The roof is a skillion-style roof with the plaster following the roof profile, rather than a suspended flat ceiling (to facilitate easy access to the internal space). The external roof dimensions are 2400×2400 mm² (including eaves), which is 5.76 m². There were two openings, one window 600×600 mm² facing north and one door 600×1850 mm² facing south. The buildings were monitored from October 2011 until November 2013.

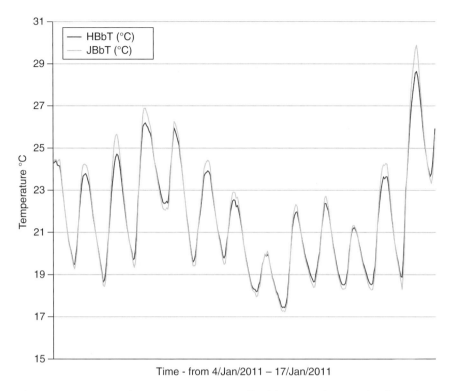

Time - from 4/Jan/2011 – 17/Jan/2011

Figure 11.13   Internal summer temperature of buildings J and H (note first letter for each line is the building – i.e. HBbT= building H Black bulb temperature).

The data collected from log-tag mobile temperature recorders before the application of the CPR showed that the two buildings were performing within 0.2% of each other. That is, the internal temperature, humidity and radiance were almost equal. The data after CRP application shows the clear difference between the two buildings, most notably the reduced internal temperatures of building H (CRP). Once the paint was applied the internal temperature showed that the application of the CPR resulted in a 2°C drop in summer temperature during the day and slightly higher at night (Figure 11.13). Interestingly, it was also found that the CRP building's internal temperature had a small increase in temperature in the winter (Figure 11.14).

The field measurements also showed that the CRP had an impact on both the roof surface temperature (by almost 20°C) and increased reflectivity (over 90%).

This study confirmed and provided additional data for a growing field of research that proves the benefit of CRP for increasing surface reflectivity, reducing roof surface temperature (Figure 11.15) as well as indoor temperature, subject to the properties of the building. This has been achieved in a tightly controlled study based on code-compliant buildings typical of Melbourne, Australia. Also, particular cool roof products can provide an insulating benefit during the night time and in winter, although the results in

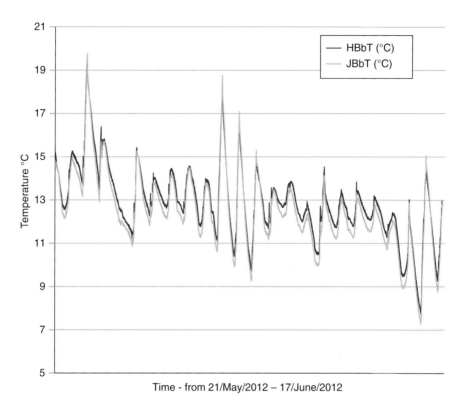

Figure 11.14   Internal winter temperature of buildings J and H.

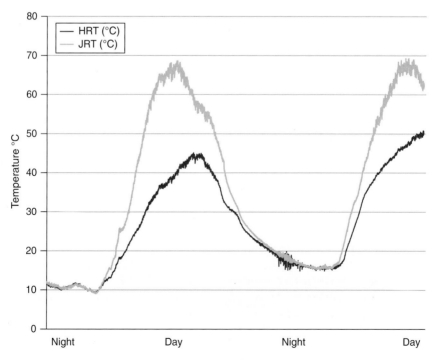

Figure 11.15   Surface temperature of buildings J and H (24 February 2012).

this study were minor and require further research to identify the reasons for the benefit. The important point, though, is that there was no negative impact of the cool roof product tested in this experiment at night or in winter. This could be attributed to the insulating properties of the nano-ceramic spheres in the paint, but this would also need to be verified by further testing.

11.4.3   Impact of CRP on PV Energy Generation

The final element of this chapter looks briefly at the preliminary outcomes of an ongoing study on the impact of the cool roof on PV panel performance due to temperature variations. It is well understood that a typical crystalline PV module is subject to power output variations in accordance with cell temperature, by increasing the conductivity of the crystalline semi-conductor, which acts to reduce the individual cell voltage. A high cell temperature reduces electrical productivity by up to 25% and a value of $-0.45\%/°C$ can be applied for crystalline silicon PV cells (Makrides *et al.*, 2009; Peck and van der Linde, 2010).

Given this effect, and the predominant rooftop location of most solar cell installations, it seems that the increased roof temperature of a dark roof will act to lower the efficiency of a solar panel. It must be noted that the panel does provide a shading effect for the roof, and therefore a roof covered in panels will not necessarily reach the same high temperature as a bare roof.

Two identical PV installations, Suntech 12 V/85 W monocrystalline panels (Figure 11.16), were installed (one per building) and linked to a series of

Figure 11.16   Buildings J and H, and test PV panels.

light bulbs in order to generate load. The PV light-bulb wiring was a closed loop with monitoring of the current and voltage only, which provided the results.

Preliminary results found that on a typical day there is a 6.7% increase in electrical output when installed over a cool roof, compared with an identical installation on a black roof, based on the scale and properties of the buildings used in the study.

11.5   Conclusions

11.5.1   Negative Impacts of Cool Roofs

The major negative impact of a cool roof is that of glare. This is an issue that needs to be considered at the initial stage of any projects, because the relatively light colours of CRPs can have a negative impact on people looking at the roof, or wall. Darker or low-glare colours should be considered if there is glare. Further, the performance of the white roof degrades over time and it is important that a maintenance regime is in place to clear the roof periodically (every one to two years depending on the amount of pollution, dust and other substance accumulation). Having said this, the technology is moving quickly, with new surface treatments being able to perform well even when soiled because of their consistency and layers (Gentle and Smith, 2015) – for example, sisalation still reflects energy away from the envelope of a building even though it is within the walls and roof surfaces.

11.5.2   Green Roofs Versus Cool Roofs

As other chapters in this book have outlined, there are many benefits to green roofs, particularly the multiple ecological benefits of provision of biodiversity, treatment of stormwater, visual amenity, uptake of emissions and so forth (see Chapters 4 to 10). The major decision point is the additional cost of a green roof versus a white roof. Sproul *et al.* (2014), during a lifecycle costing study of green roofs, black roofs and white roofs, reported that thin extensive green roofs can cost \$108–248/m² (\$10–23/ft²) while heavier, deeper intensive green roofs can cost \$355–2368/m² (\$33–220/ft²). Based on 22 case studies, Sproul and colleagues used a mean of \$172/m² (\$14/ft²) in their analysis. A CRP, in contrast, they report at \$22/m². Other considerations for green roofs are the maintenance aspects, load-bearing requirements and availability of water for those roofs that need irrigation.

Yet, as mentioned above, there are often intangible benefits to green roofs including wellbeing and productivity benefits for those looking at and/or having access to a green roof. These biophilic benefits are well documented in the work of Stephen Kellert and others, including Chapters 9 and 10 of this book.

11.5.3   Cool Roofs and Retrofits

The four experiments are limited in their extent and scope, but they repeatedly show a benefit to using the cool roof treatments in the temperate Melbourne climate. Benefits have been shown to be greater further north in Australia (Miller *et al.*, 2014, 2015). In summary, the circumstances whereby the cool roof option is most beneficial are:

- industrial buildings that have no heating or cooling;
- buildings that mainly have a cooling load;
- buildings with a large roof-to-total-surface-area ratio;
- buildings with roofs that are not overshadowed for more than 20% of the time;
- buildings with roofs that have a pitch above 23° (mainly due to increased surface area);
- buildings with a PV solar array on them.

As outlined above, the circumstances whereby the cool roof option is favoured over a retrofit green roof alternative are where there are significant aspects of cost, maintenance (including availability of water), structural load and roof pitch.

11.5.4   Barriers and Stakeholders

This research was done in collaboration with the industry – both building owners and cool roof paint providers. The key barrier identified was that of accurate reputable information on benefits (actual benefits, in the field). Both for CRPs and green roofs, data is still being collected for different climate zones. Specifically, the CRP providers often found that the modelling may not correctly identify the existence and extent of potential benefits.

Acknowledgements

This study was part of the 'Energy Saving Benefits of Urban Trees' and 'White Roofs' collaborative research effort between the Melbourne School of Land & Environment, the Melbourne School of Engineering and the Faculty of Architecture, Building and Planning. This research was funded by Nursery and Garden Industry Australia (NGIA) and special thanks go to Anthony Kachenko for his support and encouragement. The white roofs were funded by the City of Melbourne and the Department of Sustainability and Environment. Thanks go to: Dr Stephen Livesley and Dr Nick Williams for field and equipment support and discussions; Lurian Klein and Kakau Foliaki for their data analysis. Final thanks go to Ross Payne, Jamie Pearson, Tshewang Lhendup and Anthony Dawkins for assisting with research infrastructure installation and basic data collection.

References

Akbari, H. and Konopacki, S. (2005) 'Calculating energy saving potentials of heat-island reduction strategies', *Energy Policy*, 33, 721–756.

Akbari, H., Kurn, D. M., Bretz, S. E. and Hanfford, J. W. (1997) 'Peak power and cooling energy savings of shade trees', *Energy and Buildings*, 25, 139–148.

Akbari, H., Menon, S. and Rosenfeld, A. (2009) 'Global cooling: increasing world-wide albedos to offset CO^2', *Climate Change*, 94, 275–286.

Gagliano, A., Detommaso, M., Nocera, F. and Evola, G. (2015) 'A multi-criteria methodology for comparing the energy and environmental behavior of cool, green and traditional roofs', *Building and Environment*, 90, 71–81.

Gentle, A. R. and Smith, G. B. (2015) 'A subambient open roof surface under the mid-summer sun', *Advanced Science*, 26 May [online].

Gentle, A. R., Aguilar, J. L. C. and Smith, G. B. (2011) 'Optimized cool roofs: integrating albedo and thermal emittance with R-value', *Solar Energy Materials and Solar Cells*, 95, 3207–3215.

Kiehl, J. T. and Trenberth, K. E. (2010) *Sustainability: Urban Heat Island*. Technical Bulletin No. 78, p. 197.

Konopacki, S. J. and Akbari, H. (2001) *Measured Energy Savings and Demand Reduction from a Reflective Roof Membrane on a Large Retail Store in Austin*. Lawrence Berkeley National Laboratory Report LBNL-47149, Berkeley, CA.

Konopacki, S. J., Akbari, H., Gartland, L. and Rainer, L. (1998) *Demonstration of Energy Savings of Cool Roofs*. Lawrence Berkeley National Laboratory Report LBNL-40673, Berkeley, CA.

Makrides, G., Zinsser, B., Georghiou, G. E., Schubert, M. and Werner, J. H. (2009) 'Temperature behaviour of different photovoltaic systems installed in Cyprus and Germany', *Solar Energy Materials and Solar Cells*, 93, 1095–1099.

Miller, W. F., Bell, J. M. and Crompton, G. (2014) 'The impact of cool roof applications on energy performance: results from Australian sub-tropical and tropical field studies'. Proceedings of World Sustainable Buildings Conference (SB14), CIB – International Council for Research and Innovation in Building and Construction, Barcelona.

Miller, W. F., Crompton, G. and Bell, J. (2015) 'Analysis of cool roof coatings for residential demand side management in tropical Australia', *Energies*, 8, 5303–5318.

Peck, S. W. and van der Linde, D. (2010) 'System integration', *Eco-structure*, September.

Sproul, J., Wan, M. P., Mandel, B. H. and Rosenfeld, A. H. (2014) 'Economic comparison of white, green, and black flat roofs in the United States', *Energy and Buildings*, 71, 20–27.

Suehrcke, H., Peterson, E. and Selby, N. (2008) 'Effect of roof solar reflectance on the building heat gain in a hot climate', *Energy and Buildings*, 40, 2224–2235.

Urban, B. and Roth, K. (2010) *Guidelines for Selecting Cool Roofs*. US Department of Energy, Energy Efficiency and Renewable Energy, Building Technologies Program.

Looking to the Future

Sara Wilkinson[1] and Tim Dixon[2]

[1] UTS, Australia
[2] University of Reading, UK

12.0   Introduction

This book has discussed a wide range of reasons why individual stakeholders might have to retrofit a green roof. These benefits include thermal performance, stormwater attenuation, species conversation, promotion of biodiversity, urban food production and provision of spaces for social engagement and interaction. Often, the primary reason for green roof retrofit is the only one considered, and the other co-benefits are not recognised. In this chapter we articulate the primary reason along with co- or secondary benefits that stakeholders might, more readily, understand the full range of benefits, including improved urban resilience, that exist in green roofs. However, it starts with a review of the latest initiatives in best practice at the city scale, before moving on to examine the complex, and often thorny, issue of whether mandatory or voluntary approaches are the best way to deliver greater uptake of green roof retrofit.

12.1   City-level Actions: Basel and Paris

Basel, Switzerland has the highest number of green roofs per capita in the world, with some 20% of its flat roof area comprising green roofs. These have been brought about by a number of financial incentives and building regulations (Kazmierczak and Carter, 2010). In Basel and other cities in Switzerland, green roofs became more popular and commonplace in the

Green Roof Retrofit: Building Urban Resilience, First Edition.
Edited by Sara Wilkinson and Tim Dixon.
© 2016 John Wiley & Sons, Ltd. Published 2016 by John Wiley & Sons, Ltd.

1970s as a test bed for green construction, and this led to the development of pilots in the 1980s. Then, in 1996 and 1997, Basel implemented a law, which encouraged and supported energy-saving measures in the city, where 5% of all customers' energy bills are put into an Energy Saving Fund, which can then be used for a variety of measures, including green roofs. As a result, in Basel, there is a clear link between energy consumption reduction and biodiversity protection.

Indeed, this incentive programme was also linked to the burgeoning interest in research into green roofs in the city, and was further strengthened by an incentive programme in 2005/2006 which also incorporated design specifications into the green roof guidelines. Moreover, in 2002, after the first incentive programme, an amendment to Basel's Building and Construction Law was passed, stipulating that all new and renovated flat roofs must be greened and that they must meet particular guidelines, for example, the growing medium must be native, natural, regional soils and vegetation should be a mix of native Basel species. This legislation was possible because of Basel's canton-based and semi-independent powers. The vision of the city has also been important in shaping this agenda. Basel is known for its '2000-W society' and its vision for sustainable energy use (i.e., a reduction in primary energy consumption in Switzerland by a factor of three from the current 6000 W per person to 2000 W). In 2001 a pilot region was launched in Basel, where the vision was realised as a co-operative project (public/private partnership) between Novatlantis, the Department of Building for the Canton of Basel-Stadt, the University of Applied Sciences for both Cantons of Basel, and the University of Basel. Since the launch of the Basel pilot region in 2001, urban development and mobility issues have underpinned the ongoing applied research, and the inherent expertise in sustainable development has been used to help enhance urban design in Basel, all of which also underpinned and linked with the growth of green roofs in the city (TCPA, 2012).

Other European and global cities have also followed Basel's example. For example, Copenhagen, Denmark passed a similar ordinance in 2010, seeking to add some 53,000 sq. ft of new green roofs per year (NASA, 2012). In Toronto, from 1 February 2010 to 1 March 2015, 260 green roofs have been created, consisting of 196,000 m² of green roof area, with a total of 444 green roofs existing in the City of Toronto (City of Toronto, 2015). Toronto is the first city in North America to have a bylaw to require and govern the construction of green roofs on new development, and the bylaw was adopted by Toronto City Council in May 2009, under the authority of Section 108 of the City of Toronto Act. The bylaw applies to new building permit applications for residential, commercial and institutional development made after 31 January 2010 and will apply to new industrial development as of 30 April 2012. In Toronto, all large new commercial institutional and residential buildings are required to have at least 20–60% of their roof space dedicated to green roofs, depending on size (Berardi et al., 2014; City of Toronto, 2015).

More recently, in 2015, France announced plans to require all new commercial buildings in the country (not just cities) to have either solar panels or green roofs. This should be seen in the context of Paris' adaptation strategy for its Climate Change Plan, which has emphasised greening since 2007, and which is also underpinned by its Biodiversity Plan (2011) as well as the Paris Rain Plan. There have been recent high-profile examples in the city of experiments in green roofs on existing buildings, which is estimated to have a green flat roof potential of 460 ha[1] (Baltus, 2015). For example, in April 2013, the largest green roof in Paris – covering 7000 m[2], equivalent to a football stadium (and the largest in Paris), and of which 700 m[2] is dedicated to shared gardens – was officially opened on top of the newly renovated 1970s Beaugrenelle shopping centre in the 15th arrondissement (Garric, 2013). The aim of this green roof garden is to provide a haven for biodiversity and limit temperature extremes inside, and outside, the building. Gecina, the owner of the shopping centre, put the retrofit cost at €450 m ($585 m). Several thousand plants and flowers, all species native to the Paris region, have been planted in order to help preserve biodiversity and provide local residents with an attractive landscape, and this habitat serves as a sanctuary for a number of species of birds (blackbirds, tits, greenfinches, robins, etc.) and also reduces the discharge of rainwater (Bouygues Construction, 2015). In this respect the targets set by the city are important. The main targets are to achieve 100 ha of green roofs and façades, a third of which is dedicated to the production of fruit and vegetables, to increase the number of trees by 20,000, to construct 'zero-waste, zero-carbon' districts, to significantly boost recycling and composting, to improve energy recovery and to strengthen the 'green' and 'blue' infrastructures endorsed by the Grenelle de l'environnement process with guidelines for land, waterway and wetlands management, and to ensure ecological continuity within the city (Mairie de Paris, 2015).

As towns and cities continue to grow, replanting vegetation has become a form of urban utopia and green roofs are spreading fast. 1. In 2012, 1 million square metres of plant-covered roofing was built in France, as much as in the USA, and 10 times more than in Germany, the pioneer in this field (*The Guardian*, 2013). In Australia, a nationwide group named 202020 Vision has a target 'to create 20% more green space in our urban areas by 2020', some of which will be green roofs (202020 Vision, 2015). Sydney is one of 39 government agencies endorsing the vision. Furthermore, the Australian cities of Sydney and Melbourne both have targets for becoming zero-net-emissions cities by 2030 and 2020, respectively (City of Melbourne, 2015). Green roofs can play a part in achieving these targets.

12.2   City-level Actions: Requirements or Inducements?

Cities vary in the way they approach the green roof policy. As Mees *et al.* (2013) point out, Chicago has promoted green roofs since 2001 through a combination of performance-based regulations for stormwater management,

---

[1] 44 ha planted (mainly on municipal buildings), 80 ha ready for planting and the remaining 380 ha requiring major adjustments.

energy efficiency and landscaping, and through a mandatory requirement for all new buildings that receive funding to be subject to review. In addition, there are limited financial incentives including a density bonus, where developers are permitted to build more units per area if their building has a green roof, and the Green Permit Program, which involves fast-tracking permissions and a fee reduction for developers installing a green roof. In contrast, London's policy is more restrained (Mees *et al.*, 2013), encouraging the development of green roofs where this is feasible. London, however, has made some progress in helping promote green roofs, with 700 green roofs in central London alone, covering an area of over 175,000 m² (17.5 ha). The City of London (2003, 2011) has published helpful guidance and case study information.[2]

Often within cities property companies also promote their innovation in green roofs. British Land, for example. In the City of London alone, green roof space has increased from around 10,000 m² of green roofs on London's Square Mile in 2004 to almost 70,000 m² in 2014 (Cary, 2015). Green roofs are now also standard on British Land's central London developments, with some 12 new green roofs being created in central London on British Land new builds since the introduction of the Sustainability Brief in 2004. Moreover, at Exchange Square in Broadgate, 2000 m² of pocket habitats were retrofitted on the building (commercial offices) in 2011.

Other cities such as Portland, OR (GLA, 2008) have also adopted varying approaches to green roof policy. In Portland, city-owned buildings are required to have a green roof covering at least 70% of the roof area. The remaining roof surfaces must be covered with energy-efficient roofing materials. Other incentives offered by the city include 'floor area bonuses' – a preferential property tax – and a 35% reduction in stormwater management charges. The city's Ecoroof initiative is intended to raise awareness of the benefits of green roofs. In Tokyo there is a law which requires the installation of green roofs in private buildings with built areas larger than 1000 m² and in public areas larger than 250 m², while integrated green roofs must not encompass less than 20% of the whole rooftop area (Berardi *et al.*, 2014).

Mees *et al.* (2013) provide a valuable and helpful comparison of green roof policies in five major cities, setting their analysis within the context of a typology of governance arrangements (Table 12.1). Their work shows that there is a dominance of 'hierarchical' arrangements (where local authorities determine strategy and policy mix to draw in private-sector action), underpinned by a strong public sector, in the early stages of green roof policies in all five cities, but that in Basel and Stuttgart this public policy dominance has prevailed throughout the whole policy process. That is not to say that interactive governance (shared responsibilities between public and private actors) or, indeed, market governance (with private-sector interests dominating) are

----

[2] See www.london.gov.uk/priorities/environment/greening-london/urban-greening/greening-roofs-and-walls/green-roof-map and www.cityoflondon.gov.uk/services/environment-and-planning/planning/design/sustainable-design/Pages/green-roofs.aspx.

Table 12.1   Implementation levels of green roof technology

Characteristic	Basel	Chicago	London	Rotterdam	Stuttgart
Policy introduced	1996	2003	2004	2008	1986
Sq. metres installed by 2010	1,000,000	700,000	715,000	40,000	1,000,000
Inhabitants	170,000	3,000,000	7,800,000	600,000	600,000
Sq. metres per capita	5.8824	0.2333	0.0917	0.0667	1.6667
% of eligible roof space covered	25%	<1%	<1%	<1%	22%
Average price/m² (euros) for a common green roof	25–35	40–80	50–90	50–90	10–40

Source: Adapted from Mees *et al.* (2013).

not important: there is evidence to suggest from the research that private responsibility also matters, especially at implementation and maintenance stages, but if London, Rotterdam and Chicago are to progress in terms of green roof implementation, a clearer and more decisive role for the public sector could help drive change.

In Basel and Stuttgart, for example, these cities have, in comparison, with London, Rotterdam and Chicago, deeper green roof implementation. This is partly because these two cities have employed the broadest mix of instruments, using coercive regulations to make green roofs mandatory on new buildings and also rewarding green roof installations with financial incentives, such as stormwater fee reduction and also (historically) with subsidies. In both cities this has been underpinned by strong parallel environmental agendas: biodiversity in Basel and air quality in Stuttgart, whereas Chicago and Rotterdam use voluntary instruments with financial incentives complemented by education and communication campaigns. As noted above, London is more restrained in both respects.

The research by Mees *et al.* (2013) suggests that local authorities need to take a clear lead throughout the green roof policy lifecycle. However, in Basel and Stuttgart three other factors have played an important role in contributing to green roof implementation. Firstly, both cities have a strong green political climate and culture, which has helped drive change. Secondly, these cities have had policies in place for green roofs over a relatively long time period. Thirdly, this might explain the lower installation costs in these cities. Sydney, Australia has a green roof and green walls policy launched in April 2014. The city is committed to increasing the number of high-quality green roofs and walls in Sydney, and to date 58 green roofs are listed on the City of Sydney website. Initially, policy documents and guides for stakeholders were supported by a full-time project officer, but this role was subsumed into planning at the end of 2014 (City of Sydney, 2015).

On a practical level, work by Lawlor *et al.* (2006) for CMHC (Canada) has suggested that there need to be six phases in the development of a green roof policy programme at city (or community/jurisdiction) level.

Phase 1: Introductory and awareness. During this phase, the overall environmental benefits of green roofs are examined. The city may hold a green roof workshop, send delegates to a green roof conference or visit another city/community with existing green roofs or a green roof policy. For example,

Green Roofs for Healthy Cities has been key in helping North American municipalities organise green roof workshops to bring local stakeholders together.

Phase 2: Community engagement. In this phase, a local champion or a green roof committee may seek to raise the profile of green roofs, including, for example, meetings with community leaders, mayors, architects, landscaping professionals, building owners and environmental groups to gain support for green roofs. Funding sources, such as government programmes, utilities or green roof manufacturers, will be explored and deals struck. The champion or committee will outline the opportunities, threats, strengths and weaknesses of green roof development in the city.

Phase 3: Action plan development and implementation. The city (or community) may establish a green roof advisory or working committee made up of key community leaders. A green roof demonstration project may be launched, perhaps with scientific monitoring equipment, depending on the need for local research data. Green roof tours and ongoing planning meetings often include site visits to buildings with different types and designs of green roofs, leading to the formation of a green roof database/inventory. A review of existing policy options and tools may be explored in this phase, and various programmes and policy opportunities identified.

Phase 4: Technical research. The local green roof advisory committee, the local champion(s) or both, along with a possible consortium of public/private partnerships, set up a research site. In some cases, the technical research consists of demonstration projects or green roof installations on prominent sites. Research typically involves assessing the ability of green roofs to manage stormwater, mitigate the urban heat island or provide other necessary environmental benefits. Often, experimental findings are shared at international green roof conferences.

Phase 5: Programme and policy development. The green roof advisory committee may expand to include more professionals, such as landscape designers, horticulturalists, designers and municipal urban planners. This phase translates local and regional research into policy options and tools. This involves establishing ways of offering incentives to contractors, developers and building owners to retrofit or plan new buildings with green roofs. This can include financial incentives, tax credits or density bonuses.

Phase 6: Continuous improvement. During this phase, a city now has a mature view of green roofs and a familiarity with green roof technology. Therefore, the effectiveness of policies and programmes is determined and policy options are explored. There is also a need to gather information and assess programme success, through constructive feedback from users, professionals and the building community. This phase typically involves exploring other policy options or further research to fine-tune existing programmes.

12.3   Tools and Information Sources

Appendix 3 provides a table of some of the key tools and information sources globally in respect of green roofs. A summary of the tool or information source is provided with links to websites.

12.4   Green Roofs: The Big Picture of GI and Future Developments

Green roofs need to be seen as one important element within a GI strategy in cities. ARUP (2015), for example, suggests that a GI-led design approach to cities needs to create a network of healthy and attractive new and retrofitted city environments, sustainable routes and places. The longer-term ambition for cities is therefore to see GI and green roofs as part of that – as creating a city ecosystem, which will benefit citizens in social, environmental and economic terms but also protect and mitigate the effects of climate change. Thinking about the bigger picture will therefore require perhaps city and local authority collaborations, new funding models and a more integrated and scaled-up approach to GI across cities.

It will also be important to ensure that guiding principles are followed when planning for climate-resilient GI. TCPA (2013), for example, suggests ten principles.

- Principle 1: GI needs to be strategically planned to provide a comprehensive and integrated network across scales.
- Principle 2: GI requires wide partnership buy-in from across disciplines, organisations and boundaries.
- Principle 3: GI needs to be planned using sound ecological evidence and baseline information on GI assets.
- Principle 4: GI needs to demonstrate multi-functionality (i.e., its ability to perform several functions and provide several benefits on the same spatial area), which may require the integration and interaction of different functions within a single site.
- Principle 5: GI creation and maintenance needs to be properly resourced, and includes costs relating to purchase, design, implementation, monitoring and management of GI.
- Principle 6: GI needs to be central to the development's design and must reflect and enhance the area's locally distinctive character.
- Principle 7: GI should contribute to biodiversity gains by safeguarding, enhancing, restoring and creating wildlife habitats and by integrating biodiversity into the built environment.
- Principle 8: GI should achieve physical and functional connectivity between sites at strategic and local levels, locally through proximity, or strategically through landscape-based connections.
- Principle 9: GI needs to include accessible spaces and facilitate physically active travel.
- Principle 10: GI needs to be integrated with other policy initiatives.

As Lennon *et al.* (2015) suggest, a GI approach to planning and design moves beyond traditional site-based approaches of protect and preserve towards a more holistic and integrated approach which recognises the complexities of social–ecological interactions. For Lennon *et al.* (2015), GI thinking is characterised by four key elements:

- treating GI assets as fundamental infrastructure;
- promoting spatial connectivity between GI elements;

- using a multifunctional approach to planning, which recognises the complexity of social–ecological relations;
- a focus on interdisciplinary collaboration, which breaks down silo thinking.

Increasingly, therefore, cities are adopting forward-thinking visions to underpin their transition to a more sustainable future. Vancouver, for example, under the leadership of Gregor Robertson since 2008 has developed a vision to make it the world's greenest city by 2020. This ambition is structured around a 2020 action plan, with a number of targets aimed at improving green spaces and access to wildlife and nature, as well as encouraging green roofs, which link with the concepts of increased urban food production and improving urban drainage systems. Similarly, in its strategy to become a carbon-neutral city by 2025, Copenhagen became, in 2010, the first Scandinavian city to adopt a policy that requires green roofs for all new buildings with roof slopes of less than 30°. The impetus for this was in 2009, when Denmark hosted the UN Climate Change Conference COP15, which helped define the framework for tackling global climate change. During that period, the focus on green roofs intensified and led to setting a goal for urban design with green roofs in the Climate Plan of the City of Copenhagen. Since then, green roofs have become integrated into different city guidelines, such as the guidelines for sustainability in construction and civil work, which mandates green roofs for all the Municipality's buildings. Green roofs are also a part of the city's Strategy for Biodiversity, and so since 2010 green roofs are mandated in most new local plans. A recent calculation based on approved new local plans mandating green roofs gives a total of 200,000 m² of green roofs to be installed in Copenhagen, which today has more than 40 green roofs. Moreover, buildings with green roofs in Copenhagen must be able to fulfil at least two of the following requirements (CesIfo/DICE, 2012):

- absorb 50–80% of the precipitation falling on the roof;
- provide a cooling and insulating effect on the building and reduce reflection;
- make the city greener;
- reduce the urban heat island effect;
- counteract increased temperatures in the city.

Green roofs also need to contribute to an aesthetic and visual improvement in urban design that improves quality of life and also helps increase the life of the roofing membrane by reducing UV impact.

Looking further into the future, it seems likely that green roofs will continue to play an important role in GI provision in urban areas. A recent report by ARUP (2015) took a forward-looking view of how buildings in 2050 might look. The report focused on structures whose components are dynamic, intelligent and reactive, and imagined a futuristic city skyscraper building in the year 2050 that includes flexible modular pods, urban agriculture, climate-conscious façades and intelligent building systems. In the building there is a strong focus on vertical farming, so that green spaces are designed as integral parts of the building, to encourage interaction with plants, birds and insects whilst utilising vertical farming techniques such as hydroponics to facilitate food production. Indeed, ARUP has piloted one particular innovation in Hamburg, which is an apartment building designed around a biomass façade, which generates heat and electricity from algae on exterior walls. The two south-facing façades are covered in a shell of bioreactors, clear containers that create a controlled environment for an algae farm. Exposed to sunlight, the algae photosynthesise, absorbing CO_2 as they grow. Nutrients and CO_2 are circulated through the bioreactors to encourage growth, and the algae are regularly collected and fermented in a nearby biomass plant, then burned to produce electricity (Forum for the Future, 2013).

12.5   Recognising the Multiple Benefits of Green Roof Retrofit

It is the case that stakeholders may decide to retrofit a green roof for one or more of the following reasons:

1. thermal performance – to improve insulation and reduce energy consumption;
2. urban heat island;
3. stormwater – attenuation of pluvial flooding;
4. biodiversity enhancement;
5. conservation of endangered flora and fauna;
6. urban food production;
7. provision of social space.

The majority of stakeholders will be concerned primarily with the building level rather than the city level. In Table 12.2 the primary and secondary benefits are identified for each type of green roof.

In Table 12.3 each green roof type is identified along with the co-benefits accruing. In decision-making, stakeholders should be aware that these secondary or co-benefits exist.

Throughout this book there has been an underlying theme that green roofs, as part of GI, can help build and develop urban resilience. Although there is no overall agreement on the meaning of the concept of urban resilience, most

Table 12.2   Green roof primary and secondary benefits

Green roof type	Primary benefit (environmental, economic or social)	Secondary benefits (environmental, economic or social)
Thermal – to improve insulation and reduce energy consumption	Environmental	Economic
Stormwater – attenuation of pluvial flooding	Environmental	Economic
Biodiversity enhancement	Environmental	
Conservation of endangered flora and fauna	Environmental	
Urban food production	Environmental/ economic	Social
Provision of social space	Social	Environmental/ economic

Table 12.3   Green-roof-type primary and co-benefits

Green roof type	Primary reason	Co-benefits
Thermal	Improve insulation and reduce energy consumption	▪ Stormwater attenuation ▪ Urban heat island ▪ Biodiversity ▪ Air quality
Stormwater	Attenuate pluvial flooding	▪ Thermal improvement ▪ Urban heat island ▪ Biodiversity ▪ Air quality
Biodiversity enhancement	Increase local biodiversity	▪ Air quality ▪ Urban heat island ▪ Thermal improvement ▪ Stormwater attenuation
Conservation of endangered flora and fauna	Provide environment for endangered species	▪ Air quality ▪ Urban heat island ▪ Thermal improvement ▪ Stormwater attenuation
Urban food production	Local food production	▪ Reduce carbon food miles ▪ Air quality ▪ Urban heat island ▪ Thermal improvement ▪ Increase biodiversity ▪ Stormwater attenuation
Provision of social space	Amenity space	▪ Thermal improvement ▪ Air quality ▪ Urban heat island ▪ Thermal improvement ▪ Stormwater attenuation ▪ Food production

definitions highlight the capacity of individuals, communities, institutions, businesses and systems within a city to thrive and survive, adapt and grow whatever what kinds of chronic stresses and acute shocks they experience (Rockefeller, 2015; Buurman and Bobovic, 2015, Meerow *et al*, 2016). The complexity of cities makes them a particularly important focus for resilience because they are constantly changing and adapting, and green roofs provide important city-wide benefits for helping develop both adaptive and mitigation capacity. In other words, the multiple benefits of green roofs also connect to the wider notion that greening our cities can make them less likely to over-heat or flood, and that when cities do suffer more severe climatic impacts they are resilient enough to bounce back from those shocks.

12.6   Overall Conclusions

Green roofs have numerous benefits, and many existing buildings in city centres are suited to retrofit, and yet relatively few green roof retrofits are undertaken. This is most likely to be a result of the majority of existing professionals having little or no knowledge of the benefits, the technology and the performance of green roofs. There are changes in university education programme content, in the amount of best-practice guides and information available on the Internet (often hosted on local or city authority websites) that will provide the knowledge and awareness of green roofs for built environment students and existing practitioners over time. This dissemination of information needs expanding into continuing professional development events for existing practitioner to upskill and educate them. A fear of the unknown is a factor in deterring existing practitioners from recommending green roof retrofit to clients. As direct experience of the technology increases, the uptake of green roofs will grow exponentially. This book is part of the attempt to increase knowledge and awareness, particularly in the wider context of improving and developing urban resilience.

Each chapter has provided a detailed overview of the primary benefits of green roof retrofit, as well as some illustrative case studies to show how the technology can be applied in practice in different countries. Clearly, given the different climate zones and geographical regions, it may be the case that saving energy through greater insulation may drive green roof retrofit in one place, whereas species conservation and biodiversity may drive adoption elsewhere. This chapter has shown the co-benefits that also co-exist with each primary driver, as well as some of the issues of retrofitting in various locations and climate zones globally.

A city-scale vision is also shown to be a method of increasing uptake and raising awareness to deliver community-wide benefits of reducing urban heat islands and improving air quality. With increasing urbanisation, such visions are going to be needed more than ever to deliver liveable cities. Furthermore, with increasing urbanisation, the potential for inhabitants of cities to become increasingly detached from the natural environment grows. This detachment, lack of understanding and knowledge of the natural environment could lead to less willingness to act to save endangered environments in the broader population. The adoption of green roofs could help to plug that gap in knowledge and understanding for city inhabitants and the community, and on this basis is seen to be a key reason to advocate more green roof retrofitting.

On an individual building basis, occupants and users can benefit where roof access is provided and/or in reduced energy consumption and lower operating costs. Owners will benefit economically in markets where green buildings command a premium in capital value. Thus, the benefits of green roof retrofit are derived at all levels from the city scale to the building scale and the individual scale.

References

202020 Vision (2015) 'Our cities need more plants and trees', available at: 202020vision.com.au/the-vision/.

ARUP (2015) *Cities Alive: Rethinking Green Infrastructure.*

Baltus, R. (2015) 'City centre rooftops: go green, classify or densify?', available at: rogerbaltuscolumn.tumblr.com/post/120762732544/to-the-point-roger-baltuss-column-city-centre.

Berardi, U., GhaffarianHoseini, A. H. and GhaffarianHoseini, A. (2014) 'State-of-the-art analysis of the environmental benefits of green roofs', *Applied Energy*, 115, 411–428.

Bouygues Construction (2015) 'Beaugrenelle Shopping Centre', available at: bouygues-construction.com.au/project/beaugrenelle-shopping-centre-france/.

Buurman, J., and Babovic, V. (2015) 'Designing Adaptive Systems for Enhancement of Urban Water Resilience', *Lee Kuan Yew School of Public Policy Research Paper No. 15–28*. Available at SSRN: http://ssrn.com/abstract=2653481

Cary, S. (2015) 'Green roofs go mainstream: British Land', available at: views.britishland.com/2015/02/green-roofs-go-mainstream/.

CESIfo/DICE (2015) 'Green infrastructure: national approaches and experiences', available at: www.cesifo-group.de/ifoHome/facts/DICE/Energy-and-Natural-Environment/Natural-Environment/Instruments-by-Environmental-Domains/gree-infr-nati-appr-expe/fileBinary/gree-infr-nati-appr-expe.pdf.

City of Melbourne, (2015) 'Green roofs', available at: www.melbourne.vic.gov.au/Sustainability/CouncilActions/Pages/Greenroofs.aspx.

City of Sydney (2015) 'Green walls and roofs', available at: www.cityofsydney.nsw.gov.au/vision/towards-2030/sustainability/greening-the-city/green-roofs-and-walls.

City of Toronto (2015) 'Green roofs', available at: www1.toronto.ca/wps/portal/contentonly?vgnextoid=3a7a036318061410VgnVCM10000071d60f89RCRD.

Forum for the Future (2013) 'A building powered by algae', available at: www.forumforthefuture.org/greenfutures/articles/building-powered-algae.

Garric, A. (2013) 'Paris shopping centre opens green roof as French cities make room for nature', *The Guardian*, 4 May, available at: www.theguardian.com/environment/2013/may/04/paris-green-roofs-building-climate-environment.

GLA (2008) *Living Roofs and Walls Technical Report: Supporting London Plan Policy*.

Kazmierczak, A. and Carter, J. (2010) 'Adaptation to climate change using green and blue infrastructure: a database of case studies', available at: www.grabs-eu.org/membersArea/files/Database_Final_no_hyperlinks.pdf.

Lawlor, G., Currie, B., Doshi, H. and Wieditz, I. (2006) *Green Roofs: A Resource Manual for Municipal Policy Makers*. CMHC, Canada.

Lennon, M., Scott, M., Collier, M. and Foley, K. (2015) 'Developing green infrastructure thinking: devising and applying an interactive group-based methodology for practitioners', *Journal of Environmental Planning and Management*, in press.

Mairie de Paris (2014) *The Paris Greening Programme*, Available at: www.energy-cities.eu/db/Paris_Programme-vegetalisation_2014_en.pdf.

Meerow, S., Newell, J., Stults, M. (2016) 'Defining urban resilience: a review', *Landscape and Urban Planning*, 147, 38–49.

Mees, H., Driessen, P., Runhaar, H. and Stamatelos, J. (2013) 'Who governs climate change adaptation? Getting green roofs for stormwater retention off the ground', *Journal of Environmental Planning and Management*, 56(6), 802–825.

NASA (2012) *NASA and Green Roof Research*.

Rockefeller Foundation (2015) 100 Resilient Cities. https://www.rockefellerfoundation.org/ourwork/initiatives/100-resilient-cities/

TCPA (2012) *Planning for a Healthy Environment: Good Practice Guidance for Green Infrastructure and Biodiversity*. TCPA, London.

The Guardian (2013) 'Paris shopping centre opens green roof as French cities make room for nature', 4 May, available at: www.theguardian.com/environment/2013/may/04/paris-green-roofs-building climate-environment.

Appendices

Appendix 1: A Checklist for Appraising the Suitability of an Existing Roof for Green Roof Retrofit

This checklist is designed for building surveyors to use in an **initial appraisal** of an existing building for green roof retrofit.

Please review the following aspects and take into account in your decision making.

1. Position of the building
   - What is the position of the building within the settlement? Is it over-shadowed by other adjoining buildings which may affect access to sunlight and the growth of plants?
     - Not overshadowed (good)
     - Partly overshadowed (maybe OK)
     - Overshadowed (may not be OK)
   - What is the quality of the building? For example, those with a high quality may experience an increase in capital value and yield as a result of having sustainability features such as a green roof.
     - High quality (in Australia, PCA Grades Premium and A) – more likely to enhance value
     - Medium quality – may enhance value
     - Low quality – unlikely to enhance value

Green Roof Retrofit: Building Urban Resilience, First Edition.
Edited by Sara Wilkinson and Tim Dixon.
© 2016 John Wiley & Sons, Ltd. Published 2016 by John Wiley & Sons, Ltd.

2. Location of the building
    -   What is the prevailing climatic condition? For example, is the building in a hot arid climate zone or a maritime zone? Each has different characteristics which favour different types of green roof solution. For example, those locations which experience heavy rainfall may favour a stormwater solution aimed to reduce as much runoff as possible.
        ○   The prevailing climate is ....
        ○   The building and roof location is exposed to
            □   High winds
            □   Medium winds
            □   Low winds
        ○   The building and roof location is exposed to
            □   High rainfall
            □   Medium rainfall
            □   Low rainfall
            □   Wide seasonal variation in rainfall
    -   Does the location favour (tick all which apply and rank in order of preference):
        ○   Stormwater design
        ○   Improving water quality entering sewer system
        ○   Thermal design
        ○   Reducing urban heat island
        ○   Reducing noise pollution
        ○   Biodiversity design
        ○   Aesthetic and social space design
3. Orientation of the roof
    -   North facing is good in the southern hemisphere, whereas south facing is better in the northern hemisphere
        ○   What is the orientation of the roof?
            □   Good
            □   OK
            □   Poor
4. Height above ground
    -   How high is the building? In some locations high buildings are subject to high winds and/or fierce heat, which can make growing plants challenging.
        ○   How high is the roof? .... floors
5. Roof pitch
    What is the roof pitch?
    -   Up to 21° is suited to green roof retrofit
    -   Exceeding 22° is too steep and not suited
    -   Minimum roof pitch less than 3°
6. Existing roof construction
    What is the existing structural form of the roof?
    -   Timber (size and spacing of beams) ....
    -   Concrete slab (depth in mm) ....

- Structural steel (size and spacing of beams) ....
- Other (describe) ....

7. Load limitations of the building
    - What is the dead load-bearing capacity of the existing roof?
    - What is the live load-bearing capacity of the existing roof?

8. Preferred planting options
    - What is the budget?
        - High
        - Medium
        - Low
    - How much maintenance is available for the green roof plants?
        - High
        - Medium
        - Low
    - Is there a water supply on the roof?
        - Yes
        - No
    - Is there a power supply to the roof?
        - Yes
        - No
    - Are there any potential environmental hazards?
        - Yes
        - No

9. Presence of plant and other equipment on the roof
    - The presence of plant such as air conditioning or HVAC may affect plant growth by creating micro-climates on the rooftop through the discharge of fumes and warm air.
        - Is there any HVAC equipment on the roof?
            - Yes (please indicate approximate area covered in sq. metres)
            - No
        - Are there window-cleaning tracks on the roof?
            - Yes
            - No
            - Partly
        - Is there a safety guardrail around the roof?
            - Yes
            - No
            - Partly
        - Are there any PV panels mounted on the roof?
            - Yes (please indicate approximate are covered in sq. metres)
            - No
        - Is there any other equipment on the roof which may affect the area that could be retrofitted?
            - Yes (please indicate type of equipment and approximate area covered in sq. metres)
            - No

10. Access for construction and installation of the roof
    Materials and equipment will have to be taken up to the roof during construction and installation. The presence of scaffolding for other external works may provide a good means of moving materials to the roof.
    - What is the access like for construction and installation?
      ○ Very good (i.e., lift directly to roof level)
      ○ OK (wide stairs to roof, say one floor below roof)
      ○ Poor (narrow/winding stair access only)
11. Levels of maintenance
    - What is the access like for maintenance to the plants? To the roof?
      ○ Very good (i.e., lift directly to roof level)
      ○ OK (wide stairs to roof, say one floor below roof)
      ○ Poor (narrow/winding stair access only)
12. Costs
    - How much is the owner prepared to pay for a green roof?
      ○ High
      ○ Medium
      ○ Low
    - Can the costs be partially offset by the improvement in thermal performance and energy savings?

Other Notes

In this section, please note down any other factors that may affect the installation of a retrofit green roof.

Final Evaluation

Based on the review of the factors above, what is the potential for green roof retrofit?

Appendix 2: Checklist for Designers of Biodiverse Green Roofs

This checklist is designed for anyone interested in creating or retrofitting a green roof for the purpose of enhancing or increasing biodiversity.

1. *Focus animal group* Which animal group(s) is the roof designed for?
    Invertebrates
    - Pollinators (bees, flies, butterflies)
    - Soil invertebrates (millipedes, collembolans, centipedes, earthworms, nematodes, mites)

- Ground-dwelling arthropods (beetles, ants, centipedes, millipedes)
- Spiders
- Snails and slugs
- All invertebrates
- Other (specify)

Vertebrates

- Small terrestrial mammals (mice, voles, rabbits)
- Bats
- Birds
- Reptiles
- Other (specify)

2. *Habitat requirements* Which of the following resources need to be provided on the rooftop to support the focal animal group? For non-flying animals, all resources must be within walking distance. Note that some invertebrates are able to survive on very little water and can often prosper from ephemeral water sources such as dew.
   - Food (ex. flowers for pollinators, flying insects for bats, etc.)
   - Water
   - Nest sites (specify type, ex. nest boxes for bats)
   - Other (specify)

   Will all habitat requirements be provided on the green roof?

   Y

   N

   If not, are these resources available within flying range?

   Y

   N

3. *Measuring success* What is the goal of your green roof?
   - To increase the number of species within a target group
   - To increase the abundance of a particular species
   - To increase the breeding success of a focal species
   - Other

   What kinds of site will be used as comparison (control) sites?
   - Adjacent ground-level sites
   - Conventional roofs
   - Other kinds of green roof

   How will you sample the taxa to measure changes in biodiversity associated with your green roof intervention?
   - Pitfall trapping (appropriate for ground-dwelling arthropods)
   - Intercept traps (appropriate for flying insects)
   - Hand netting (appropriate for many pollinators)
   - Pan trapping (appropriate for flying insects and pollinators)
   - Visual count surveys (appropriate for birds and some pollinators)
   - Acoustic monitoring (appropriate for bats)

   When and how often will you sample the green roof and comparison sites?

   I will sample ... times, starting ... after roof constructions

Do you require specialist help in identifying members of your focus group?

 Y* (if yes, contact specialists immediately; museums and universities are good contacts)

 N

* *Note:* 'yes' will be the case in most invertebrate surveys, unless the designer has training in invertebrate taxonomy.

4. *Habitat complexity* How will you increase the habitat complexity (particularly for invertebrate biodiversity)?

- Use of diverse substrates (rocks of different sizes, wood piles, wood chips, etc.)
- Planting complex, multi-level vegetation
- Planting a variety of flowers with different flowering periods
- Planting native species
- Planting both nectar and pollen-providing plants
- Use of topographic features such as slopes

Appendix 3: Tools, Information Sources and Mapping/GIS for Green Roofs – Some Examples

	Country	Summary	Website
Tools			
Green Roof Energy Calculator Information Green Building Research Laboratory	USA	This model incorporates a vegetation canopy and soil transport model that represents the following green roof physics: – long and shortwave radiation exchange within the canopy (multiple reflections, shading) – effect of canopy on sensible heat exchange among the ambient air, leaf and soil surfaces – thermal and moisture transport in the growing media with moisture inputs from precipitation (and irrigation if desired) – evaporation from the soil surface and transpiration from the vegetation canopy	greenbuilding.pdx.edu/GR_CALC_v2/CalculatorInfo_v2.php
Green Roof Construction Standards – Toronto	Canada	The purpose of the Toronto Green Roof Construction Standard is to govern the design and construction of green roofs by setting out minimum requirements that meet the city's objectives and the Ontario Building Code requirements Mandatory provisions are included in the Toronto Green Roof Construction for the following areas: – green roof assembly – gravity loads – slope stability – parapet height and/or overflow scupper locations – wind uplift – fire safety – occupancy and safety – waterproofing – drainage – water retention – vegetation performance – plant selection – irrigation – maintenance	www1.toronto.ca/wps/portal/contentonly?vgnextoid=77420621f3161410VgnVCM10000071d60f89RCRD

(Continued)

(Continued)

	Country	Summary	Website
Green Infrastructure Valuation Toolkit	UK	Since December 2008, a project steering group including Natural Economy Northwest, the Northern Way, Natural England, the Commission for Architecture and the Built Environment, Design for London and Tees Valley Unlimited has been working with consultants (Genecon LLP) with support from the Department for Environment, Food and Rural Affairs, the three Regional Development Agencies in the North of England, Advantage West Midlands and the London Development Agency on the development of a valuation framework for assessing the potential economic and wider returns from investment in green infrastructure and environmental improvements Now that the project is complete, the Green Infrastructure Valuation Toolkit is being made available as a prototype and free open-source resource	www.greeninfrastructurenw.co.uk/html/index.php?page=projects&GreenInfrastructureValuationToolkit=true
Greening the Grey	USA	Website built and maintained by Virginia Tech's Center for Leadership in Global Sustainability and the National Association of Regional Councils with support from the US Forest Service as a portal and resource bank for information about green infrastructure in its broadest sense. Provides information about the full range of reasons why cities, communities and regions have decided to invest in green infrastructure, some of the financing strategies for doing so, case studies of innovative policies, tools and programmes to advance green infrastructure, innovative tools and research being developed around green infrastructure, and much more	www.greeningthegrey.org/tools/
Information			
Green Roof Technology	USA	Professional consultants, architects and engineers who are specialised in the specification and design of any type of living technology, particularly in ground remote locations. Green Roof Technology adheres to a strict ethics code that offers unprejudiced service without affiliation with any product or manufacturer. Furthermore, the CEO of Green Roof Technology has developed multiple green roof systems and advanced technical green roof solutions for many system providers and roofing manufacturers in the USA and Germany	www.greenrooftechnology.com/

	Country	Summary	Website
International Green Roof Association	International	The International Green Roof Association (IGRA) is a global network for the promotion and dissemination of information on green roof topics and green roof technology. Owing to its status as a multinational, non-profit organisation, IGRA offers the platform and infrastructure for independent 'pro green roof' lobby work with political decision-makers and investors. IGRA members are national green roof organisations, green roof research institutes and green roof companies. IGRA also welcomes persons and green roof experts who support the ecological green roof idea to join the green roof network	www.igra-world.com/index.php
Green Roofs.com	USA	Provides a listing of links to educational, governmental, media, NGO/private (non-governmental), non-profit and professional organisations promoting green roof-related and general environmentally friendly activities and programmes worldwide	www.greenroofs.com/resources.htm
Living Roofs	UK	An independent organisation that promotes green roofs and living roofs in the UK and is the UK member of the European Federation of Green Roof Associations Livingroofs.org provides an in-depth resource for all things to do with green roofs and living roofs. From their benefits to exemplar case studies, from policy to plants, livingroofs.org aims to raise awareness of the need for green roofs in new developments and the need to retrofit vegetation on the existing building fabric in our cities across the globe. Livingroofs.org promotes and highlights companies and suppliers, professional designers, consultants and individuals involved in ensuring ecosystem services and green infrastructure are the future of our cities	www.livingroofs.org/

(Continued)

(Continued)

	Country	Summary	Website
GIS/mapping			
London Green Roof Map	UK	This shows that there are around 700 green roofs in central London alone, covering an area of over 175,000 m². That is 17.5 ha, or around 25 football pitches! You can click on a green roof to see a short description of the green roof type and an estimate of the area it covers. You can also search by postcode and switch between a map and aerial photograph	www.london.gov.uk/priorities/ environment/greening-london/ urban-greening/greening-roofs-and-walls/green-roof-map
Toronto Green Roof Map	Canada	The city's Green Roof Bylaw applies to new commercial, institutional and many residential development applications. You can find out which developments require a green roof, get information on the Green Roof Construction Standard and find out what you need to know if you are going to build a green roof in Toronto	www1.toronto.ca/ wps/portal/contentonly? vgnextoid = 3a7a03 VGnVCM10000071 d60f89RCRD

Index

Page numbers in *italics* refer to figures; page numbers in **bold** refer to tables/boxes. This index is ordered letter-by-letter (ignoring hyphens and spaces)

Green Roof Retrofit: Building Urban Resilience, First Edition.
Edited by Sara Wilkinson and Tim Dixon.
© 2016 John Wiley & Sons, Ltd. Published 2016 by John Wiley & Sons, Ltd.